A BIOGRAPHY OF A MAP IN MOTION

A Biography of a Map in Motion

Augustine Herrman's Chesapeake

Christian J. Koot

NEW YORK UNIVERSITY PRESS

New York

NEW YORK UNIVERSITY PRESS
New York
www.nyupress.org
© 2018 by New York University
All rights reserved

ISBN: 978-1-4798-3729-8

For Library of Congress Cataloging-in-Publication data, please contact the Library of Congress.

Manufactured in the United States of America

10 9 8 7 6 5 4 3 2 1

Also available as an ebook

For Jennifer

CONTENTS

LIST OF FIGURES

A NOTE ON THE TEXT

Original spellings have been preserved except in the use of inter-
changeable letters like i/j and u/v. In these cases spellings have been
modernized. Abbreviations have also been silently expanded for clarity.
In the text, dates have been modernized as per the Dutch seventeenth-
century usage, though the notes preserve original dates. Like many
seventeenth-century Europeans' names, Augustine Herrman's name
appears spelled differently in period sources, and this has carried over
to modern historical works. In the text I have chosen the spelling that
appears on his map but have maintained original spellings in quotations
and in the notes.

Introduction

Located in the back of the second court of Magdalene College in Cambridge, England, and accessed through a cloister that runs by the college's formal dining room is the Pepys Library, an early eighteenth-century building that holds Samuel Pepys's library. Famous for the meticulous diary he kept from 1660 to 1669 capturing the daily life and political intrigue of Restoration London, Pepys was a government bureaucrat and voracious consumer of London's high and low cultural attractions. Bequeathed at his death to the college he attended, Pepys's collection numbers more than three thousand volumes and includes his diary. The volumes are housed in a second floor reading room, where they are encased in a series of twelve book presses that Pepys had built specially for them. The room is wide and shallow; five windows span the front side, and the book presses line the back wall. At the center of the room is a large desk that may have been Pepys's own. The library's contents match Pepys's various interests and range from poetry and political treatises to popular ballads and sheet music. Particularly notable are Pepys's holdings relating to the growth of England's navy, which include more than one thousand seventeenth-century maps and charts.[1] Among these maps is one of five extant copies of *Virginia and Maryland as it is Planted and Inhabited* (1673) (Figure I.1). Reproduced widely in the seventeenth and eighteenth centuries, *Virginia and Maryland* is one of the most famous images of the Chesapeake, but its story has never been told.

Created by a colonial merchant, planter, and diplomat named Augustine Herrman and engraved by Londoner William Faithorne, this extraordinary map depicts the seventeeth-century Mid-Atlantic stretching from what is today southern New Jersey to northern North Carolina.

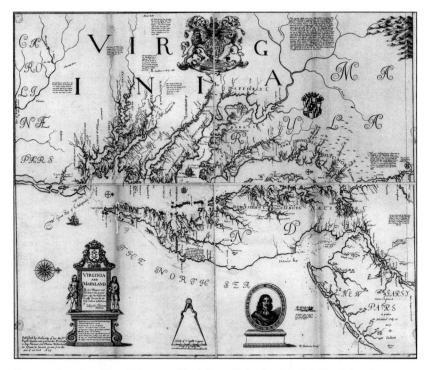

FIGURE I.1. Augustine Herrman, *Virginia and Maryland As it is Planted and Inhabited this present Year 1670 Surveyed and Exactly Drawne by the Only Labour & Endeavour of Augustin Herrman Bohemiensis; W. Faithorne, sculpt.* London, 1673. Courtesy of the Library of Congress, Geography and Map Division.

While early modern European nations rushed to make maps as they expanded their empires overseas, the colonial Chesapeake engendered few distinct cartographic depictions. Its waterways were complex and difficult to chart; so, too, were its imperial permutations as the Dutch, English, and Swedes jockeyed for control of the Native American lands that surrounded the bay. The imperial rivalry between the Dutch and English ultimately led to *Virginia and Maryland*'s creation, but the map speaks to more than European empires' claims for political ownership. It illuminates a densely connected interimperial world as experienced and captured by its maker. Born in Bohemia, Augustine Herrman arrived in New Netherland (now New York) in 1644 and spent the next two decades traveling between the Dutch colony and the English Chesapeake before eventually settling in Maryland. As the following pages will reveal, Herrman's *Virginia and Maryland* played an important role in England's imagination of and halting dominion over the Chesapeake, and yet, at the same time, the map preserves the intercolonial perspective of its maker.

Encountering *Virginia and Maryland*

On a sunny and brisk Tuesday at the end of March, the Pepys Library was quiet save for the deputy librarian who opened the space so that I could examine Pepys's copy of *Virginia and Maryland*. The map is bound at the end of a large folio volume of sheet maps drawn largely from the first and third volumes of London map dealer John Seller's *The English Pilot* and his *The Coasting Pilot*.[2] Because of its size, *Virginia and Maryland* is folded in four pieces, and to view it you have to fold out the left and right sides and then fold the top up from the bottom. When finally opened to its full extent, the map is striking. Of the five existing copies—others are held in the British Library, the Richelieu Library of the Bibliothèque Nationale de France, the Library of Congress, and the John Carter Brown Library in Providence, Rhode Island—the copy at Magdalene College is in the best condition. Sheltered inside an oversize folio volume since at least the latter years of Pepys's life, the thick white paper is still largely free of the yellowing of age, and the ink remains a rich dark black; it looks very much as it did when it came off the press in 1673 or 1674.

Imagine yourself standing beside Pepys and a small group of his friends and colleagues as they gather before a small table like the one I used in the Pepys Library. Perhaps that table was also was positioned in front of a window so the volume of maps on its surface would catch the light as Pepys turned the pages, stopped on *Virginia and Maryland*, and folded open the map. Measuring roughly three feet by two and a half feet, the map would take up nearly the entire desk when fully opened. Standing over, it your eye would instantly seek out the darkest lines. First you would likely notice the word "VIRGINIA" and the massive and beautifully rendered Arms of Great Britain that together dominate the top center of the map. As your eye then traveled downward, it would quickly take in the more subtly rendered "MARYLAND," the Calvert coat of arms, and the cartographic image of the Chesapeake, before settling on a striking portrait of Augustine Herrman depicted in a vaguely classical manner. After you had inspected the portrait, the map's cartouche—viewable out of your peripheral vision to your left— would draw you quickly to that side of the engraving to examine the ornamental plinth, which is flanked by two Native American figures and on which the title appears. Having absorbed these figurative elements, your eye might then travel back up the paper and finally begin to take in the map's cartography.

Your gaze would most likely settle initially on the "North Sea" (sometimes used on maps to denote the Atlantic Ocean in the seventeenth century) at the bottom of the map or the "Great Bay of Chesapeake" between Cape Henry and Cape Charles and then follow the ship depicted there into the bay itself. You might then begin to read the names of the major rivers of the Chesapeake—the James, the York, the Rappahannok, and, finally, the "Patowmeck." Since it is printed in a relatively small font, you might have to lean down to see this final name clearly, and suddenly more detail would come into view. From a standing height, you would already have noticed the scores of toponyms that cover the map, but stooped over it, you are suddenly greeted with a blizzard of town, plantation, and waterway names. Perhaps more striking are the tiny marks scattered along the coastline, which had been almost invisible when you were standing, but now bring the map to life as they detail sandbars, marshes, the depth of waterways, and the locations of towns and plantations. Once you have become familiarized with the structure of the map, this information is yours, allowing you to choose which direction to travel, following rivers inland to read narrative blocks that tell some of history and geography of the region or skirting around the plantations of the shoreline as you see fit. Because most of the interior space is barren, you will likely stick close to the region's rivers and inlets but there is plenty there to digest before Pepys calls you away to examine another of his treasures.

As you (our imagined viewer) discovered, *Virginia and Maryland* operates at two scales. Viewing the map from distance, an effect only enhanced when displayed on a wall as the Lords of Trade did with their copy, the map would have allowed English viewers to picture possessing the region. Crowned by Great Britain's arms and prominently scattered with the names of familiar English places (New Kent, Middlesex, Northumberland, Dorchester), those associated with the Royal family (Charles and Carolina) and with Lord Baltimore and the Calverts (Anne Arundel, Cæcil, Baltimore), the map is familiar and nonthreatening. Seen from afar, it depicts wide rivers and open land with mountains visible only in the distance. This is a place that can be understood, inhabited, and easily incorporated into the English Empire. Looking more closely, however, another, more bewildering, world appears as hundreds of waterways, inlets, and streams, dangerous shallows and sandbars, and dozens of plantations and Indian towns reveal themselves. Though mapped and measured, this close-up view, which emphasizes the specificity of local conditions, brings out the challenges inherent in fully comprehending the colonial world at a distance.

The two scales at which a viewer sees *Virginia and Maryland*—the local and the metropolitan—offer insight into the ways the British Empire was constructed and experienced. As symbols of authority and possession, maps occupied a critical space in seventeenth-century empire-building and were especially important in the Americas, a region rife with overlapping claims and unclear borders. By naming territory within the Atlantic, displaying the boundaries of empires, and describing the features of distant lands, maps were a central aspect of the process of colonization and territorial acquisition; they enabled metropolitans and colonists alike to comprehend and lay claim to distant lands.[3] At the same time, most of these maps, like Herrman's, largely ignore Native American nations, and thereby reveal the ways that the colonial project depended upon the erasure of native spaces by the 1670s. Though firmly situated in this context, Herrman's map is unusual in the way it pictures the English Chesapeake. Not overly concerned with depicting land and its boundaries, Herrman devoted the majority of his map to delineating the waterways and the coastline, the areas with which he had great familiarity as a merchant. Neglecting borders (both European and Native American) but including precise navigational data, Herrman's map was shaped by Dutch mapmaking traditions and eschewed imperial divisions in favor of openness. This is a map of access, not of repulsion, and it reveals that even as empires divided the region, many colonists imagined the Mid-Atlantic to be a unified whole. Inscribed in *Virginia and Maryland* was the colonial idea of a linked multinational European world, a view that had shaped not only the map, but also the mapmaker who produced it and the empire he represented.

Herrman's decision to concentrate on the Chesapeake's hydrographic system reflects the ways that the waters of the Mid-Atlantic flowed together to allow economic and social integration between Dutch and English colonists even while political power remained centered in colonial and imperial governments. As Europeans struggled for control of early North America, the central place they interacted—the Mid-Atlantic—was not only a zone of contest but also a space of cooperation. Surely colonists and government officials in New Netherland, Maryland, and Virginia—taking their lead from commercial companies, government officials, and proprietors in the seat of empire—clashed over territorial and commercial control, but at the same time they accommodated a large degree of economic and social integration on the ground. Around the Atlantic world, ties between colonies of different empires were strong in the seventeenth century, before imperial administrators could successfully circumscribe and manage overseas empires. This interconnectedness was particularly true in the Mid-Atlantic, where Dutch, English, and Swedish colonists interacted regularly. Close study of the intercolonial trader and diplomat Herrman's life alongside his map of *Virginia and Maryland* uncovers the influence Anglo-Dutch interaction

had on the development of the Mid-Atlantic by explicating the interconnectedness of Dutch and English colonies and the ways that colonists
working out distinctive local strategies for success fabricated empire.[4]

Yet the meaning assigned to Herrman's map changed over time and
varied over space. In London this colonial object became an imperial one
reinscribed with the need to claim and circumscribe dominions abroad.
As Herrman's map traveled across the Atlantic into the workshop of an
engraver and into the hands of consumers, it was transformed, literally
from manuscript to printed map and metaphorically as it acquired new
meanings and associations different from those it held in the colonies.
Confirming its new status as an imperial object, the Lords of Trade purchased a copy of *Virginia and Maryland*, which they had colored and
mounted on cloth. Samuel Pepys acquired his copy in the same years
to add to his burgeoning collection of maps and books, which allowed
him to chart the expanding empire. Sponsored by Lord Baltimore, the
proprietor of Maryland, endorsed by the king, and used by metropolitan
elites, the map became an apparatus of empire by which policymakers
and polite Englishmen could project their authority abroad. *Virginia
and Maryland*, then, is more than an engraved and printed version of
Herrman's map; it is an altogether new creation.

The dual meanings Herrman's map held at different times across the
English Empire coincide with the complex way that the seventeenth-
century English Atlantic developed. The empire was produced at two
scales simultaneously, and *Virginia and Maryland* captures both of these.
At the scale of the local, the map was an expression of the commercial
and cultural links that bound the English Chesapeake to Dutch New
Netherland, a vision that prompted colonists there to regard the Mid-
Atlantic as an interimperial, and increasingly, European space. From
the perspective of merchants and state-builders in London, however,
Virginia and Maryland was a statement of empire that would help government officials and other elites to both manage and imagine an expanding empire. For them the region was not a unit in and of itself but
rather one part of a much larger empire. It is impossible to understand

the history of the Mid-Atlantic without an Atlantic perspective, which includes the rest of the British Empire, but at the same time, it is also important to be aware of the fact that this empire was fabricated out of smaller regional units, each of which had their own distinct histories. Recovering the local meanings of Herrman's map reminds us that colonists' experience of empire on the ground in their own communities shaped their Atlantic world.

Recent scholarship has suggested the profitability of examining the biographies of individuals who moved across and between empires and has revealed the extent to which early modern empires were not created by "inanimate forces" or states' ability to project absolute power abroad, but instead were also made by the "decentralized" and improvisational decisions of individuals geographically and politically distant from metropolitan institutions.[5] This book provides an example of how local stories should factor into our understanding of the way Atlantic empires were constructed and underscores the negotiated nature of empire-building.[6] In order for English officials to make sense of and manage their ever-expanding empire, they depended upon a Bohemian-born immigrant from a Dutch colony to render their lands accurately, just as the communities that colonists were building in North America depended upon settlers from all over the Atlantic to succeed. Even though this map was conceived by a unique colonial individual who moved seamlessly across colonial borders and possessed extraordinary business, diplomatic, and cartographic skills, his labor alone was not sufficient to bring the map into existence. For Herrman's work to become an engraved and printed map available for sale in London, he needed metropolitan collaborators. Without Lord Baltimore's and King Charles II's patronage and without a network of engravers, map sellers, and elite consumers, the map would have remained a series of individual manuscripts tucked into Herrman's account books or circulated among a small group of associates and would be lost to us today. These men and women's involvement, however, was not neutral; on the contrary, their participation remade the map. For them a printed map of the Chesapeake served political purposes, helping to reinforce Lord Baltimore's control of his province, tying the proprietor closely to the Stuart king, and aiding Restoration efforts to advance England's geographic knowledge and enhance its maritime empire. Paying attention to how the politics of empire in London remade Herrman's manuscript into a new object with an imperial narrative captures the ways that the developing machinery of empire in England reprocessed colonial goods and information to fit metropolitan needs.[7] Grounding the process of empire-building in an object that was both colonial and imperial, this book reveals how colonists established a sense of local place even as their actions forged an empire. A complex object produced by multiple actors and consumed by many more, the map holds in tension the countervailing levels on which the early modern British Empire was fashioned and experienced—the colonial and the metropolitan, the local and the Atlantic, the economic and the political. *Virginia and Maryland* offers an exceptional opportunity to recapture the sometimes complementary and sometimes conflicting forces that created the British Empire.

Maps as Objects

This book begins with the premise that maps are not objective documents; rather, they are multivalent material objects that have meanings far beyond the cartographic signs they contain. Maps do not simply represent geographic knowledge; instead they have the power to generate meanings.[8] In the early modern period, for example, maps of overseas territory not only reflected expanding state authority, but also helped generate colonial order by making the distant and unfamiliar accessible. Consequently, we can read maps backward to gain insight into the larger ideologies their makers and users held. At the same time as they served as iconographic texts, maps were also complex objects created in a particular time and place, yet which transcended that original context to survive into the present. This means that in order to uncover a map's power, it is necessary to study how its makers and consumers made, used, and understood it. In order to capture the interplay between map as text and map as object and the complicated role makers and users played in this process, this book is structured as a dual biography of Augustine Herrman and *Virginia and Maryland*. The idea of a "cultural biography of things" promotes study of the ways that objects, such as maps, can be put to different cultural uses by actors in disparate places and how those uses change over time based upon users' needs. Such an approach is useful in drawing out the multiple meanings this cultural artifact generated as it circulated across the empire.[9] This book's narrative thus shifts from New Netherland to the colonies of Virginia and Maryland as it traces Herrman's intertwined commercial, diplomatic, and cartographic careers alongside the comingled histories of these places to reveal how New Netherland traders like Herrman aided the development of the Chesapeake colonies. It then follows the map from the waterways of the Mid-Atlantic, where Herrman collected the data and drew the manuscript, to the workshops of London, where engraver William Faithorne turned it into a print. The scene then shifts to the fashionable 'Change Alley, where it was sold, and finally to the coffee-houses, government offices, and private homes of Restoration London, where it was consumed alongside other elements of the burgeoning information economy as elite Englishmen and women worked to build and imagine an empire. As the narrative moves from the colonies to London it pays close attention to the context of the map's production and consumption, detailing the practice of navigation and mapmaking, the emerging discourse of geography in early modern England, and the individuals both within and outside the government who promoted new maritime technologies as they constructed an empire.

It is in an imperial context that we most often see maps, thus understanding them as instruments of power, as tools used to mark territory and claim space. In the early modern Atlantic, as European empires struggled to gain sovereignty over native peoples and competed with one another, maps became one of the key technologies that allowed Europeans to picture and manage empires. *Virginia and Maryland* surely served this function, and many of the map's final consumers probably saw it in this way as well. But tracing the production and consumption of the map further indicates that what we often think of as maps are really the processed metropolitan versions of local geographies (or the engraved and printed synthesis of earlier manuscript maps). The two trajectories of the map (the local and the metropolitan) intersect at the moment of the map's drafting, engraving, and printing, which makes us think they are the same. But really what we see when we examine a map like *Virginia and Maryland* are two different objects that were born separately and continued to live separate lives as users consumed them in different ways.[10]

Maps can bridge disparate views of empire because of their unique multiplicity of form. With many artifacts there is a single producer (artist/craftsman) and a solitary moment of creation. With maps, however, not only are there often multiple producers—the person who amasses the cartographic information, the individual(s) who drafts the manuscript, the engraver(s), and the printer(s)—but there also are several moments of creation. *Virginia and Maryland* was in effect created and created again many times over the course of a century, as a manuscript, as a printed map, and as the basis for subsequent derivatives, and at multiple sites, the Chesapeake and London. By tracing the creation and consumption of *Virginia and Maryland* in both the colonies and in London, this book uncovers the ways multiple actors shaped and understood the geography of the expanding English Empire. At the same time it indicates that many similar maps contain underlying colonial articulations of empire as well.

Recreating the process by which multiple actors produced *Virginia and Maryland* allows insight into how maps, one of the central technologies of the Atlantic world, were produced. Key to understanding the settling of British America is uncovering the multidirectional flows between colonies and across the Atlantic. While the emphasis of Atlantic historians over the last three decades on the movement of goods, people, and ideas along transatlantic networks has become part of how we un-

derstand early American empires, there has been decidedly less attention paid to the practices and technologies that generated the knowledge
about distant places and made Atlantic empires possible, or to the connection between local information gathering and transatlantic circuits
of knowledge. This is particularly true when considering the role of locals, both indigenous and European, who collected the data that formed
the basis for maps of the Americas.[11] Looking closely at the production
and consumption of Herrman's map, the individuals involved, and the
historical contexts in which they operated allows us to understand the
process of acquiring and disseminating vital geographic information
about the Chesapeake.

* * *

Maps' mobility, the seeming effortlessness with which they crossed
empires and accrued new interpretations, while retaining their ability
to connote the accurate and objective, requires careful analysis to determine what these artifacts meant at a specific time in a given location.
As a manuscript, Herrman's map was a relatively inflexible object that
still carried the colonial context of its creation. This book demonstrates
that the acts of engraving, printing, advertising, selling, and consuming
Virginia and Maryland in London remade Herrman's original chart into
a new object. This process largely severed *Virginia and Maryland* from
its colonial past, allowing a variety of Englishmen to use it in ways that
Herrman could no longer control. Through the universalizing language
of cartography, *Virginia and Maryland* translated the Chesapeake's innumerable waterways into a knowable space; the map did not merely stand
for these places—it became them. As an object rather than a tangle of
waterways, the Chesapeake was no longer fearsome. As jarring as this
transformation was, though, it was not fully complete. For fundamental
to the object's authority was its ability to represent the colonial world
"exactly"—meaning that the replication process had to retain the role
Herrman played in gathering the map's precise data. In other words, to
be successful, the engraved *Virginia and Maryland* had to preserve the

moment of its creation in the colonies while also presenting that world in a manner that was appealing to its metropolitan audience.

Drawing power from its status as a technical, scientific, historical, and aesthetic object, *Virginia and Maryland* functioned like many other contemporary encyclopedic efforts to picture, rename, and categorize colonial places and things; it made the alien familiar and thus knowable. But maps, like all these forms of empirical knowledge, relied upon the individuals who gathered, organized, and presented the information. In this way, though transported to London, engraved in copper, printed on fine paper, and consumed by London's elites, a trace of the colonial would always remain.[12] The tension between local and imperial present in *Virginia and Maryland* mirrors the tension that existed in the British Empire itself. For that empire to succeed, it relied upon colonial actors to make their lands, and by extension the empire, itself productive. By the 1650s, however, it was clear that colonial and metropolitan goals often diverged, and thus the history of the development of the empire in the seventeenth century was one of complex negotiation between a multiplicity of colonial and metropolitan interests. Examining the process by which English craftsmen and consumers reshaped Herrman's colonial map into an imperial text fit for reading and display while keeping in mind the instabilities present in the final product offers a chance to recreate the process by which a collection of colonies was turned into an empire and the critical role of maps in that process.

1

The Merchant

On Sunday, October 12, 1659 the secretary of the colony of Maryland, Philip Calvert, welcomed Bohemian Augustine Herrman to his plantation, "Pope's Freehold," near St. Mary's City. Herrman was one of two emissaries whom Director-General of Dutch New Netherland Petrus Stuyvesant dispatched to Maryland to settle a border dispute between the Dutch colony and Maryland. Just two months earlier, Maryland Governor Josias Fendall and his council had demanded that the settlers living in Dutch New Amstel on the west bank of the Delaware River (in present-day Delaware) depart immediately from what Maryland's proprietor Cecil Calvert, the second Lord Baltimore, considered his territory. Lord Baltimore claimed a vast province. Running from the Potomac River north and east across the Chesapeake Bay and "unto that Part of the Bay of Delaware on the North, which lieth under the Fortieth Degree of North Latitude," the colony spanned more than twelve million acres. Baltimore was especially eager to shore up the borders of his province in the late 1650s because the colony had only just been fully restored to the family after the Calverts found themselves on the losing side during the English Civil Wars (1642–1651). As far as Stuyvesant, the Dutch West India Company (WIC), the City of Amsterdam (which operated New Amstel), and the States General of the Dutch Republic were concerned, however, the lands along the Delaware (what they called the South River) were rightful Dutch territory by virtue of Dutch discovery and exploration, WIC patents and maps, land purchases from Native Americans, and three decades of occupation.[1]

Resuming a conversation they had begun several days before, the Dutch and English negotiators quickly fell into a debate about the history of the settling of the Chesapeake and the validity of land claims.

Aiming to settle their dispute, Philip Calvert called for the dinner dishes to be cleared and dramatically produced a set of "charts or maps," three of "which he laid on the table. One was printed in Amsterdam at the direction of Captain Smith, the first discoverer of the great bay of Chesapeack or Virginia; the second one also appeared to be printed in Amsterdam at the time of Lord Balthamoer's patent"; and the third was an unattributed manuscript map. Calvert's theatrical production of his maps called upon early modern Europeans' understanding of the power of maps, which more than passively illustrating space, maps' accurate representations of borders and their recording of place names constituted acts of possession. But Calvert's maps did not "indicate the extent of Baltamoer's boundaries" as well as he had hoped. Examining the printed maps, Herrman—a merchant with extensive experience in the Chesapeake—quickly declared that the charts not only "all differed from one another" but also clumsily depicted the Chesapeake Bay, making it appear "crooked" too far "to the northeast." With his cartographic evidence effectively discounted, Calvert reverted to an argument based on first conquest, claiming "the English had first discovered and possessed all of these territories." His contention gained little traction with Herrman, who countered by asserting Dutch evidence of first discovery and habitation—two key Anglo-Dutch legal standards for possession. The conversation soon became "more and more heated" and was finally "dropped." The subsequent negotiations achieved similar results as both sides subscribed to incompatible narratives of settlement and occupation and each held conflicting land patents. Herrman eventually became so frustrated by these debates and colonial officials' reliance on inaccurate maps and documents that he resolved to construct a map of the region himself.[2]

Though the border negotiations had reached a stalemate, Herrman's meetings with Maryland's governor and council were not completely unproductive. In several "private conversation[s]" Herrman endeavored "to move [New Netherland] towards a firm relationship and confederation of trade and exchange" with Maryland. Though Maryland's councilors made it clear that "the majority of them [were] favorably disposed" to such an arrangement, they did not have the "power" to formalize it, having "no other commission than to defend Lord Balthamoor's lawful patent." On the final day of the meeting Herrman raised the possibility of establishing "trade and commerce overland between Maryland and Delaware." Meeting this time privately with Philip Calvert, Herrman assured the secretary that such a trade would benefit not only "his province" but also him and his brother, Lord Baltimore, "personally."[3] The men came to no formal agreement, but the discussions indicate that while each colony's leadership disagreed sharply—and eventually violently—about who had a rightful claim to settle the Delaware Bay, individual colonists could put these differences aside for personal or collective profit.

This comingling of imperial rivalry and interimperial trade was typical of the relationship between Dutch and English settlers in the Mid-Atlantic, where proximity on the ground, conflicting land patents, and mutual opportunities for trade encouraged both conflict and cooperation.[4] As the October 1659 meeting between New Netherland and Maryland indicates, defining colonial borders and establishing authority was important for European settlers eager for a stable legal regime that could sanction their land claims and commercial contracts, but clear borders did not preclude profitable interimperial alliances. Colonial governments simultaneously enforced borders and allowed those same borders to be permeable, especially when their porousness accommodated economic exchange. This culture of permeability was most apparent in the daily lives of colonists like Herrman, who built cross-national families, traded across imperial boundaries, and moved between empires at will. Examining the interimperial lives that Dutch and English colonists pursued, alongside the rich artifactual residue of their trade, allows us to see the everyday comingling that formed the basis of a shared Mid-Atlantic community. A resident of New Netherland and Maryland, a planter, trader, and diplomat, and part of an important intercolonial family, Augustine Herrman embodied the intimate cross-national networks that made the Dutch and English Empires possible in early North America.

Origins

Like many residents of New Netherland in the 1640s and 1650s, Augustine Herrman was not native to the Dutch Republic but was born in Bohemia in either 1621 or 1622. Located in what is now the Czech Republic, Bohemia was a kingdom of the Holy Roman Empire and part of the Habsburg Monarchy. The region was ethnically diverse, and its rulers allowed the Protestant Reformation to flourish there. Herrman's father, probably a Protestant minister, initially benefited from this environment, but after Protestant elites led a failed revolt against Holy Roman emperor and king of Bohemia Ferdinand II in 1621, the elder Herrman was forced to flee with his family amid increasing religious persecution. After a brief stay in Saxony, the Herrman family eventually relocated to the Netherlands where they probably arrived in the early 1630s. The Dutch Republic's expanding economy and its religious pluralism made it a welcoming destination for this Protestant minister's family and an exciting environment for a young man on the cusp of adulthood.[5]

Beyond these broad elements of his family's travels, no additional details of Herrman's youth are known until June 1644, when he arrived in New Netherland as the twenty-three-year-old agent for the Amsterdam mercantile firm of Peter Gabry and Sons and, for a short time, for Haarlem trader Coenraet Coymans. While little is known about Coymans, the Gabrys were one of many Dutch firms who traded occasionally in North America into the early 1650s.[6] Herrman mingled work for the Gabrys with undertakings of his own. In just his first decade in New Netherland, Herrman dealt in furs on the Hudson and Connecticut Rivers, delivered supplies to Dutch settlements on the Delaware River for the WIC, sold "divers goods" to New Sweden Governor Johan Printz in exchange for beaver pelts, exchanged Dutch goods for tobacco in the Chesapeake, and journeyed to the Dutch Republic and back. Meanwhile in New Amsterdam he invested in a privateering venture against Spanish ships and purchased a building next to the WIC Pack Huys (*warehouse*) where he stored, among other things, Chesapeake tobacco. Soon Herrman was well known not only in New Netherland but also in neighboring English and Swedish colonies in New England, the Delaware Bay, and the Chesapeake.[7]

Herrman's rapid rise during the 1640s and 1650s coincided with New Netherland's ascent from a colonial backwater to an important fur colony and regional commercial hub, which tied together European settlements from New England to Virginia. When Herrman arrived in New Netherland in 1644, the colony had just two thousand residents and its small size was indicative of its first tumultuous decades. Dutch interest in the Americas began in the late sixteenth century during the United Provinces of the Dutch Republic's long struggle for independence from the Habsburgs. Since 1611 a number of independent Dutch companies had been sending vessels to the river that Henry Hudson had first explored in 1609 to purchase beaver pelts from Native Americans in what today is New York. These activities were formalized in 1615, when the States General, the Dutch Republic's legislature, gave the New Netherland Company sole permission to outfit four voyages over a period of three years to the North (Hudson) River. Although the company's charter for exclusive trade expired in 1618 and was not renewed, the New Netherland Company continued to send fur-trading expeditions to the region through 1623, when the newly formed West India Company received a monopoly over all Dutch Atlantic trade.[8] Dutch traders were already present elsewhere in the Atlantic, most notably in West Africa, where they engaged in an active spice and gold trade, in Portuguese Brazil, where they bought sugar, and along the so-called "Wild Coast" of Spanish America (between what is today Venezuela and Suriname) and in the Caribbean, where Dutch merchants obtained salt and traded with indigenous nations. Hoping to bring order to this tangle of independent and often competing commercial interests, the States General saw the WIC as a way to consolidate Dutch interests in the Atlantic into one official trading company that could also advance martial aims as they had done with the East India Company (VOC).[9]

Despite early difficulties in raising capital and outfitting sufficient vessels, the WIC had its initial successes through warfare and conquest.

In 1624 the company captured several trading stations along the Gold Coast and the Congo River in West Africa, giving the company a foothold in the gold and slave trades. The conquest of Portuguese Brazil in 1630 further expanded the company's interests, as well as providing it direct access to Brazilian sugar, a welcome development for growing refinery businesses in Amsterdam and Rotterdam. Profitable as a plantation colony, Dutch Brazil also became an entry point for Dutch trade to the Spanish Caribbean. The settling of the Caribbean islands of St. Eustatius (1625), St. Martin (1630), and Curaçao (1634) gave the company a well-placed base for the transit trade with emerging Spanish, English, and French West Indian colonies. Soon dozens of Dutch vessels were crisscrossing the Caribbean, exchanging Dutch manufactured goods, foodstuffs, and livestock for salt, sugar, tobacco, and dyewoods, which they carried back to the Dutch Republic.

The growing potential of this transit trade, the successful West African slave trade, and a planters' revolt against Dutch rule that began in Brazil in 1645 made it clear to many in the Netherlands that an Atlantic empire based on commerce and warfare, rather than agriculture, best played to the republic's strengths. However successful the WIC's goal of building an Atlantic trading empire was in the Caribbean, the company initially failed to transfer that success to North America. As conceived in its first charters, New Netherland was to straddle three great rivers and their tributaries, allowing ready access to eager trading partners among the region's Native American nations. The central of these waterways was the North (Hudson) River, which was flanked by the South (Delaware) River and the Fresh (Connecticut) River (Figure 1.1). Aiming to capitalize on these "wide and deep" rivers well "adapted for the navigation of large ships" and the protected bays, good anchorages, and sandy shores that lined the coastline between them, the WIC's first settlements in New Netherland were small riverine trading posts designed as rudimentary bases from which to direct the fur trade. Seeking a more permanent settlement, the WIC eventually established a trading fort at the island of Manhattan in 1626. New Amsterdam, as the city would come to

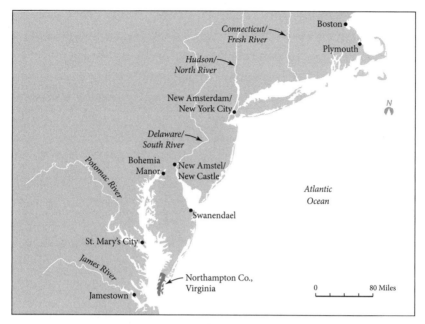

FIGURE 1.1. Map of the Mid-Atlantic in the Seventeeth Century.

be called, was situated so as to provide quick access both to the interior along the North River and to the Atlantic from its sheltered bay. Over the next half-century more towns that functioned similarly as trading hubs would come, most importantly Beverwijck, the town that grew up outside of the fur-trading base of Fort Orange on the North River, and Fort Casimir (later New Amstel), the company's outpost on the South River. While New Netherland initially concentrated on the fur trade, some in the WIC had high hopes for its agricultural possibilities, believing that in time the colony could produce grain and lumber to relieve, or even replace, Dutch dependence on imports from the Baltic states. Others saw great potential for New Netherland to function in tandem with Curaçao, supplying the island with provisions, agricultural goods, and lumber for the transit trade. But despite some success, New Netherland's farms would never meet their boosters' expectations. Instead, the fur trade and New Amsterdam's position as a commercial hub would drive the colony's economy. The Dutch men and women who populated New Netherland were what historian Donna Merwick has called an "alongshore people." Dutch colonists knit together their colony not by transforming this "very pleasant . . . though wild" land into contiguous agricultural settlements, but by successfully navigating the waterways that made trade possible. Control of rivers and coastal estuaries established a Dutch presence and would make the fortunes of New Netherland, New Amsterdam, and merchants like Herrman.[10]

Building a Regional Entrepôt

Herrman's first glimpse of New Amsterdam in the late spring of 1644 must have shocked him. Unlike the bustling metropolis he had just left, Manhattan boasted fewer than 450 colonists. They were temporarily huddled in Fort Amsterdam and afraid "to move a foot to fetch a stick of fire wood without an escort" to protect them from the Munsee-speaking peoples who largely controlled "the Island of Manhattans, killing our people [the colonists] not a thousand paces from the Fort" while the colonists' crops still lay "standing and rotting" in the fields. Meanwhile the dilapidated fort consisted only of "mounds, most of which had crumbled away," thus allowing anyone to enter "the fort on all sides."[11] The pitiful state of New Amsterdam mirrored the larger state of the colony twenty years after the WIC had taken charge. As per its original commission, the WIC held a monopoly on exporting furs. This policy created revenue for the WIC, but because it also stifled opportunity for private residents, the monopoly discouraged immigration and thereby hampered agricultural production and stalled economic diversification. Under pressure from a States General that was eager to improve the colony to counter growing English imperial competition, the directors of the WIC relinquished their fur monopoly in 1639. This decision created new openings for Amsterdam mercantile firms, which would soon dominate New Netherland's trade, and for the agents whom these trading houses sent to New Amsterdam to manage their affairs. Like

Herrman, many of the Europeans who arrived in New Amsterdam after 1639 (the colony's population roughly doubled in the next five years) were not natives of the Dutch Republic. Since its founding, the WIC had been unable to recruit sufficient employees from the republic and turned increasingly to Germans, French Huguenots, Scandinavians, and enslaved Africans to populate the colony. These residents from beyond the Netherlands (many of whom passed through the Dutch Republic on their way to the colony) made up perhaps a quarter of the population. At least one other prominent New Amsterdam trader, Frederick Philipse, was also of Bohemian ancestry.[12]

As new capital and migrants arrived in New Amsterdam, the city's prospects improved. However, continuing clashes between the WIC and private residents, incompetent leadership, and a series of devastating wars with neighboring Munsee-speaking Algonquians forestalled expanded trade and threatened to destroy the colony. What became known as Kieft's War (1642–1645) had its origins in growing tensions between coastal Munsees, who had traded largely peacefully with the Dutch for several decades, and the expanding colonial population that encroached on their lands. Adding to the climate of instability was a regional downturn in the fur trade that put added pressure on Native American trading networks and contributed to the decision by Director-General William Kieft and his council to demand payments from Manhattan's Native American neighbors to support WIC fortifications and troops. The result was a series of acts of violence carried out by both Native and European peoples. Kieft's poor leadership and his decision to launch preemptive raids turned these isolated incidents into a bloody and widespread war, which disrupted the regional alliances that made the fur trade possible, ground trade to a halt, destroyed the lives of hundreds, and threatened New Amsterdam itself. It was in this miserable situation that Herrman found New Netherland when he arrived in 1644.[13]

The turning point for New Netherland, and indeed for Herrman's success in the colony, came with the 1647 appointment of Director-General Petrus Stuyvesant who had previously served the WIC in the

Caribbean. Friction between private and WIC interests that revolved
around the proper balance between local rights and privileges and company authority persisted in New Netherland, yet Stuyvesant navigated
these successfully enough to foster prosperity, especially for New Amsterdam traders. Aware that he owed his position to the directors of the
WIC and ultimately the States General, Stuyvesant doggedly advanced
metropolitan interests. He also realized, though, that the colony's greater
success depended upon the success of New Amsterdam and its mercantile residents. Stuyvesant recognized that the best way to ease conflict
between the WIC and city residents was to give the latter a role in administering civil law, and thus he convened an advisory body called the
Nine Men in 1648. Made up of three members each from the merchants,
farmers, and burghers (resident citizens), this body offered guidance to
Stuyvesant and his council when asked. Kieft had assembled two similar committees during his administration, but he largely ignored them
and disbanded the groups when they used their position to assert bur-
gher interests. In contrast Stuyvesant understood the steep challenges
he faced in rebuilding trust between the company and the citizenry and
literally in rebuilding the crumbling city. Convening the Nine Men was
a step to accomplishing both these goals. Herrman's rapid rise to prominence in the colony and his blend of Amsterdam and local commercial
connections likely prompted Stuyvesant to see the Bohemian as someone who could help him to balance local, metropolitan, and company
interests, and so the director-general appointed Herrman to the body.[14]

Despite Stuyvesant's best efforts to work with the community, his
obligations to uphold the WIC's authority meant that residents were
unhappy when he clamped down on smuggling and more rigorously
collected company duties in an effort to protect company revenues. New
Amsterdam residents, chafing under what they saw as neglect and indif-
ference from the WIC, took advantage of their new political institution
and pushed the Nine Men to bypass the WIC and appeal directly to the
States General in Amsterdam for greater autonomy over commercial
policy. In a series of petitions that Herrman signed, the Nine Men called

for additional inducements to encourage settlement, an enhanced role in civic government, greater investments in security, and, most crucially for the local merchants whom Herrman represented, economic reforms. At the top of the Nine Men's list was relief from trade duties—especially the 5 percent duty the company placed on goods imported from surrounding English colonies—and enhanced "permission to export, sell, and barter grain, timber and all other wares and merchandise, the produce of this country, every way and every where" that was at peace with the Dutch Republic. As the chief representative of the WIC in New Netherland, Stuyvesant did not overtly support these appeals but neither did he fully oppose them; instead, he signaled his passive acquiescence to enhanced local control, which came in 1653, when the States General issued the city a municipal charter.[15]

Where Stuyvesant had the greatest direct success in merging local and company interests was in improving the colony's overall commercial position. Most important for Herrman's evolving career was Stuyvesant's support for local merchants' aims to expand their coastwise trade to New England and to the Chesapeake, a goal that would expand New Netherland's regional power as well. Key to New Amsterdam's evolving role as a regional entrepôt had been the decision to give the port the so-called staple right when the WIC had lost its trade monopoly in 1639. This provision guaranteed that "all produce and wares" exported from New Netherland or imported either from Europe or from other colonies had to pass through the city, placing the colony's trade in city merchants' hands. The same document also specified that city traders had the right "to sail and trade to the entire coast, from Florida to Newfoundland," meaning they had explicit permission to organize regional trade.[16] Looking to further enhance the power of New Amsterdam merchants, Stuyvesant proposed that the WIC raise the duties on goods sent directly from the Dutch Republic to Virginia and New England so as to divert them to Manhattan and into city traders' warehouses and vessels. Company directors in Amsterdam, eager to protect the interests of metropolitan merchants, rejected this plan, but they allowed all goods sent first to New Amsterdam and then to New England or Virginia to "pass duty free." Together these provisions meant that as New Netherland's trade with surrounding regions expanded, it would be New Amsterdam merchants who would benefit.[17]

Before regional trade could flourish, however, New Netherland needed to improve its relationships with surrounding English colonies, especially with those in New England. As early as 1627, WIC officials in New Netherland had approached Governor William Bradford of Plymouth with the hope of inaugurating profitable trade, indicating to the governor that they would send "any goods" they received from their "native countrie" that "may be serviceable unto you" in return for "either beaver or any other wares or marchandise that you should be pleased to deale for." Within a few years New Netherland was shipping "suger, linen cloth, Holland finer and courser stufes" and wampum to Plymouth in exchange for tobacco with which Plymouth had begun to experiment. The presence of wampum—or to the Dutch, zeewan—on the list of goods sent from New Netherland to Plymouth was important as these ropes of small white and purple beads strung into measured lengths would come to undergird regional trade for the next three decades. Made by native craftspeople from quahog and whelk shells found along the beaches of Long Island Sound, wampum acted as a form of currency in the fur trade and in securing strategic alliances throughout the European and Native American communities of the northeast and Mid-Atlantic. In the years following their arrival Dutch traders and their native allies controlled zeewan supplies, but after the Pequot War (1637–1638), a conflict partially motivated by New Englanders' desire to gain control of wampum, Dutch merchants were forced to purchase more of their wampum from English colonists, who in turn received it as tribute from the Native communities of southern New England. The centrality of zeewan to New Netherland's (and much of eastern North America's) economy, combined with New Englanders' growing population and appetite for trade, guaranteed that Dutch and English colonial traders were a constant presence in each others' colonies, even as each jockeyed for imperial control in coastal New England. By the 1640s English colonists especially looked to their Dutch neighbors to provide European manufactures imported from the Dutch Republic including textiles, metal goods, tobacco pipes, and ceramics as well as provisions carried from Europe and from other colonies, including sugar and fortified wines. In return New Netherland received wampum and furs together with New England–produced salted fish and corn, livestock, and tobacco imported from the Chesapeake and the West Indies.[18]

As trade between the colonies flourished, however, rising tensions over territory and Anglo-Dutch conflict in Europe threatened mutual prosperity. By the time Stuyvesant arrived in New Netherland, English colonists from Connecticut and Massachusetts who had begun flooding into the Connecticut River Valley and eastern Long Island after the end of the Pequot War were already pressuring Dutch territory. Since his arrival in 1647 Stuyvesant had corresponded with Governors John Winthrop of Massachusetts and Theophilus Eaton of New Haven in an attempt to improve relations and enhance regional trade despite growing imperial tension. Although the tone of the men's letters could often be acrimonious when touching on territorial borders, they nonetheless worked to find common ground, with the Dutch director-general going so far as to suspend the "ten per centum formerlie demanded and paid" on goods imported from New England to encourage trade.[19] As war flared between the Dutch and English in Europe, these interimperial connections became vital to preserving "trafffick[,] trade[,] & commerce" between New England and New Netherland.[20]

In 1653 local concerns merged with imperial affairs to threaten peaceful commerce. As news of conflict in Europe between the Dutch Republic and England reached New England, rumors began to spread that Stuyvesant was busy building an alliance with the region's native inhabitants in order to launch a devastating attack on New England. Key to this supposed plot was Ninigret, a Narragansett sachem, who traveled to New Amsterdam in January 1653 to allegedly meet with Stuyvesant. Although both the Narragansett sachem and the Dutch leader later denied the meeting, many New Englanders were nevertheless convinced that a combined force of Dutch and Narragansett troops meant to invade. The allegations soon found their way back to England where they became another part of London printers' pamphlet war against the Dutch and helped to fuel anti-Dutch sentiment and to aid Oliver Cromwell's decision to authorize a later abandoned attack on New Netherland. Meanwhile in eastern North America all of Stuyvesant's diplomatic skills would be needed in the coming months to reassure New Englanders that he had no intention to begin a war. Key to these efforts were Stuyvesant's relationships with New England governors. In a series of missives sent in early 1653, Stuyvesant urged continued friendship between the colonies and explained that "there shall never any appeerance of truth be found" in the rumors "touching" on a "Conspiracye with the Natives or Barbaros wild people." Instead of focusing on conflict Stuyvesant urged his English neighbors to pursue the "Continnuation of peace[,] Correspondency[,] negotiation[,] and Naighbourly frindship as formerly wee have had, with[out] taking notice of any of the differences and warrs arisin in Europe betwixt both nations."[21] The courier Stuyvesant chose to deliver this message signaled his desire that commerce remain open and his understanding that mutual economic interests provided the best hedge against conflict. That messenger was Augustine Herrman.

As important as the peaceful ties that could promote coastwise trade with New England were, it was the Chesapeake that offered the brightest prospects to New Netherland traders like Herrman, and Stuyvesant hoped to encourage this connection as well. Dutch involvement in the Chesapeake stretched back even farther than it did in New England. Dutch vessels first called at Virginia soon after that colony began to produce tobacco in the 1620s as an extension of their emerging trade in the Caribbean. Many of these early voyages were speculative offshoots of the Caribbean transit trade. Dutch shipmasters (based largely in Amsterdam and Rotterdam) loaded cargoes of household manufactured goods such as textiles and ceramics along with foodstuffs and luxury goods and sailed to the Americas. Over the course of many months the vessels cruised the Caribbean and the Chesapeake, calling at numerous ports to exchange their cargoes for tobacco. English planters welcomed the Dutch vessels not only because they supplied "all sorts of domestic manufactures, brewed beer, linen cloth, brandies, or other distilled liquors, duffels, coarse cloth, and other articles for food and raiment," but also because Dutch captains were often willing to pay more for tobacco than their English rivals. Key in allowing them to best English shipmasters was Dutch firms' access to Amsterdam's efficient capital and insurance markets, superior ship technology, and innovative industrial production.[22] Wharf-side exchanges like those used in the cruising trade could be profitable, but they were also cumbersome because they often required vessels to spend an extended period of time in port as shipboard factors or captains sought trading opportunities. In December 1642, for example, the *De Spiegel* of Rotterdam arrived near St. Mary's City in Maryland with a cargo of "sugar, strong waters, lemons, hats, shirts, stockings, frying-pans, &c." Although colonists at St. Mary's were eager to trade, it took more than two months for the captain and crew to sell their cargo and to load more than 100 hogsheads of tobacco (more than 31,000 pounds) from a number of Maryland planters, including Governor Leonard Calvert. Other times shipmasters found that they had arrived at the wrong time for trade or that without a permanent presence they could not easily collect debts.[23]

Hoping to resolve these problems and to take advantage of increased tobacco production and a shortage of shipping during the English Civil War, Dutch merchants looked to enhance the efficiency of their operations. First, some Dutch merchants migrated to the Chesapeake, where they bought land and assembled networks of planters to supply them with tobacco. Most successful of these early migrants were the brothers Arent and Dirck Cornelisz Stam, who represented the interests of a number of Amsterdam merchants. As historians Victor Enthoven and Wim Klooster have found, by 1641 their yearly trade of roughly 100,000 pounds of tobacco "greatly exceeded that of any single London merchant." Metropolitan Dutch firms also began to employ agents resident in New Amsterdam who could travel regularly to the Chesapeake to manage their trade. This is how New Amsterdam's Govert Loockerman, a longtime associate of Herrman, made his fortune. Loockerman began his career in New Netherland in 1633 working for the WIC. By 1641 he had left the company to become the local agent of powerful Amsterdam merchant Gillis Verbrugge and his son Seth. Running one of the four Amsterdam firms that dominated New Netherland's trade, the Verbrugges were regular traders to Virginia, sending more than fourteen vessels there in addition to the almost thirty they sent to New Netherland between 1641 and 1664. Key to their success was the work of Loockerman who was able to coordinate the purchase of tobacco, arrange for the dispersal of European cargoes, and perhaps most importantly offer the Verbrugges accurate and timely information about market conditions and planters' needs. In turn, working as agents gave traders like Loockerman the experience and contacts that would in time enable them to dominate Anglo-Dutch trade in the Chesapeake.[24]

As was the case for New Netherland's trade with New England, local governors supported and extended metropolitan Dutch merchants', New Netherland agents', and English planters' Anglo-Dutch trade through diplomacy. Just months after he had arrived in America, Stuyvesant approached Virginia governor William Berkeley with a plan to encourage trade, sending him a "horse of the Spanish breed" as an inducement. Stuyvesant found a willing partner. Since at least the 1620s Virginia's governors and its assembly had been doing what they could to promote Dutch trade. In March 1643, for example, the assembly passed an act that both declared "that it shall be free and lawfull for any merchant, factors or others of the Dutch nation to import wares and merchandizes and to trade or traffique for the commoditys of the collony" and relaxed earlier laws requiring that Dutch traders enter bonds for the payment of duties in England. Then, in the spring of 1647, just weeks before Stuyvesant's overture, Berkeley issued a remarkable declaration further welcoming Dutch traders to Virginia. Responding to a recent missive from Parliament that encouraged American colonists to favor English traders above foreigners, Berkeley reiterated his colony's desire for Dutch trade and pledged his defense of it.[25] Unlike Berkeley and the Virginians, Maryland's government gave a more mixed welcome to Dutch traders. In recognition of their active presence in Maryland and the benefits they brought to the colony, Lord Baltimore authorized the granting of land to some Dutchmen in 1649. The same year, however, the government imposed an export duty of sixty pounds of tobacco for each hogshead of tobacco that Dutch vessels took away as part of a larger effort to erase the colony's debts. The tax did little to discourage trade, though it must have been a disincentive: in the two years after its passage the law raised more than 12,000 pounds of tobacco.[26] Not as accommodating as those in Virginia, Maryland's laws nevertheless acknowledged the importance of Dutch traders and residents in the Chesapeake.

Building an Anglo-Dutch Network

The stability Stuyvesant brought to New Netherland and the connections he helped forge with the colony's English neighbors directly benefited Herrman. As agent for the Gabrys, Herrman managed the firm's American trade, taking charge of European shipments, distributing those goods, acquiring cargoes of furs and Chesapeake tobacco, organizing their shipment to the Netherlands, and reporting intelligence on American affairs. Though none of Herrman's correspondence with the Gabrys remains extant, it would have resembled the letters that Loockerman and the Amsterdam-based Gillis and Seth Verbrugge exchanged in the same years, albeit without the kinds of family news that cousins Govert Loockerman and the Verbrugges shared. Most critically these letters included invoices and accounts that detailed the outcome of ventures, recorded the movement of ships on which goods had been freighted, reported changing market conditions, and described the general political and commercial situation in New Netherland and in the Dutch Republic. In 1648, for example, Loockerman explained to his employers that his efforts "so far" were "gaining but little profit, even though I am one of those who have profited most" from the fur trade on the South River. He also called for them to send him a "chest with Faroese stockings" because those "are the best goods to wet people's appetite for the ship's cargo." Later that year he sent the Verbrugges a list of the prices of fifty items sold at New Amsterdam, ranging from wine, brandy, and other foodstuffs to textiles, thread, and household goods like tin chamber pots and wooden chairs.[27] This kind of precise market information, available only through an on-the-ground representative like Herrman or Loockerman, would have been vital for the Gabrys' or Verbrugges' success or failure in their New Netherland ventures. Herrman might even have requested maps or navigational guides to aid his trade on the Gabrys' behalf as Loockerman did.[28]

As a relative novice in trade, Herrman would probably have been scolded for not including exactly the information that his Amsterdam employers were looking for, just as Loockerman was in March 1648, when his cousin Seth Verbrugge offered an unsolicited lesson in letter writing. Noting that Loockerman's last letter contained too much "about the state of the country" and not enough "about the trade" that was most "dear to our hearts," Verbrugge reminded Loockerman that "it will take a whole year before we will have more of the next news" so it was imperative to learn as much as possible from each letter. To make these missives most valuable, Verbrugge instructed Loockerman to begin each letter in a "draft book . . . 14 days beforehand." Then as he thought of things necessary to the letter he could periodically add them before finally "formulat[ing] from this draft a letter in final form. This letter," Verbrugge continued, "will then be easier for you to read and more useful for the person who receives it. But that you, who has such great things at hand, would write us letters at the last minute! It is impossible, in such a short time, to think about everything and write up everything in detail for the common good."[29] In following such instructions agents, like Loockerman and Herrman translated shifting market conditions and complex business transactions into familiar forms of writing—letters and accounts—that enabled their distant employers to gauge how (and how well) their capital was being deployed.

Although we can only speculate about the contents of Herrman and the Gabrys' letters, we know more definitively that the men clashed over their business, a matter that resulted in a protracted legal dispute. The first hint of conflict between the parties emerged in April 1651, when the brothers Carel and Jean Gabry (who took over for their father after his death) requested that Herrman explain inaccuracies in his accounts with the company. There is no record of Herrman's response, but his decision later that summer to convey the deed for his brick three-story house and lot in New Amsterdam valued at 8,500 guilders to the estate of the recently deceased Peter Gabry indicates that he could not fully account for all the goods the Gabrys had dispatched to him. Declaring that he was then "not able, nor as long as he lives" would he "be able, to make any better payment in satisfaction of . . . [his] obligation," Herrman hoped the property would settle the matter. The Gabrys, however, felt the house and lot insufficient and a year later the States General interceded on the Amsterdam merchants' behalf, ordering Stuyvesant to "lend a helping hand to the Petitioners [the Gabrys] or their attorneys, that they may receive from Augustin Herman, their factor in those parts, due account, proof and remainder of the goods which he hath had to dispose of from the Petitioners and their co-partners." Looking to recover their investment, the Gabrys eventually went so far as to request that the tobacco that Virginian Edmund Scarborough owed to Herrman be impounded in Virginia until their account with Herrman was settled. In the spring of 1653 Herrman and his employer finally resolved their dispute, and the council of New Netherland publicly acknowledged that Herrman had settled with his creditors.[30]

Herrman's tenure as an agent for an Amsterdam firm embroiled him in complex legal affairs, but it also provided him an entrance into the commercial community of the Mid-Atlantic. In the same years that he traded in New Netherland and the Chesapeake on the Gabrys' behalf, he also began to erect his own commercial network as was common for representatives of Dutch firms. Things initially did not go smoothly for the ambitious young merchant. In what was likely one of his earliest (and boldest) ventures, Herrman invested in the second voyage of the New Amsterdam privateer *La Garce*. Joining with a number of other New Amsterdam traders and officials, including Director-General Kieft, Herrman must have had high hopes his investment would succeed as the privateer had successfully captured a rich Spanish vessel on its first voyage. Unfortunately for Herrman *La Garce*'s second voyage would prove a disappointment when its most valuable Spanish prize was declared invalid because it had been taken after Spain and the United Provinces concluded peace.[31] Two years later Herrman suffered another damaging commercial setback. In 1651 Herrman's vessel was anchored in a cove at the mouth of the Connecticut River near Saybrook when he encountered Englishman John Dyer and three Mohegan men. When the Mohegans approached Herrman's "Dutch vessell," they inquired if the merchant had any "coates" for sale. Herrman did have a store of coating—a heavy woolen cloth that was often used for blankets—and he replied that he was willing to sell the Mohegans "coate of two yards" for "twenty shillings . . . or two bushells of wheat." This exchange of Dutch textiles for New England wheat was unremarkable for residents from the two regions; the problem for Herrman in 1651 was that New Haven prohibited unlicensed trade with Native Americans. When some Saybrook residents suspected Herrman might also be selling guns to the Mohegans, they seized his vessel. Though Dyer later testified before the general court in Hartford that Herrman "did not trade gunns, powder and shott," the merchant was forced to pay £40 to redeem his vessel and cargo. There was no clear evidence to support the charge of arms trading against Herrman, but the fact that this man, who was no stranger to protracted legal battles, chose not to fight the fine raises the possibility that he was indeed selling more than "coates" and was happy to admit to a lesser offense so as to reclaim his vessel and cargo.[32]

The trouble Herrman encountered in Saybrook was costly, especially when combined with his failed investment in the *La Garce* and his debts to the Gabrys. But Herrman's early failures were not indicative of his skills, nor did they dull his ambitions. Later in 1651 he did the best thing that any young merchant could do to improve his prospects: he married well. Already favorably connected in New Netherland, Herrman solidified his regional and Amsterdam ties when he married Jannetje Varleth (var. Varlet) in December 1651. Jannetje's uncle was the prominent Amsterdam merchant and WIC director Pieter Varleth, and her father, Caspar Varleth, was an Amsterdam silk merchant who in 1650 had brought the family to New Netherland and established himself as an important local trader. His son Nicolaes held a post as an administrator in the WIC in New Amsterdam before launching a prosperous trading career of his own and marrying Petrus Stuyvesant's sister Anna. Meanwhile a third sibling, Anna Varleth, had recently moved with her husband, the German-born Dr. George (var. Joris) Hack, to Virginia, from where she organized a steady trade between the Chesapeake and New Netherland. Marrying into the Varleth family provided Herrman entrance into an important network that stretched from Amsterdam to New Netherland and from there to Virginia and New England. Herrman's connection to the family must have been close as he and his father-in-law, Casper Varleth, helped Casper's daughter Maria Varleth and Johannes van Beeck "secretly depart . . . for New England between 26 and 27 February [1654] in order to marry there, it is presumed, without the knowledge and against the prohibition of . . . Johan van Beeck'[s] father." The ties that bound these families together were more than just commercial; they were intimate, and as such, they were all the stronger.[33]

Though not "the first beginner of the Virginia tobacco trade" as he later claimed, Herrman was nevertheless an important link between New Netherland and the Chesapeake, and his marriage into the Varleth family was central to this success. The marriage facilitated trade with his sister-in-law Anna Varleth (who managed her own trade) and her husband, George Hack, and gave Herrman access to their Virginian networks. He also relied upon brother-in-law Johannes van Beeck to help him organize shipments of tobacco to the Dutch Republic.[34] No longer an agent for the Garbys, Herrman needed to further improve his access to tobacco and thus followed the Varleth-Hacks to Northampton County on Virginia's Eastern Shore. Purchasing a plantation in there in 1655, and then transporting servants and goods to the property (though he never intended to relocate permanently) gave Herrman a firm foot-hold in the Chesapeake and further aligned him with the locally in-fluential Varleth-Hacks.[35] The investment was also well timed to take advantage of a series of Atlantic-wide disruptions in the Chesapeake tobacco market.

The first of these came as part of the fallout from the English Civil War and the subsequent efforts of Parliament to harness overseas trade for the needs of the state. During the war most colonies stayed neutral but Virginia (along with Barbados, Bermuda, and Antigua) remained Royalist and refused to recognize the Commonwealth government. In order to subdue the Royalist colonies Parliament imposed a full trade embargo on them in 1650, banning all English and foreign vessels from their waters. The next year Parliament extended its power to regulate co-lonial trade, which it had enunciated in the Act of 1650, to the remainder of the empire with the Act of Trade and Navigation. In response to the belief that Dutch control of England's and its colonies' carrying trade was damaging England's commercial interests, this law specifically tar-geted Dutch control of Anglo-Dutch commerce. From the perspective of the Chesapeake, it required that the bulk of colonial produce (including tobacco) pass directly to England on English vessels and that colonial imports come directly from the nation where they were produced or from England. Effectively, then, the law made English colonists' trade with the Dutch illegal as many of the goods colonists imported origi-nated outside the Dutch Republic.[36]

Almost immediately those most invested in maintaining interimpe-rial commercial connections between the Chesapeake and the Neth-erlands objected to these new nationalist laws. In a fiery speech to the House of Burgess, which was later published in the Dutch Repub-lic, Berkeley denounced the Act of 1650, arguing that by eliminating

Dutch trade, it would set back the colony and "bring us to the same poverty, wherein the Dutch found and relieved us." Dutch merchants, with their long experience in the Chesapeake, concurred. In 1651 a group of nearly fifty of them (including Jean Gabry) petitioned the States General to intercede on their behalf. For "upwards of twenty years past" the traders pointed out, they had provided Virginians "with food and raiment" in return for "beavers and other eastern furs, [and] considerable tobacco," a trade that not only made them wealthy but contributed "to the support of several thousand people."[37] These appeals did little to bring the two nations to an accommodation. After talks for a planned union between them collapsed the next year and with popular opinion in both nations turning against the other, the commercial conflict erupted into a naval war. Fought mostly in northern European waters, the First Anglo-Dutch War (1652–1654) discouraged Dutch merchants from chartering ships to the Chesapeake and raised the costs of those who persisted.[38]

Together the acts of 1650 and 1651 and Atlantic warfare reversed the inroads that metropolitan Dutch firms and their agents had made in organizing Virginia's and Maryland's tobacco trade in the 1640s. Merchants based in the Dutch Republic would still occasionally venture vessels (often disguised as English ones) to the Chesapeake until at least the 1690s, but after 1652 many Amsterdam and Rotterdam merchants retreated from bilateral trade with the region, creating new opportunities for traders based in New Amsterdam. As Berkeley's 1651 address indicated, planters in the Chesapeake, even more so than those in New England, remained eager for Dutch trade because of their dependence on tobacco. Tobacco prices had been falling since the 1640s and this, combined with insufficient English shipping, made them more eager than ever to find whatever advantage they could.[39] Based in close proximity, with contacts in both the Chesapeake and the Dutch Republic, and able to use small vessels that could more easily evade authorities, New Amsterdam traders quickly redirected much of the region's Anglo-Dutch trade through the Dutch colony.

Coming exactly as these events were unfolding, Herrman's marriage into the Varleth-Hack family and his purchase of land on the Eastern Shore of Virginia positioned him well to benefit from the reordering of the tobacco market. Particularly important to his success in the tobacco trade was the geography of his chosen lands in Northampton County. The county is a twenty-mile-wide peninsula that makes up the tip of the Delmarva Peninsula. The eastern side of the county borders the Atlantic and consists of sandy soil, salt marshes, and small islands—meaning that the bulk of the population in the seventeenth century lived, as its does today, in the western portion of the county along the Chesapeake Bay. Here the soil is rich, and beginning in the 1620s English colonists began to clear its pine forests and to plant tobacco along the points of land that stretch between the small creeks and bays that line the bay. Northampton County was lightly populated until the influx of colonists to Virginia in the mid-1630s began to spill across the bay. Between 1635 and 1650 its population rose from less than four hundred European inhabitants to about one thousand. With few roads and paths connecting these plantations, with every plantation bordering a waterway, and with less than 10 percent of the population owning a horse, the English settlers of mid seventeenth-century Northampton County lived in a maritime world that would have felt familiar to a trader from the Dutch Republic like Herrman.[40]

His purchase of land there in 1655, however, was likely driven not by his comfort with the landscape but by the opportunities for trade that Northampton County offered. The expanse of the Chesapeake Bay separated the county (which was referred to as Accomack until 1642) from the rest of Virginia. This division led to political neglect but also insulated colonists from government oversight, especially when it came to enforcing trade laws. In addition to being distant from the seat of authority in Jamestown, the dispersed nature of settlement made it difficult to regulate trade. In 1641, the Virginia Assembly had tried to mandate that all tobacco be stored at two central locations from which the county's trade was to be managed. Residents, however, ignored this provision and traded from their waterside plantations. The resulting settlement pattern meant that it was virtually impossible to stop illicit trade in Northampton. Residents based along the innumerable bays lining the bayside shore regularly landed illegal cargoes and loaded tobacco without being detected. The relatively short distance across the bay meant that they could easily reach the James, York, and Rappahannock Rivers and help facilitate Dutch trade there as well. Using small vessels that could take advantage of the county's geography by operating close to the shore, permanent or temporarily resident Dutch traders like Herrman and the Varleth-Hacks came to play a central role in Northampton's tobacco economy.[41]

Herrman's investment in Northampton County solidified his ties to a thriving interconnected Anglo-Dutch community. In the 1640s and 1650s the Eastern Shore, including Northampton County, probably had the largest collection of merchants with Dutch ties in Virginia. Some of these individuals, such as Jan Michielsz (var. Michael) and John Cornelius, were Amsterdam or Rotterdam traders who decided to take up residence after traveling to the region for years. Other migrants from the Dutch Republic, such as John Custis, were not ethnically Dutch but rather were English and hailed from families who had migrated to the Dutch Republic earlier in the seventeenth century. Still others who managed Anglo-Dutch trade were Virginians who had traded to the Netherlands for years. Some of these men traveled regularly to the Netherlands, including William Waters and Argoll Yeardley, the latter of whom married John Custis's sister Ann in Rotterdam. Yeardley was the son of a former governor, a council member, and a close associate of Berkeley, and he both participated in Anglo-Dutch trade and helped protect it politically. Edmund Scarborough, similarly politically powerful and one of the largest landholders in Northampton County, did not marry into a Dutch-connected family but gained his entry to Anglo-Dutch networks through long-term commercial contacts with New Amsterdam traders and frequent travel to the Dutch colonial port. The final key group who managed Anglo-Dutch trade in Northampton County were migrants from New Amsterdam, who, like the Varleth-Hacks, retained strong ethnic and family ties there.[42] It was from among these men and women that Herrman would find his trading partners and construct an interimperial network.

Herrman prospered from trade with his new Virginia connections in the decade following his marriage, supplying salt, horses, slaves, manufactured goods, and lumber to them in return for tobacco. He traded indiscriminately in regard to nationality with a variety of contacts in Northampton County, including Englishmen John Custis, John Stringer, and Edmund Scarborough, as well as with those who had migrated from New Netherland like Anna Varleth. Well-connected on the Eastern Shore, Herrman also made inroads across the bay in nearby Hampton Roads, where Rotterdam merchant Simon Overzee owned a plantation and where he traded with Englishman Major John Billingsey who lived in Nansemond County, Virginia (just across the James River from Hampton). When both men moved to Maryland, they continued to deal with Herrman. A series of lawsuits resulting from Herrman's trade with Overzee, with whom he eventually entered into a "firme Coepartnership and Comon fellowship of trade and traffique for three yeares," describe a significant trade in tobacco. When he died, Overzee owed Herrman more than "fifteen thowsand pounds of good sound well condition Tobacco and Caske." Herrman assembled tobacco cargoes from planters like Overzee at a number of central locations on the Eastern Shore and shipped them to New Amsterdam, where merchants such as Van Beeck purchased the tobacco and re-exported it to the Netherlands.[43]

The geography of the Chesapeake and its dispersed population meant that Herrman spent considerable time in the region arranging trade and traveled widely. In the process he became familiar with the topography, perfected his English, and created the social bonds that tied Dutch and English colonies together and made it possible for both empires to benefit from successful trade. One lawsuit from Northampton County reveals the complex mechanics of Herrman's Chesapeake trade, the connections that facilitated it, and the obstacles he encountered. In the spring of 1657

Herrman and John Custis agreed to assemble a quantity of tobacco from Northampton County for shipment to New Netherland. Over the course of several weeks Herrman purchased tobacco from a number of planters, including the widow Mrs. Grace Vaughan with whom he also left "5 or 6 hogsheads" of his own tobacco to be collected with hers. Because Vaughan's tobacco was not yet ready, Herrman requested that she "send downe her tob[a]cco with his unto Some Convenient place in the County" and "then he would send . . . it unto the Dutch plantation [New Amsterdam] with his owne." It was Custis's job (together with mariner Robert Burwell) to collect the tobacco Herrman had purchased from Vaughan and other plantations in the area, store it at his house, and then deliver it to "John Green's house," leaving it there "until Such time as Augistiens [Herrman's] Vessel" arrived. Three months later Vaughan still "had heard nothing from Mr Augustine concerning the transportation of it [her tobacco] unto the dutch plantation" so she ordered Custis to detain her "15 hogs[heads] of tobacco" which he had been storing for her "at his house." As Vaughan would later discover, Custis had not cared properly for the tobacco: he'd left it "in a Very neglective [neglected] Condition" with "Some of the hog[head]s upon the ground without any thing Under them," resulting in a significant loss for the widow. In this case Herrman failed to collect the tobacco quickly enough and failed to coordinate the operation with the timely arrival of his vessel from New Netherland, but the fact that this example stands out as an exception suggests that he got the timing right more often than not.[44]

One way that Herrman hoped to avoid problems like those he encountered with Vaughan was by owning the vessels he used. As early as 1651, Herrman operated a galliot piloted by Simon Joost between New Amsterdam and Beverwijck. This might be the same vessel that Herrman took to New Haven that same year. Herrman also deployed the *Beginning* in the Chesapeake before he and fellow New Amsterdam merchant James Cade sold the vessel to John Stringer of Northampton County in August 1656 for "Seaven Thousand ponds of good, sound merchantable Virginnia leafe Tobco." Perhaps Herrman was willing to sell the *Beginning* because earlier that year he had purchased the *Mary*, another bark he used in his Virginia trade. Ten years later Herrman partnered with Ann Varleth (who was now married to Nicholas Boot, another New Amsterdam tobacco trader living on the Eastern Shore and with whom Herrman also did business) to commission James Fookes of Virginia to construct a "sloope which shall Carry thirty five hogsheads of Tobacco to bee builded all of Barrell worke with a Sufficient Cabbin." Though the terminology used to denote different types of vessels was not always consistent in the seventeenth century, the vessels—a galliot, a bark, and a sloop—that Herrman owned were all relatively similar. All would have been small and flat-bottomed; they would have likely been powered by only one small sail and possibly oars; and they would have been easily maneuverable and thus well-suited to small rivers, bays, and even creeks, yet were still seaworthy enough for coastal trade in the western Atlantic.[45]

Although he devoted most of his attention to building his Chesapeake network in the 1650s, Herrman remained on the lookout for other opportunities. One way he found these was by parlaying personal connections with those in power into business opportunities. Never an employee of the WIC, Herrman nevertheless clearly won Stuyvesant's favor. In addition to his being named as one of the Nine Men in 1648, a position that enhanced his commercial reputation, Herrman's connection to Stuyvesant likely paved the way for him to trade at the WIC's Fort Nassau on the east bank of the South River in 1649.[46] This venture familiarized Herrman with the market there, and the next year he returned, this time selling "158 ½ good merchantable winter-beavers and one guilder" worth of "divers merchandizes" to Governor Johan Printz, commander of the Swedish Fort Christina.[47] In 1658 he again called upon Stuyvesant to smooth his entrance into new markets, requesting both permission to trade to the French and Dutch colonies in the Caribbean and letters of introduction to governors there. Stuyvesant not only furnished the letters, but also hired Herrman to trade on the WIC's behalf while in the Caribbean. In April 1659 Herrman arrived in Curaçao on the WIC galliot *Nieuw Amstel*. There Herrman was to procure "as much salt" as the *Nieuw Amstel* could carry, but when he realized that "the salt" was "too heavy to take on alone as a full load," he acceded to the vice-director Mathias Beck's wishes that he load dyewood in lieu of a portion of the salt. When finished in Curaçao, Herrman took the *Nieuw Amstel* on to French St. Christopher, where he combined work for the WIC with trade of his own, procuring almost 4,000 pounds of sugar for his brother-in-law Nicholas Varleth and one barrel of sugar and two barrels of molasses for himself before departing for New Amsterdam. On the return trip, the vessel called at Dutch New Amstel on the South River, where Herrman acquired "14 bear skins, 10 tanned deer hides, 2 fox, 1 lion skin, 2 half beavers, 12 untanned deer skins, [and] 4 elk skins" for himself. The next spring the final part of Herrman's Caribbean cargo arrived: an enslaved woman he had requested of Beck.[48]

Key to Herrman's success in these years was the elaborate web of regional connections he could call on to support his trade. But as his work in the Caribbean, on the South River, and in Virginia shows, his personal presence on the ground was equally vital. Herrman spent much of the 1650s in motion, traveling throughout the Mid-Atlantic to manage his trade. Never able to stay in one place long, Herrman entrusted his wife, Jannetje Varleth, with handling his business affairs in New Amsterdam. While Dutch law resembled English law in limiting married women's economic activity, in practice many Dutch wives participated actively in commerce as agents for their husbands, as partners of their husbands, and, once given verbal or written permission from their husbands, on their own behalf. This was especially true in New Netherland, where the exigencies of colonial life meant that courts and husbands were more permissive in allowing space for women to function as traders. Unlike her sister, Anna Varleth, Jannetje Varleth was never active in trade on her own account, but she would have been an important node in Herrman's network as she helped manage his correspondence, provided news, collected or paid bills, and represented his interests in court. Born into a trading family and married to a merchant, Jannetje Varleth was probably familiar with account books, contracts, and legal processes. Her experience allowed Herrman's extensive intercolonial travels and helped make his mercantile, diplomatic, and eventually cartographic, activities possible. Jannetje Varleth's work reminds us that women's labor undergirded Atlantic networks of trade and information.[49]

Laws may have instructed otherwise, but instead of trying to impede his constant border-crossings, both Dutch and English authorities valued Herrman's skills and called upon his interimperial experience to help them maintain productive relationships with one another. In March 1660, for example, Maryland authorities named Herrman to a board to solve a legal dispute in that colony. In New Amsterdam he was prized for his expertise as well, working as an interpreter in court cases involving English traders. His language skills and ease moving between cultures were the same attributes that Stuyvesant prized when he sent him to negotiate with Maryland in 1659 and to Rhode Island on a similar mission a decade earlier.[50] These attempts to harness Herrman's expertise and connections in numerous colonies reveal how important New Amsterdam and Chesapeake traders such as Herrman were in building mutually beneficial interimperial alliances. By connecting resource-starved Chesapeake planters to Dutch markets and vice versa, and by skillfully traversing North American borders to build a larger community, these men and women enabled residents of both empires to prosper.

The Anglo-Dutch Material World

Early American settlers like Herrman moved fluidly between English and Dutch colonies to build families and commercial careers that spanned political borders and united communities in both places, even as they quarreled over borders and swore allegiance to feuding countries. To the modern reader accustomed to thinking in terms of the nation-state, it may seem discordant that colonists in the Mid-Atlantic held these seemingly opposing views simultaneously. But the very everydayness of colonists' interactions belies such a perspective. Encouraged by close religious, political, and cultural ties that had bound England and the Dutch Republic together in Europe since the Protestant Reformation, English and Dutch colonists in the Chesapeake and New Netherland lived interimperial lives and belonged to a linked Atlantic community. They owned land, organized business, and used courts in multiple empires. Likewise they married, socialized, and built families across those same borders. These interimperial interconnections and networks were so routine that they were rarely commented upon in the seventeenth century.

One particularly revealing way to glimpse Dutch and English settlers' seamless construction of a shared community is to examine the material remnants of their lives. At virtually every seventeenth-century site inhabited by European colonists that archaeologists excavate in the Chesapeake, they find earthenware, clay pipes, floor tiles, and glassware that can be identified as "Dutch" because of these artifacts' place of manufacture, their form, or their decoration. Though considered "Dutch," it is not always clear where and how these pieces arrived in the Chesapeake. It is almost impossible, for example, to know if numerous Dutch-produced tin-glazed earthenwares discovered in St. Mary's City arrived there directly from Dutch vessels calling at the city, if New Netherland traders like Herrman brought them, or if they had reached the colony from England after having been manufactured there by Dutch immigrants. The difficulty in determining the source of these Dutch objects is precisely the point: Herrman's English customers in the Chesapeake, for example, did not think of the goods they bought from him as particularly "Dutch." Instead they likely wove these inexpensive utilitarian items into their daily routines without a second thought. Despite ongoing Anglo-Dutch wars and changing metropolitan injunctions against trade, Virginians and Marylanders ate from Dutch stoneware, smoked tobacco from Dutch pipes, and sat in front of hearths decorated with Delft tiles.[51] In their very everydayness the objects that Dutch traders like Herrman brought to the region embody the deep-seated intercultural, commercial, familial, and personal ties that bound the region's residents together in practice despite those imperial divisions that separated them in principle. Always in plain sight but rarely demanding attention, these objects serve as a metaphor for Anglo-Dutch interaction in Early America.

One extraordinary piece of Virginia furniture from the middle of the seventeenth century, first discussed by furniture scholar Robert A. Leath and now in the collection of the Museum of Early Southern Decorative Arts (MESDA), is particularly useful for understanding the entangled Anglo-Dutch community of the Mid-Atlantic. Blending Dutch and English features, the piece is almost certainly a product of cross-cultural collaboration and might even be linked to Anna Varleth (Figure 1.2). This wardrobe or "close[s] cupboard" stands almost square, measuring a massive 61 ½ inches high by 61 ¾ inches wide and 20 inches deep. In size and form the piece resembles a kas or kast, a distinctly Dutch furniture form that appeared in the Netherlands at the beginning of the seventeenth century for textile storage. Typically more than six feet tall and almost as wide, Dutch kasen borrowed their design from classical architecture. Though slightly smaller in size, a mid-seventeenth-century example at Winterthur Museum, probably produced in New Netherland or New York, is typical of those crafted in North America (Figure 1.3). Two large rectangular doors made of fielded panels separated by a narrow rail dominate the piece. Each is framed by long, narrow stiles divided into three sections. Topping the entire piece is a heavy cornice that projects outward at a sharp angle. The rough finish on the kas's top suggests the maker did not intend this surface to be seen and that the kas once stood taller. Elaborate on the exterior, the kas's interior was strictly functional. It now contains only one of the two original shelves that supported the folded or rolled linens and other textiles, ceramics, and other valuables that were once stored in it. Like kasen made in the Netherlands, this New Netherland example's sheer size—especially its almost two-foot depth—and interior volume mean it would have stood prominently in a low ceilinged seventeenth-century house, serving almost as a room within a room.[52]

FIGURE 1.2. Clothes Press or Cupboard, 1680–1700, Williamsburg or Eastern Shore, Virginia. Walnut with yellow pine; HOA: 61-5/8", WOA: 61-1/4", DOA: 20-1/4". Collection of the Museum of Early Southern Decorative Arts (MESDA), Acc. 2024.1, Gift of Frank L. Horton.

FIGURE 1.3. Kas, Unknown Maker, 1650–1700, New York. 1957.0087.001. Courtesy of the Winterthur Museum, Garden, and Library.

The Virginia clothes cupboard now at MESDA shares a design and mode of construction that tie it closely to Dutch kas and the New Netherland example at Winterthur. Instead of rectangular carved stiles, the maker of the Virginia piece used carved spindles, but he carried the design across the three stiles in the manner of Dutch kasen. As in the New Netherland kas, the maker created the doors' symmetrical moldings by working with a plane directly on the wood of the doors themselves (a Dutch trait). Most indicative of Dutch influence are the Virginia cupboard's fielded door panels (they consist of a flat central surface surrounded by four beveled sides), which are held together with mortise-and-tenon joints and the piece's dovetail joinery; all three practices were used by Dutch craftsmen but rarely by the English. Finally, the unknown maker formed the Virginia piece's back with a nailed backboard much like the back and top of the New Netherland kas. As similar as it is to Dutch kasen in exterior form, the Virginia clothes cupboard differs in its interior fittings. Rather than consisting of one large chamber with several shelves, it has two distinct sections behind the doors. The larger right-hand portion had pegs on three sides from which presumably its user would have hung his or her clothes. The left side, by contrast, more closely resembles a kas in that it holds three simple shelves. As a whole, then, it represents a marriage of Dutch craftsmanship and English consumers' demand.[53]

A 1668 contract between Herrman's sister-in-law Anna Varleth Boot (who had only recently moved to Maryland after her marriage to Nicholas Boot) and furniture-maker John Rickards suggests how such a Dutch form may have acquired English features. Rickards, by all indication an Englishman who had previously been indentured to Varleth and her husband, agreed to make an impressive array of furniture for Varleth, including "Eight bedsteads, Nine tables & ten formes, five close Cupboards, five Courth Cupboards, one Courth Cupboard, . . . Six Spinne wheels, five chaire Tables, [and] four chests."[54] Varleth and Rickard's contract offers no details about the design of these articles but specifies that they will be "very handsome according to Mrs. Boote['s] . . . directions," indicating that the English Rickards and the Dutch Varleth collaborated in creating what would have been distinctive Anglo-Dutch objects. The sheer number of pieces Rickards fabricated and his location on the Eastern Shore of Virginia, not Maryland where Varleth was then living, means that these objects were likely not meant for the Dutch Varleth herself but for sale to English Virginians. Blending English and Dutch design, created by an English man, and retailed by a Dutch woman to English neighbors, these objects belie simple definitions of empire and discrete cultures. As with interimperial trade hidden behind façades of seeming national identity, the pieces Rickards produced embody a complex Anglo-Dutch cultural world that defies neat imperial categorizations.

Although unique in its specificity and its detail, this contract is only one example of Anglo-Dutch collaboration in furniture design in the region. According to Leath, fully one quarter of the fewer than twenty-four pieces of furniture that survive from the seventeenth-century Chesapeake show some Dutch cultural influence. Additionally several period probate inventories (listings of a deceased individual's property) indicate the ways that Dutch forms were modified to fit English storage practices, just as in the case of the MESDA clothes cupboard. A 1671 inventory of Norfolk County, Virginia, resident Captain William Moseley, for example, notes that he kept a "greate dutch Cash [kas]" in his hall valued at five hundred pounds of tobacco. This kas likely resembled large expensive Dutch kasen. Unlike those found in Dutch homes in the Netherlands or New Netherland, Mosely's kas was not a storage place for household linen, which he kept mainly in a separate "great dutch trunck," but rather held "his [personal] woolen waring apparel" including "one old Cloaths Suite." The Dutch Simon Overzee's English wife similarly used the top portion of her kas to store her dresses and the bottom drawers for her bodices and other smaller parts of her costume.[55] These brief glimpses testify to the ways that English men and women adapted Dutch objects to fit their own needs.

Like the prevalence of Dutch ceramics, pipes, and tiles throughout Maryland, the presence of Dutch-influenced kasen in Virginia testifies to the strong cultural and economic ties that bound the Dutch and English Mid-Atlantic together. Any visitor to a Virginia household with one of these kasen would have been unable to ignore such a significant object whose very bulk as well as its status as the most expensive case piece would have demanded attention. Yet as with the Delft tiles that surrounded many hearths and the Dutch earthenwares that graced the table, their users did not think these forms out of place. Instead English Virginians incorporated them into their routines, using Dutch goods as they did Dutch trade to meet their varied needs. Hailing from different empires, holding divergent religious beliefs, and often competing over the same lands and access to Native American trade, English and Dutch colonists in the Mid-Atlantic belonged to one larger cross-national community. That they did so does not mean that they rejected their national identities and imperial rivalries but rather that their shared experience living at the peripheries of European empires meant that imperial competition and imperial cooperation did not preclude one another. Anna Varleth had every reason to expect that her neighbors would be willing to put a piece of Dutch furniture in their English houses without feeling that they were losing their Englishness in the process.

A "Perfect Map"

In the first fifteen years Augustine Herrman lived in North America, he traveled from New Amsterdam to Dutch and Swedish outposts on the Hudson and Delaware Rivers, to English settlements in New England and the Chesapeake, and to the Dutch and French West Indies. He worked as a trader, as a diplomat, and as a politician, and he counted important merchants, governors, planters, and mariners among his partners and acquaintances. Through trade, marriage, and travel, he constructed a network of Dutch and English correspondents similarly well-versed in working across imperial borders. In short, Herrman lived in an integrated cross-national Mid-Atlantic, and these experiences as a border-crosser would frame his mapmaking, helping him to see the wider connections that bound New Netherland and the Chesapeake together. Even as he visualized an interconnected Mid-Atlantic, Herrman nevertheless understood imperial politics, and just as he did in the October 1659 border conference, he stood ready to exploit these to advance his own fortunes when the moment came.

In his report to Stuyvesant at the conclusion of his meeting with Maryland's governor and council Herrman expressed his frustration that Marylanders had refused to accept Dutch sovereignty over the South River, and he advised Stuyvesant to urge the directors of the WIC to press their case directly "to Lord Baltimore to see whether an agreement could not be made quietly with him" rather than with his assignees in the colonies. To make the Dutch case as strong as possible, Herrman continued, "the South river and the Virginias, with the lands and kills [rivers] between both, ought to be laid down on an exact scale as to longitude and latitude, in a perfect map, [so] that the extent of country on both sides may be correctly seen . . . for some maps which the English have here are utterly imperfect and prejudicial to us."[56] Herrman's hope was that an accurate map would force Baltimore to acquiesce to Dutch territorial claims. He must also have realized that a "perfect map" of the region would also greatly benefit trade. When Stuyvesant ignored Herrman's advice, the Bohemian recognized that such a map would equally appeal to New Netherland's rivals and made a similar proposal to Lord Baltimore.

Sometime in September 1660, Herrman contacted Baltimore (either directly or through his half-brother, Philip Calvert) and offered to make "an Exact Mapp of the Country" in return for land and "the Priviledges of a Mannor."[57] Several months later, in January 1661, the Governor's Council of Maryland issued letters of denization—the formal providing of trading and property rights to foreigners—for Herrman. Identifying him as a "Manhatans Marchant," the council noted that it issued the papers because Herrman "for our satisfaction and the bennefitt of trade hath drawne a Mapp of all the Rivers Creekes and Harbours thereunto belonging."[58] The Calverts were eager to establish the borders of

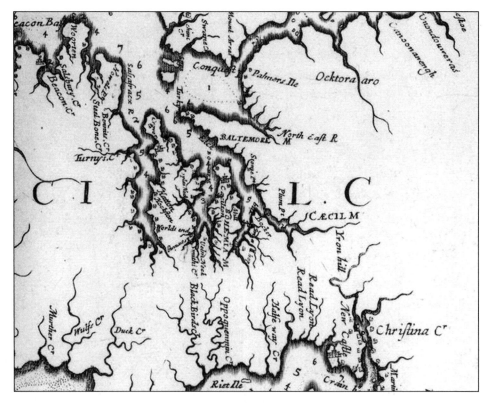

FIGURE 1.4. Augustine Herrman, *Virginia and Maryland* (detail). Herrman's property was along the Oppoquimimi (Bohemia) River in Northern Maryland. Courtesy of the Library of Congress, Geography and Map Division.

their colony more clearly: in addition to clashing with New Netherland over the Delaware River, the colony was mired in similar disputes with Virginia. Thus they also met Herrman's other demands, offering him manorial control and the permission to purchase a tract of four thousand acres (he soon added another of one thousand acres to this original purchase) along the Oppoquimimi River (which Herrman renamed the Bohemia River) in what is today Cecil County, Maryland (Figure 1.4). Here he hoped to build a plantation and town called "Caceleus" (or Cæciliton) on the Middle Neck, a spit of land nestled between two creeks he renamed the Great and Little Bohemia Rivers. Fertile and relatively unoccupied, this portion of the Upper Chesapeake had been only recently confirmed as part of Baltimore's grant after a long dispute with Virginia. Settling Herrman here, the proprietor believed, would strengthen his claim to this part of the colony. What Baltimore almost assuredly did not know, but which Herrman (and Philip Calvert) did, was that this estate sat at the western end of what would become a vital overland trading path connecting the Chesapeake and Delaware Bays. Seeking to quickly capitalize on his new lands, Herrman "took Possession and Transported his people from Manhattans . . . to seat and inhabit" the land in 1661, which he named Bohemia Manor after his distant homeland. The same year he began to construct the map that would make his name.[59]

2

The Mapmaker

In order to understand why Augustine Herrman's *Virginia and Maryland* looks the way it does, it is necessary to examine the three key factors that shaped its production: Herrman's on-the-ground experiences in the region; the Dutch cartographic, geographic, and visual traditions from which he worked; and the manner in which he constructed the map. In particular Herrman's practical understanding of the wider Mid-Atlantic, which he acquired in the course of more than two decades of travel in service of mercantile and diplomatic duties, influenced his mapping. Herrman transferred the interimperial outlook that drove these affairs to his cartographic project. As we have seen, Herrman's professional experiences led him to view the greater Chesapeake as an interconnected multi-imperial unit. Dutch and English authority surely mattered in creating the legal climate that allowed Herrman to benefit from trade and diplomacy, but as Herrman discovered, the boundaries between Dutch and English territory in the region were porous. At the same time that he built an intercolonial network, Herrman was shaped by the Dutch traditions he had acquired living in the Dutch Republic and New Netherland. As a result, Dutch nautical chart-making and the emphasis that Dutch geographers placed on mapping waterways shaped his way of imaging space and provided the cartographic language that Herrman used to create *Virginia and Maryland*. Finally Herrman's own extensive shipboard experience as a merchant prompted him to borrow navigators' tools and techniques to construct his map. Together the perspective and skills his mercantile background gave him and the larger Dutch geographic and cartographic traditions he carried from Europe led Herrman to construct a unique map that captures a distinctive colonial geography.

Most scholars have understood early modern European maps as instruments of political empire, used by governments to claim sovereignty and to comprehend the possibilities of new territories.[1] Herrman's work points to the simultaneous but overlooked underlying local meanings that were also embedded in these documents. Engraved, printed, and consumed primarily in Europe, colonial maps were nevertheless as much local as they were imperial. Recovering the ways that locals gathered and processed the cartographic information upon which maps rested is therefore critical to fully understanding this mode of representation and its importance on both sides of the Atlantic. Drawing attention to Herrman's practice of mapmaking reinserts *Virginia and Maryland* into a particular historical context that includes both the Mid-Atlantic in the seventeenth century and the techniques mapmakers used to represent space. These frames of reference matter because they determined the particular geography of the Chesapeake that Herrman produced; the making and the meaning of *Virginia and Maryland* are inseparable.[2]

Imperial Mapmaking: Seventeenth-Century Depictions of the Chesapeake

Oriented with north to the right-hand side of the map, *Virginia and Maryland* situates viewers with the Atlantic behind and the Chesapeake unfolding before them (see Figure I.1). When seen from afar, the map captures the geographic diversity of the Chesapeake in one glance. *Virginia and Maryland* presents these colonies as well as the southern half of New Jersey, ranging from the Atlantic Ocean through the tidewater counties to the foothills of the Appalachian Mountains. Water structures the map, from the Chesapeake Bay that makes up the strong horizontal void at is center to the rivers that converge there, piercing the landmass to form the transportation network which unified the region. Not limiting himself to the Chesapeake, Herrman also faithfully represented the southeastern coast of New Jersey, the Delaware Bay, and much of the Delaware River and its tributaries. Capturing a wide expanse of territory Herrman also chose to communicate meticulous detail. Ranging along nearly every shoreline are a series of minute soundings marking depths, while stipple marks and shadings cluster together to indicate shoals and isobaths (lines connecting points of equal depth on a map). On shore, where tiny icons represent plantations and Native American towns and where almost every point and bay bears a name, the precision is equally exhaustive. Confidently picturing in one sweep the terrestrial and hydrographic features of the bay that structured settlement and trade in the Mid-Atlantic, *Virginia and Maryland* is a striking cartographic work. Herrman's map marked a significant departure from previous maps of the region. To grasp his achievement it is necessary first to understand how previous mapmakers approached the region and what elements of its geography they privileged.

The most famous seventeenth-century map of the Chesapeake is John Smith's *Virginia Discouvered and Discribed*, which William Hole engraved in England in 1612 (Figure 2.1). Copied widely throughout Europe, Smith's map was the template for most depictions of the Chesapeake produced before 1673. Though his map is remarkably accurate in capturing the shape and relative size of the Chesapeake Bay and the major rivers of what would become colonial Virginia, Smith focused most of his attention on the general topography of the region (which takes up the majority of the printed surface) rather than the details of the bay's jagged coastline that most concerned Herrman. Even when mapping the particulars of the bay's hydrographic system, Smith neglected to depict the coast in any detail, leaving the viewer to wonder about the connection between land and water; he pictured them both, but left them isolated. Hole's engraving reinforced this inattention. Instead of guiding the viewer onto the landscape, the vivid black outlines of the coastline (the darkest elements on the map) serve to suggest a division between land and water. Further testifying to their interests in land rather than water, Smith and Hole allowed for iconographic confusion by allowing the banners that proclaim "Virginia" across the top of the map and label the map's scale to trail away in a manner that resembles the rivers of the region. Blurring the line between decoration

FIGURE 2.1. John Smith, *Virginia Discouvered and Discribed by Captayn John Smith Graven by William Hole*. London, 1612 [1624]. Courtesy of the Library of Congress, Geography and Map Division. Drawn in 1608, this map was first engraved and published in 1612.

and hydrology, these small details corroborate Smith's relative lack of interest in waterways.[3]

Certainly, Smith's map shares some conventions with nautical charts, as the presence of a compass rose and markings around the border to indicate latitude and longitude reveal. But these similarities seem more schematic than integral. The rhumb lines, for example, extend only a short way beyond the compass rose in the bottom left corner before they are swallowed by landmasses, making them as much decorative as useful. Meanwhile the Chesapeake Bay itself is covered with a dense network of stipple marks that effectively highlight the smooth white edge of land but preclude the inclusion of useful navigational information. Even the suggestion of navigational hazards, like the shoals between Watkins and Mumford Points on the border between Maryland's and Virginia's Eastern Shore, are pictured with such a lack of precision that they make the area seem completely impenetrable. The presence of a sea monster—commonly used to fill blank or unmapped spaces—interrupting the lettering for "Chesapeak Bay" emphasizes the fantastical over the practical. The interplay between text and image further diminishes the riverine features of *Virginia Discouvered and Discribed*. Because much of the text is small, dense, and dark, the viewer's eyes abandon it at first glance and instead gravitate to the dramatic and larger scaled iconographic indigenous figures and scenes in the top corners of the map. Even if the viewer peers closely at the crowded toponyms, the dense type intrudes upon the region's rivers and obscures their geography. It is not only the Chesapeake Bay and its rivers that received scant attention. Smith consigned the Atlantic Ocean to the bottom left-hand corner, where it serves only as a border to set off the landmasses. In fact the four icons arranged from left to right across the bottom edge of the map—a compass rose, a ship, a scale and dividers, and Smith's coat of arms—overwhelm and minimize the colony's connection to the Atlantic. The cumulative effect of all of these features is that land and people dominate Smith's print, and water is relegated to a place of secondary importance.

Created both as a separate publication and to illustrate his promotional pamphlet, *A Map of Virginia with a Description of the Country, the Commodities, People, Government and Religion*, Smith's map was intended to encourage settlement and to claim Virginia as an English colony. His goals were both cartographic—to "present to the eye the way of the mountains and current of the rivers"—and perhaps more importantly, ethnographic—to clearly illustrate the "several habitations" of Native Americans in Tsenacommacah (the Powhatan's name for their territory) and their commercial possibilities. The sheer quantity of ethnographic data Smith presented (there are more than forty named Native towns along the Rappahannock River alone) commands viewers' attention.[4] Moreover, the massive and elaborately figured Susquehannock warrior (borrowed from a Theodor de Bry engraving) in the upper right-hand corner and the textual and visual recounting of Smith's encounter with Wahunsonacock in the upper left immediately proclaim the centrality of ethnography in Smith's rendering of Virginia's geography. As exotic as these native peoples appear, however, the large central banner renaming Tsenacommacah "Virginia" and the royal coat of arms superimposed just above the label "Powhatan" reassure viewers that the English were coopting Tsenacommacah and that Native Americans would soon accept the authority of the English crown. Underlying this narrative of conquest (as opposed to discovery) is the depiction of Virginia's boundaries to match those of Tsenacommacah not the larger landmass detailed in the Virginia Company's charter. Smith's political and ethnographic interests reinforced one another elsewhere as well. Smith and Hole covered the land's surface with dense type that located 166 Native American communities, and they dotted the area with icons for trees and hills that marked the region's terrain. By demonstrating Smith's seemingly indisputable geographic command of Virginia, his map claimed this place for England.[5] *Virginia Discouvered and Discribed* is a map of possession designed to draw the viewer quickly away from the Atlantic to the continent itself so that he or she can imaginatively possess it.

Smith's was a marvelous achievement, and it was wildly popular. In an exhaustive study Colie Verner has found that just two decades after it first appeared, Hole's original plate had been reworked eleven times to meet unprecedented consumer demand. Meanwhile, Dutch atlas makers Willem Janszoon Blaeu and Henricus Hondius incorporated Smith's cartography in their own work, ensuring the map's wide distribution across Europe.[6] Though not all imitators maintained Smith's focus on ethnography, many nevertheless preserved his emphasis on terrestrial over hydrographic features. The unknown maker of *Nova Terra-Mariæ Tabula*, for example, employed Smith's depiction of the general shape of the Chesapeake while sweeping aside Smith's ethnographic information to meet new imperatives (Figure 2.2). This map, which was included

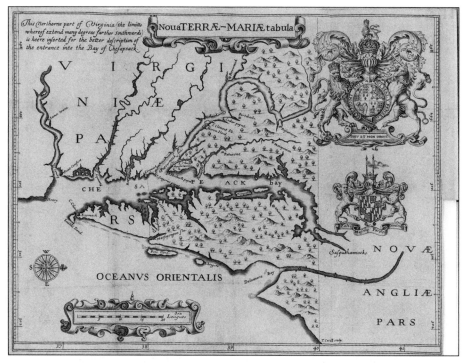

FIGURE 2.2. *Nova Terra-Mariæ Tabula.* [London, 1635.] Courtesy of the John Carter Brown Library at Brown University.

with Lord Baltimore's 1635 promotional tract, *A Relation of Maryland*, highlighted the territory encompassing Baltimore's new patent and took particular care to delineate the borders of the still mostly uninhabited colony. Designed to attract settlers to Maryland and present the new colony to Englishmen, the map was often bound so that it would open opposite Chapter 2 of the pamphlet, "A Description of the Country." In addition, in order to reinforce the textual description of the colony offered in the pamphlet, the maker of *Nova Terra-Mariæ* removed most of Smith's Native American settlements and erased the terrestrial icons within Virginia's borders.[7] In sweeping aside Smith's ethnographic information as well as eliminating the trees and mountains from Virginia while leaving these icons in Maryland, the map suggests that Virginia has already been cleared and occupied and prospective colonists should turn their attention to Maryland, an untapped land ready for settlement.

In thus promoting Maryland, the maker of *Nova Terra-Mariæ* paid little attention to the bay's hydrographic system. More inviting than Smith's darkly colored Chesapeake Bay, the opening of the bay is generous, but as the viewer's eye moves along it toward Maryland, the bay begins to close up as textual labels, islands, and dark shading intrude into the waterway. The result is that much of the bay is pictured as a relatively narrow channel pinched between Virginia and Maryland, an effect that diminishes its importance. The maker also offers little additional navigational information or tools beyond a standard compass rose to communicate the importance of water to the region. The scales of latitude and longitude at the map's borders are likewise unconnected to navigation, serving mainly to clearly mark the northern and southern latitudes (40 and 38 degrees) of Baltimore's grant. Like Smith's *Virginia Discouvered and Discribed*, *Nova Terra-Mariæ* is typical of early seventeenth-century English maps of the Americas in its efforts to claim land, mark borders, and encourage settlement.

Whereas the maker of *Nova Terra-Mariæ* eliminated *Virginia Discouvered and Discribed*'s detailed iconography to more clearly picture Maryland, Ralph Hall, the engraver of *Virginia* (1635), took the opposite approach (Figure 2.3). While this map also derives from Smith's, Hall was uninterested in representing the geography of Virginia with any precision. Instead, Hall used the colony as a tableau across which to narrate fantastical scenes of the wonders of the Americas.[8] Hall anchors three of the four corners of the map with relatively crude interpretations of De Bry's engravings of native peoples. At the center of the image, Hall engraved a hunting scene in which two colonists fire muskets at a menagerie of exotic animals including boars, a panther, deer, numerous birds, and a sea monster. Three Native American figures, two with their bows drawn, either join the hunt or—because of their position—may be soon to engage the colonists in combat. Lost in these vignettes of adventure is any detailed sense of the Chesapeake's geography.

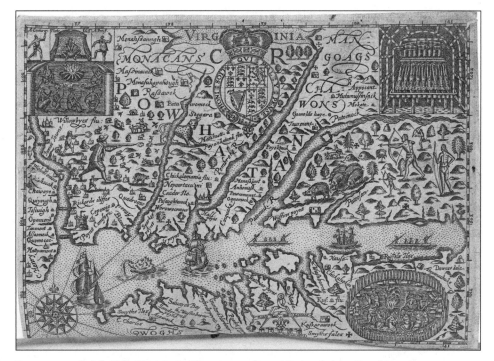

FIGURE 2.3. Ralph Hall, *Virginia*, in *Historia mundi; or, Mercator's Atlas*. London, 1635. Courtesy of the John Carter Brown Library at Brown University.

While these three maps underplay the centrality of the water to development of the region by understating their depiction of the Chesapeake Bay, a fourth mid-seventeenth century map of the region largely eliminated the importance of that body of water altogether. John Ferrar's *A mapp of Virginia discouered to ye Falls* (1651), included in the third edition of Edward Williams's *Virgo Triumphans*, is one of the region's most extraordinary maps (Figure 2.4). Largely following Smith in his hydrography of the bay, Ferrar added an oddly curving Hudson River to his map. Located at the right edge, it dramatically sweeps upward to join the St. Lawrence and form a northwest passage to the Pacific. An early officer in the Virginia Company, which had hoped to find a passage to the East Indies, Ferrar claimed through his map that one could reach the "peaceful Indian Sea" in "ten dayes march . . . from the head of Jeames River, over those hills and through the rich adjacent Valleyes." Reviving the already dismissed notion that the Pacific coast lay just beyond the mountains of Virginia, *A mapp of Virginia* depicts the region as a staging ground for trade to the east. In highlighting the Pacific Ocean lurking just to the west, Ferrar suggests that Virginia is most important not as a plantation colony but rather as a link to the East Indies. In such a scenario the Chesapeake Bay becomes not a vital connection to a range of profitable, if widely dispersed, settlements but rather an intermediate zone for global trade.[9] Simultaneously Ferrar's fantastical reimagining of North America's geography reveals the ways these maps captured English men and women's hopes for colonization as much as its reality. Designed to promote colonization, describe English adventurers' discoveries in the Americas, and

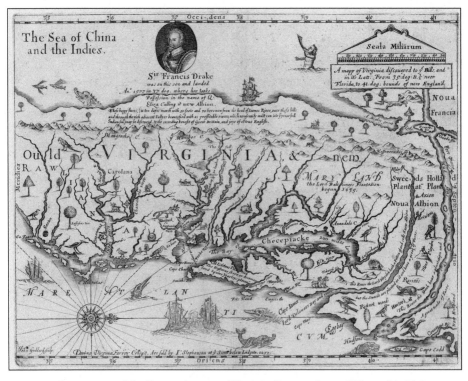

FIGURE 2.4. John Ferrar, *A mapp of Virginia discouered to ye Hills, and in it's Latt: From 35 deg: & 1/2 neer Florida to 41 deg: bounds of new England.* London, 1651. Courtesy of the John Carter Brown Library at Brown University.

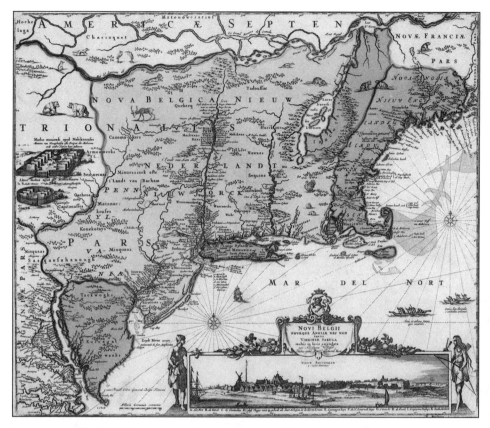

FIGURE 2.5. *Novi Belgii Novæque Angliæ: Nec non partis Virginiæ tabula.* Amsterdam, 1655 [1685]. Courtesy of the Library of Congress, Geography and Map Division.

incorporate the region into the empire, these four early English maps of the Chesapeake spoke primarily to metropolitan consumers.

Dutch maps of the mid-Atlantic, such as the so-called Jansson-Visscher map series, also obscured the size and expanse of the Chesapeake Bay, though from the perspective of different imperial concerns. Intended to show the entire eastern seaboard stretching from Cape Henry in Virginia to the St. Lawrence in New France, the first of these maps was engraved in 1650 or 1651 by Jan Jansson and later published as *Novi Belgii Novæque Angliæ: Nec non partis Virginiæ tabula* by Nicolas Janszoon Visscher (Figure 2.5). The Visscher map incorpo-

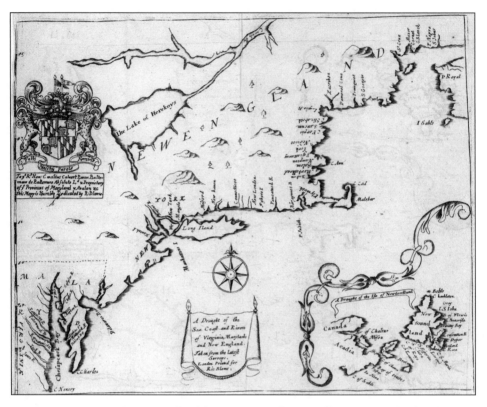

FIGURE 2.6. *A Draught of the Sea Coast and Rivers, of Virginia, Maryland, and New England, Taken from the latest Surveys.* London [1672]. Courtesy of the John Carter Brown Library at Brown University.

rated elements of Smith's map of Virginia as well as his 1614 *Map of New England*, but because the scale of the Jansson-Visscher maps is much smaller than that of Smith's works, they do not contain the same level of detail. Included in the popular atlases produced by Jansson, Johan Blaeu, and others, these Dutch maps place New Netherland at the center of the continent, emphasizing this colony's prominent position between New England and Virginia and Maryland from which it could prosper through trade with both English regions. The Chesapeake Bay is forced to the bottom left of the map, a position of secondary importance.[10]

During the 1670s a number of English mapmakers took a similar wide-angled approach to mapping the North American coast. The unidentified English maker of *A Draught of the Sea Coast and Rivers, of Virginia, Maryland, and New England* (1672) replicated the framing of the Jansson-Visscher map series, but this time, with the English having conquered New Netherland, the map celebrated the removal of Dutch colonies from continental North America (Figure 2.6). Significantly, he altered the shape of the Chesapeake, opening the bay and narrowing the Delmarva Peninsula to highlight the bay's expanse and the prominence of its rivers. But he did so in only a schematic way that related little detail to its viewers beyond the location of Maryland's border and still privileged the New York region. Robert Morden and William Berry's *New Map of the English Plantations in America* (1673) likewise heralds the growth of the English Empire after the Restoration (Figure 2.7) showing, "all the English Plantations in *America*," and "their true Scituation and [the] distance for Trade, either from *England*, or one with another; as also their chief Townes, Ports, Harbors, Rivers, &c."[11] In picturing the entire English Atlantic on one sheet, Morden and Berry followed Richard Blome's lead in representing a mature empire ready for growth. Published just prior to Herrman's *Virginia and Maryland*, these two English maps epitomize the typical cartographic representation of this region in the late seventeenth century. Despite their claims to originality, however, neither of these maps improves on earlier depictions of the region. As with all of the predecessors to *Virginia and Maryland* discussed here, the information about the Chesapeake they presented continued to be derived largely from the data Smith collected more than six decades earlier. Metropolitan cartographers might reframe older renderings of the Mid-Atlantic according to new imperial conditions, but without new data their depictions of the Chesapeake remained static.

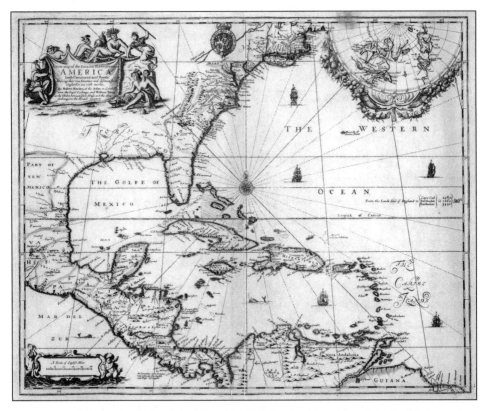

FIGURE 2.7. Robert Morden and William Berry, *A New Map of the English Plantations in America both Continent and Ilands, Shewing their true Situation and distance, from England or one with another*. London, [1673]. Courtesy of the John Carter Brown Library at Brown University.

Breaking from Tradition: Herrman's Map of the Chesapeake

A resident of the Chesapeake, Augustine Herrman could conduct the long-term information gathering that allowed him to distinguish his map from contemporary English and Dutch examples. Unlike earlier maps, whose makers based their work on the efforts of prior cartographers, intense but relatively short-term observational trips, and secondhand data gathered from mariners and explorers, Herrman's map was a

product of his long experience in the region. Herrman drew the Chesapeake as he visualized it and used it in his trading career. Not overly
concerned with depicting land and its boundaries, Herrman chose to
leave much of the continent's interior blank, labeling only the colonies
and counties and selected Native American settlements (see Figure I.1).
Instead, he devoted most of his map to an incredibly detailed depiction
of the waterways and the coastline, the areas with which he as a trader
he had great familiarity and a decision that emphasized commercial
development and, through their absence, diminished Native American
spaces in favor of an interconnected Anglo-Dutch trading community.

Herrman employed at least four cartographic techniques uncommon
in period maps of the Americas to achieve a comprehensive image of the
Chesapeake's hydrography. First, he included extensive soundings marking the depth of shipping lanes at the entrance to the Chesapeake Bay and
at other critical places. Robert Dudley, an English cartographer working
in Florence, had incorporated some of this information in his 1646 map
of the Chesapeake, *Carta Particolare Della Virginia Vecchia e Nuoua*—
part of his 1646 atlas, *Dell'Arcano del Mare* (Mysteries of the Sea), and the
first map of the Chesapeake to employ the Mercator projection—but his
soundings and depictions of shoals are scattered and imprecise compared
with Herrman's careful and comprehensive work (Figure 2.8). Dudley,
for example, indicated the depth of the opening of the bay between Cape
Henry and what he called Cape Smith at the southern tip of the Delmarva
Peninsula, recording two depths (of 10 and 15 fathoms) in this region. Farther south, near Cape Hatteras, he labeled depths more frequently, but
they are still few in number. In contrast with Dudley, Herrman included
nearly fifteen soundings at the mouth of the bay. And whereas Herrman's
readings extend into the bay and mark almost every major inlet, Dudley
included no information within the bay itself.

Herrman paired these soundings with a series of markings designed to
indicate marshes, shoals, and sandbars (Figure 2.9). Common in Dutch
and English charts of the coastlines of Europe, these isobaths and their
accompanying soundings enabled Herrman to indicate the precise lo-

FIGURE 2.8. Robert Dudley, *Carta Particolare Della Virginia Vecchia e Nuoua*, in *Dell'Arcano del Mare*, vol. 2. Florence, 1646. From the Lionel Pincus and Princess Firyal Map Division, New York Public Library.

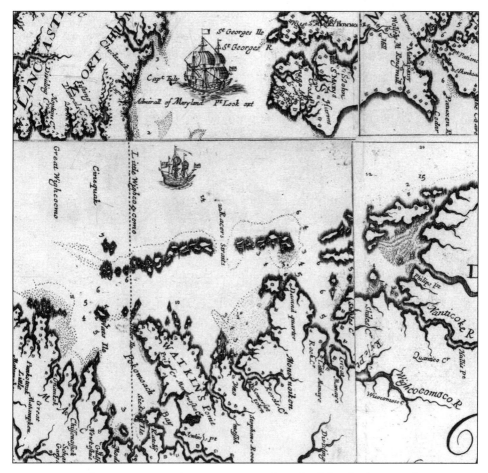

FIGURE 2.9. Soundings in Augustine Herrman, *Virginia and Maryland* (detail). The numerals seen here indicate water depth.

cation of navigable shipping channels and supplied unsurpassed information about access points to mariners. Dudley's map, which contained by far the most complete navigational information on the region before Herrman's, also pictured shoals and sand bars. But again, they are more schematic than precise. Surrounding every peninsula in Virginia from Point Comfort north, for example, Dudley marked sandbars with stipple lines in a double semicircle formation. These markings suggest the presence of shoals, but unlike Herrman, Dudley made no effort to capture the exact (often irregular) shape these shoals actually took. Reinforcing its precision, *Virginia and Maryland* distinguished between various types of underwater obstacles, such that a dotted pattern indicates sandbars, for example, and a collection of short lines marks marshes (Figure 2.10).

Herrman's decision to diligently record the sites of plantations (designated by small icons) made his inclusion of information about shallow water approaches all the more useful for the traders and shipmasters who might transfer the data from *Virginia and Maryland* (or perhaps from the manuscript versions of the map that might have circulated within the Chesapeake) to their own maps. In constructing the map, Herrman employed the same equirectangular projection—in which lines of latitude and longitude are straight, equally spaced, and intersect one another at right angles—used by mapmakers such as Smith to systematically locate each of these places. Though only the markings for latitude are extant on the border of *Virginia and Maryland*, four manuscript charts based on Herrman's work, which include a longitudinal scale and his original proposal, specifying that the map would be drawn according to "an exact scale as to longitude and latitude," make clear that the Bohemian's original manuscript must have included both scales.[12] While equirectangular projections often result in significant distortions if used to map a large area (since the projection cannot account for the convergence of longitudinal lines the longitudinal scale does not remain consistent at the poles), this projection is useful for regional maps, and it allowed Herrman to display the relative location of features lying on different, parallel planes to one another. Herrman's plotting and the map's projection would have permitted users to accurately gauge the distances between plantations scattered along many rivers. Mariners could then plot complex courses to travel more efficiently between nonsequential points, something that many earlier maps did not easily allow.[13]

Finally, in addition to *Virginia and Maryland*'s navigational features and its projection, its size allowed Herrman to locate topographic elements with an impressive degree of precision. Measuring 37 ¼ by 31

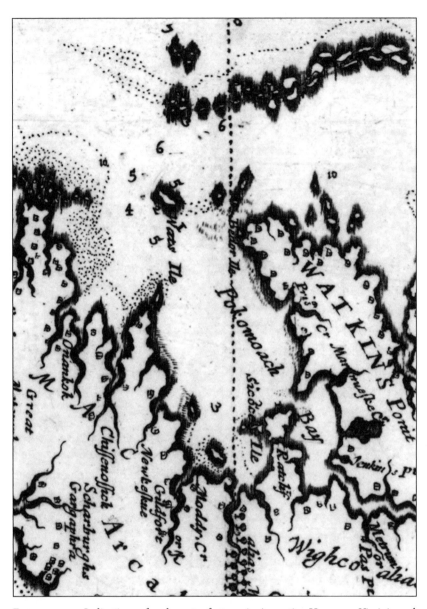

FIGURE 2.10. Indications of underwater features in Augustine Herrman, *Virginia and Maryland* (detail). The dotted pattern indicates sandbars and a collection of short lines marks marshes.

¼ inches, the map dwarfs many of its contemporaries, which were designed for inclusion in books and atlases. This large format—common for sea charts—made it possible for Herrman to use a scale of one inch per 7.5 English miles compared with the one inch per 42 English miles Dudley employed and the one inch per 110 miles Jansson used. To be sure, mariners most likely would not have directly used such an expensive map as a navigational tool aboard their vessels. However, shipmasters could have taken tracings from it, a common practice for making more inexpensive and mobile versions of maps, which they could easily transport.[14] The extraordinary information about waterways and coastlines *Virginia and Maryland* contained reflects the accumulated and collected knowledge of a navigator with long experience in the Chesapeake. Taken together, the features of Herrman's map not only communicate his understanding of the Mid-Atlantic as an integrated and mutually dependent whole but also aided others in entering this cross-national commercial space. Far from a static image of Native communities, waterways, and English plantations, the map equips viewers with the tools needed to link the parts of the Chesapeake together.

Dutch Cartographic Traditions

In his concentration on coastwise navigation, Herrman worked closely within a Dutch mode of mapmaking that he likely first encountered as a young man in Amsterdam while training to become a merchant. The first topographic depictions in this tradition can be more accurately called hydrographic charts than maps. Until 1584, when Dutch engraver and former pilot Lucas Janszoon Waghenaer published the first printed atlas of sea charts, *Die Speighel de Zeevaert* (The Mariner's Mirror), most northern European mariners navigated not by maps, which were largely useless in charting precise courses, but by referring to printed descriptions of coastlines and ports called "rutters" by the Dutch and "waggoners" by the English. Produced by collating experienced mariners' observations, rutters had created a common corpus of

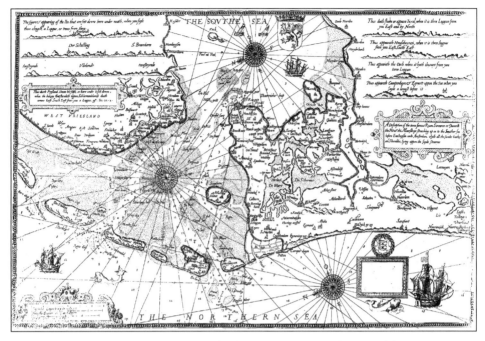

FIGURE 2.11. Lucas Janszoon Waghenaer. *The mariners mirrour*. London, 1588. (2) 1v-2r. Courtesy of the Henry E. Huntington Library and Art Gallery. One page of Waghenaer's guide to sea charts, this map pictures the coastline of North Holland.

Netherlandish navigational knowledge by the sixteenth century. Using these textual guides in conjunction with compass bearings and estimates of their speed, pilots navigated by marking their progress between a series of fixed points, a form of navigation known as dead reckoning. Waghenaer's sea charts enhanced mariners' rutters by adding a series of detailed coastal depictions that contained depth data for shoals, sandbars, and tidal variations; inserting intersecting rhumb lines (lines of constant compass bearing radiating out from one or more points); and adding multiple distance scales. Waghenaer also paired his charts with detailed inset maps of the mouths of rivers and harbors and panoramic views of the coastline, such as those visible on either side of the landmass in his chart of the Dutch Republic (Figure 2.11). A pilot himself, Waghenaer did more than compile this information; he completed many of these sketches himself just as navigation manuals instructed all pilots to do as they traveled. So-called *paskaerts*, or passage charts, greatly improved navigation by collecting textual and visual information in one place and linking it together. But because most *paskaerts* did not account for the earth's curvature, they did not represent coastlines accurately enough for mathematical navigation, and thus pilots still had to sail sequentially from point to point using dead reckoning. [15]

During the next few decades, however, Dutch cartographers continued to develop new techniques that would further heighten maps' utility to sea masters. When Waghenaer published *Die Speighel de Zeevaert* in the 1580s, Amsterdam lagged behind Antwerp and other Low Country cities in cartographic production. The Dutch Republic's war with Spain and increased overseas trade soon helped to reverse this deficit by galvanizing residents' desire for maps. Aided by the immigration of experienced cartographers and engravers fleeing from Ghent and Bruges as Spanish armies invaded the Low Countries, Amsterdam quickly became the center of European mapmaking. Foremost in Amsterdam mapmakers' success may well have been their willingness to quickly adopt a new projection that Geradus Mercator, a Flemish cartographer working in Germany, introduced in 1569. The use of Mercator's projection—a way to project the curved lines of latitude and longitude onto a flat surface so that they represented a line of constant compass bearing—quickly transformed Dutch navigational maps. Before Mercator, mapmakers could choose either a projection that allowed them to easily plot courses directly on the chart or one that accurately represented nonsequential points in relation to one another; they could not do both. If makers designed their work for navigators, they selected a rectangular form with intersecting rhumb lines upon which to plot their map. But if their intent was to serve educational or display purposes, they often employed a Ptolemaic (or equirectangular) structure of equidistant longitudinal and latitudinal lines. The first of these formats allowed mariners to trace out routes of constant compass bearing along the rhumb lines and to move from line to line as they progressed toward their destination. But, unlike evenly gridded Ptolemaic maps, charts based on intersecting rhumb lines did not accurately locate nonsequential points with respect to one another. Meanwhile, Ptolemaic maps captured such features in relation to one another but were largely useless for sailors because they did not account for the curvature of the earth, a particular problem in northern Europe, where proximity to the North Pole intensified these distortions. Moreover, with a Ptolemaic projection, straight lines on the map were not of one constant compass bearing, meaning that if a navigator used them to plot a route, he would have had to constantly adjust the ship's bearing as he sailed, an almost impossible task. The Mercator projection was so valuable because it bridged these technologies, uniting the best features of equirectangular and rhumb line projections. Made up of a grid of parallel equally spaced longitudinal meridians that intersect latitudinal parallels at right angles like equirectangular projections, Mercator charts are distinct in that the parallels are spaced increasingly distant from one another as they approach the poles. The result is that straight lines on the map are of one compass bearing. Mercator's projection therefore better accounted for the earth's curvature than other period projections, enabling mariners to sail from point to point by simply following the bearing of a straight line connecting those points on their map while other users could easily locate points according to latitude and longitude.[16]

In the first decades of the seventeenth century, Amsterdam's mapmakers, led by Petrus Plancius (often called the father of Dutch cartography) and Jodocus Hondius (who acquired the Mercator plates in 1604), embraced Mercator's projection along with other cartographic innovations to produce Europe's finest atlases. Published first in 1606, the Mercator-Hondius atlases contained uniform maps derived from Portuguese, Spanish, and Dutch sources all engraved in the same style. Beautifully rendered and containing the most up-to-date topographic data, these atlases appealed to navigators seeking technical information, state builders crafting empires, and consumers who desired them as luxury goods. The end result was that they thrust Amsterdam to the forefront of northern European cartography.

While large expensive atlases dominated Amsterdam's market, makers also produced numerous specialized maps intended for specific audiences. The Dutch East India Company (VOC), for example, sponsored an active cartographic program, instructing captains and supercargoes to transmit their manuscript maps and other navigational data to company-employed chart-makers who collated the information and produced new maps (many on the Mercator projection) of the East Indies for use on subsequent ventures. Lagging behind the East Indies in importance to the Dutch Republic, the Atlantic largely did not get similar detailed attention until the formation of the Dutch West India Company (WIC) in 1621. Building on earlier collections of narrative descriptions and coastal charts, Willem Janszoon Blaeu published the first map of the Atlantic on Mercator's projection in 1629, and others soon followed. Mathematically projected maps, however, did not simply displace earlier navigational aids; the two forms worked in tandem with the former allowing for accurate trans-Atlantic crossings and the latter for precise sailing along coastlines. Throughout the 1620s and 1630s, the WIC sponsored the production of detailed hydrographic charts for American coastlines under the leadership of Hessel Gerritszoon. These charts—which still included detailed narrative and visual descriptions of coastlines, prevailing winds, and shoals drawn from mariners' experiences—were combined with projected maps to offer some of the most complete navigation manuals in Europe.

Among the most prized mid-seventeenth-century Dutch works to depict the Mid-Atlantic in this tradition of navigational charts were Johannes Vingboons's sea charts. One of the leading Dutch cartographers of the early seventeenth century, Vingboons—who worked with Gerritszoon—produced hundreds of charts, mostly of the East and West Indies. Initially designed to help Dutch mariners working for the VOC and the WIC, these charts circulated in manuscript form before many were printed at the end of the seventeenth century. Typical of Dutch sailing charts of the period, Vingboons's *Carte vande Svydt Rivier in Niew*

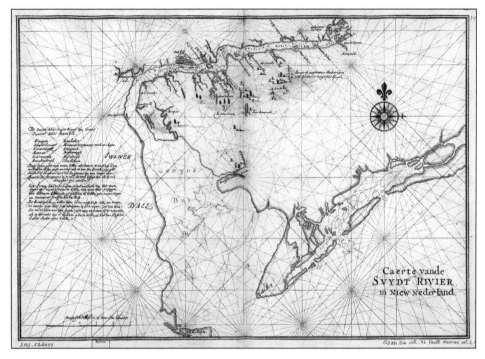

FIGURE 2.12. Johannes Vingboons, *Carte vande Svydt Rivier in Niew Nederland*, 1639.
Courtesy of the Library of Congress, Geography and Map Division.

Nederland (Figure 2.12) offers what was unsurpassed detail about the
Delaware River when it was completed around 1639. Its most prominent features are the soundings and markings indicating the presence
of shoals within the Delaware Bay and River. Vingboons also employed
compass roses and intersecting rhumb lines to help mariners navigate
to these places. Probably constructed based on information gathered
from Dutch mariners as well as other charts of the region, this map
would have facilitated Dutch trade in the Mid-Atlantic, and if using
it in conjunction with another Vingboons chart that covers the whole
region from New France to Virginia, *Pascaert van Nieuw Nederlandt,
Virginia, ende Nieuw-Engelandt*, a mariner would be able both to sail
long distances accurately and to navigate complex waterways with preci-

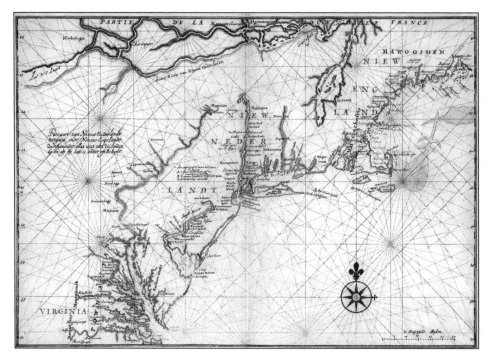

FIGURE 2.13. Johannes Vingboons, *Pascaert van Nieuw Nederlandt, Virginia, ende Nieuw-Engelandt*, 1639. Courtesy of the Library of Congress, Geography and Map Division.

sion (Figure 2.13).[17] Not quite as detailed as Herrman's map and already based on out-of-date information by the time Vingboons completed them, these maps nevertheless help explain why Dutch traders and shipmasters had such commercial advantages over those from other empires in the seventeenth century.

Charting the Chesapeake and the Art of Navigation

In constructing *Virginia and Maryland*, Herrman worked in this Dutch cartographic tradition, producing a technologically advanced map based on detailed local information that was useful for accurate navigation. Herrman probably also labored in the same manner as Dutch chart-makers, approaching his task from the perspective of a navigator rather than of a land surveyor. Instead of collecting information from returning captains, as was common in the Netherlands, Herrman did much of the work himself, routinely sketching the coastlines and harbors of places where he traded and combining these with detailed logbook entries, measurements of distances between points, soundings, and a set of intersecting compass bearings that recorded the major features of the entrances and coastlines of rivers and bays.[18] Because Herrman and other colonial mapmakers left no detailed account of how they worked, the evidence for Herrman's methods is necessarily circumstantial. But given his long commercial experience, it is reasonable to believe that he drew upon the navigational skills most merchants who went to sea possessed. Despite numerous historians' assumptions, there is no evidence that Herrman ever trained or worked as a surveyor. Of the many recorded efforts he made to secure and protect his various estates, none mentions his own efforts to survey his land, and in fact Herrman often hired surveyors. Rather than approaching his work from the tradition of surveying, Herrman most likely learned his mapmaking by working on the sea.[19]

Buttressing the argument that he worked from the perspective of a mariner is that Herrman's map differs significantly from those surviving examples individuals skilled in land-based surveying produced. Completed and published just over a decade after Herrman's map, William Reid's *A map of the Rariton River* (1685) is a good example of the way surveyors depicted space (Figure 2.14). Reid, a trained surveyor possibly sent to New Jersey in response to the governor's 1684 complaint that "an exact Mapp of the Countrey is not yet drawn," spent about four years delineating the settlements of East Jersey.[20] His map includes waterways and a number of soundings in the Rariton Bay that resemble Herrman's work, but Reid lavished the most attention on his representation of boundaries. The largest of these, between East and West Jersey, were drawn distinctly at the top of the map and labeled with precise measurements. Even more prominent are the marked plats of land, the products of individual sur-

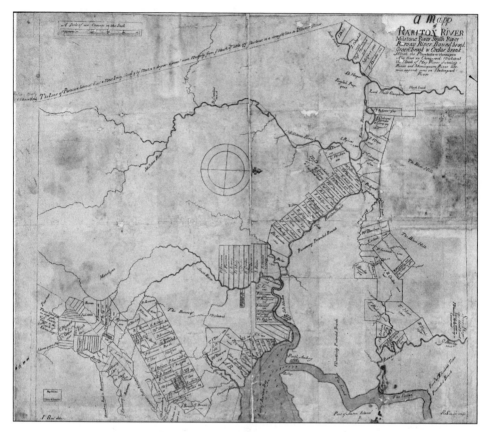

FIGURE 2.14. William Reid, *A map of the Rariton River, Milstone River, South River,*
1685. Courtesy of the Library of Congress, Geography and Map Division.

veys, many of which are designated with their owner's name, the plat
number, and their size. Reid's property-focused *A map of the Rariton
River* reveals a distinct difference between the ways a surveyor and a
navigator conceptualized space.[21] Working on land, Reid transferred the
boundaries settlers marked with trees and rocks into lines on his image,
while Herrman, working from the water, transposed the navigational
points used by mariners to set their courses onto his map.

Although they conceived of the landscape differently, the mathematical skills that Reid and Herrman possessed would have been similar.

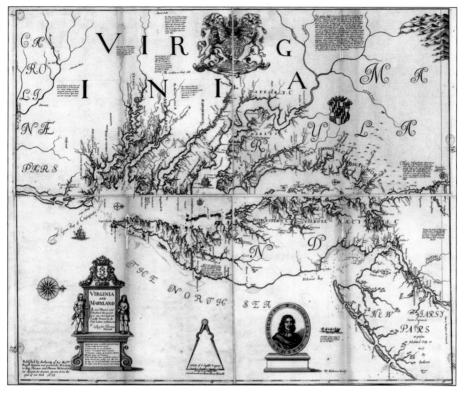

Augustine Herrman, *Virginia and Maryland As it is Planted and Inhabited this present Year 1670 Surveyed and Exactly Drawne by the Only Labour & Endeavour of Augustin Herrman Bohemiensis; W. Faithorne, sculpt.* London, 1673. Courtesy of the Library of Congress, Geography and Map Division.

Augustine Herrman, *Virginia and Maryland As it is Planted and Inhabited* (Detail.)

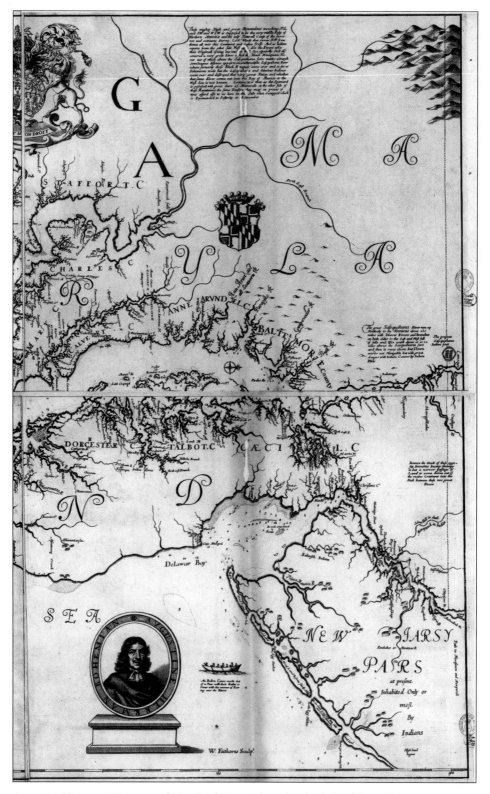

Augustine Herrman, *Virginia and Maryland As it is Planted and Inhabited* (Detail.)

Clothes Press or Cupboard, 1680–1700, Williamsburg or Eastern Shore, Virginia. Walnut with yellow pine; HOA: 61-5/8", WOA: 61-1/4", DOA: 20-1/4". Collection of the Museum of Early Southern Decorative Arts (MESDA), Acc. 2024.1, Gift of Frank L. Horton.

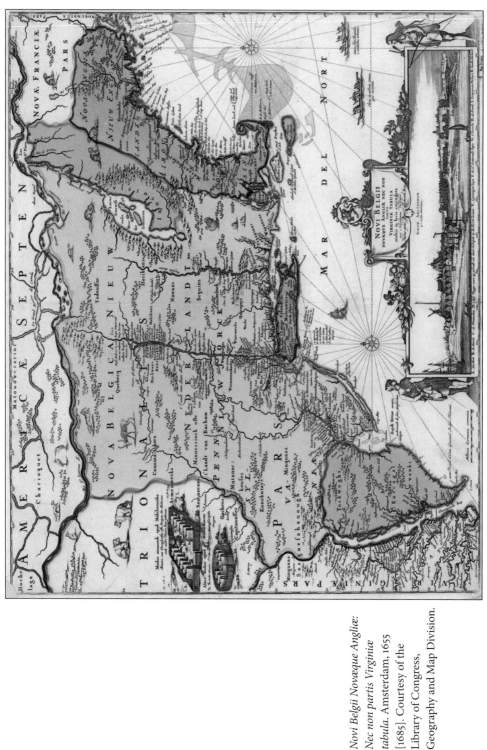

Novi Belgii Noveque Angliæ: Nec non partis Virginiæ tabula. Amsterdam, 1655 [1685]. Courtesy of the Library of Congress, Geography and Map Division.

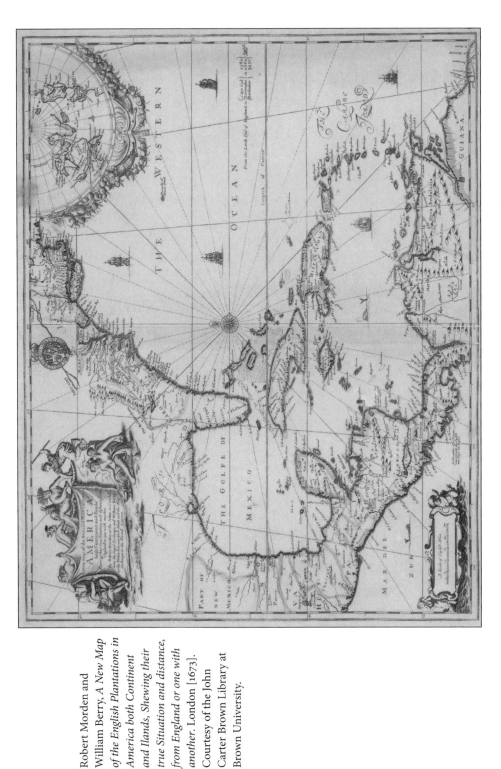

Robert Morden and William Berry, *A New Map of the English Plantations in America both Continent and Ilands, Shewing their true Situation and distance, from England or one with another.* London [1673]. Courtesy of the John Carter Brown Library at Brown University.

Robert Dudley, *Carta Particolare Della Virginia Vecchia e Nuoua*, in *Dell'Arcano del Mare*, vol. 2. Florence, 1646. From the Lionel Pincus and Princess Firyal Map Division, New York Public Library.

Johannes Vingboons, *Carte vande Suydt Rivier in Niew Nederland*, 1639. Courtesy of the Library of Congress, Geography and Map Division.

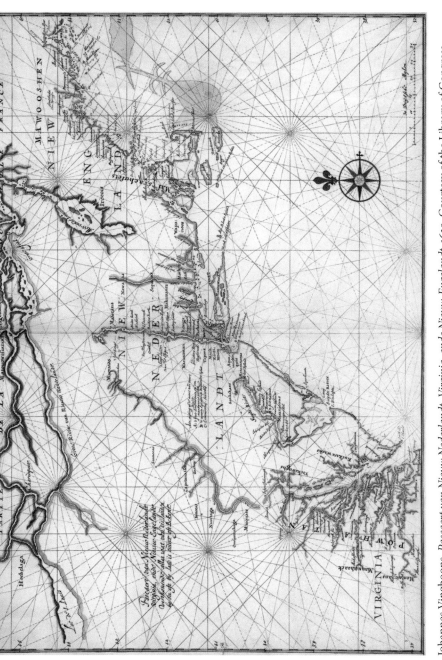

Johannes Vingboons, *Pascaert van Nieuw Nederlandt, Virginia, ende Nieuw-Engelandt*, 1639. Courtesy of the Library of Congress, Geography and Map Division.

View of New Amsterdam (New York) made on the spot, ca. 1650, perhaps by Augustijn Heerman. Courtesy of the Austrian National Library, Vienna, Picture Archive, E 23.652-C. This image is most likely one of Herrman's topographical views. Director-General Stuyvesant noted that Herrman had completed such as view in 1656 or 1657. It is perhaps the view that appears as an inset in the Jansson-Visscher map series.

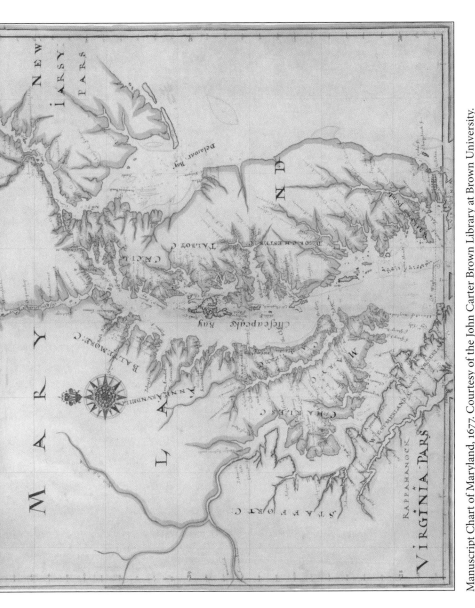

Manuscript Chart of Maryland, 1677. Courtesy of the John Carter Brown Library at Brown University.

Manuscript Chart of Virginia, 1677. Courtesy of the John Carter Brown Library at Brown University.

Frontispiece by William Faithorne, after Gilbert Soest, to John Kersey's *The Elements of that Mathematical Art Commonly Called Algebra*, 1673. © National Portrait Gallery, London.

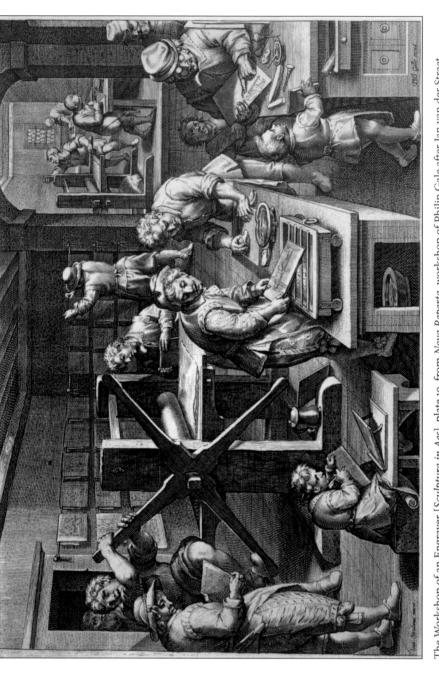

The Workshop of an Engraver [*Sculptura in Aes*], plate 19, from *Nova Reperta*, workshop of Philip Gale after Jan van der Straet published by Philips Galle, ca. 1600. Courtesy of the Metropolitan Museum, Harris Brisbane Dick Fund, 1953. www.metmuseum.org.

Theodor de Bry, title page from *A briefe and true report of the new found land of Virginia.* Frankfurt, 1590. Courtesy of the John Carter Brown Library at Brown University.

View of Pepys's library in Buckingham Street, showing his juxtaposition of books, maps and portraits. By permission of the Pepys Library, Magdalene College, Cambridge.

As part of his training to be a merchant Herrman undoubtedly studied mathematics, navigation, and the use of sea instruments. He would therefore have been familiar with navigational texts such as Martín Cortés's 1551 *Breve Compendio de la Sphera y de la Arte de Navegar* (The Art of Navigation), the introduction to Waghenaer's *Die Speitghel de Zeevaert*, and Willem Janszoon Blaeu's *Het Licht der Zeevaert* (The Light of Navigation, 1608), which included information on mathematical principles, chart-making, perspectival drawing, and basic surveying techniques. English authors produced similar books, sometimes translating Spanish or Dutch imprints, as in William Bourne's *A regiment for the sea* (1574), which was a loose translation and reworking of Cortés's work, and more famously an English edition of Waghenaer's volume, which Ashley Anthony brought out in London, entitled *The mariners mirrour* (1588). Other English writers produced their own manuals. Among the most popular of these were William Cuningham's *The cosmographical glasse* (1559), John Davis's *The Seamans Secret* (1595), and in the later seventeenth century, John Seller's *Practical navigation* (1680). Designed as practical guides that blended theory with hands-on application, these books went through many editions and were widely available throughout Europe. Herrman almost certainly would have had access to some of these works as a youth in Amsterdam. Similar books were also available in New Netherland and Maryland. When the former Swedish merchant turned American colonist Jonas Bronck died in New Netherland in 1643, for example, he owned Willem Janszoon Blaeu's *Zeespiegel* (1623) as well as two other navigation manuals, a sea atlas, and a navigational guide that included instructions for calculating longitude and latitude.[22]

These manuals offered general instructions for those for hoping to learn "the perfect skill and science of Navigation," a group that included merchants and gentlemen as well as men training to be sea captains. Thus *The mariners mirrour* directed the student of navigation to "Diligently . . . marke, What buildings, Castles, Towers, Churches, Hil[l]s . . . Downes, Windmills, or other marks [that] are standing on the land" as he traveled by sea. Being sure to "pourtray with his penne . . . [each

place's] beare[ing], and how fare Distaunt" each was one from one another, the mariner could then create an accurate picture of the coastline.
Supplementing these observations, the budding navigator should also
"Diligently indevour to seeke out and finde the true Depth and channel"
of ports and their approaches. Taking time to "often cast the Lead," he
should "exactly note in his Compt-booke, how farre off, all the shoals
and sands lie from the shoare." Keeping such a record of both coastlines
and sea bottoms would not only aid the captain or merchant in the future, but, according to Waghanaer, if those doing so took the time to
"print and publish" these sailing instructions, they would help "the fur-
derance of safer sea-faring" for all.[23] The habit of sequential observation
Herrman garnered from such manuals would have provided him with
the skill set he needed to navigate unfamiliar waters and a foundation
for constructing his map.

A vital part of learning to navigate from texts like Waghenaer's was
mastering navigational instruments such as the cross-staff and astrolabe.
These tools enabled Herrman to locate places in relation to each other,
allowing him to accurately depict winding rivers and permitting users of
the map to gauge the distance between many features. Charles Calvert,
the third Lord Baltimore, highlighted exactly this feature of Herrman's
map in 1678, writing, "[the] Longitude and Latitude of this Provynce
are well described and . . . sett forth in a Late mapp or Chart of this
Provynce . . . lately made and prepared by one Augustine Herman."[24]
Because Herrman's probate inventory does not survive, it is impossible to say for certain, but he probably owned or had access to a basic
set of navigational instruments. These likely included those that John
Davis recommended for seamen in 1595—namely, the "Sea Compass,
Chart[,] and Cros-staff," as well as the mariner's astrolabe, circumferentor (used to measure angles), and quadrant (used for estimating latitude).[25] Though not always reliable when used on the deck of a rolling
ship, these instruments were standard parts of the skilled navigator's and
chart-maker's collection. In *The general historie of Virginia* John Smith
described his fine brass and ivory sea compass and reflected upon the

advantages that a cross staff offered for navigation.[26] When Richard Norwood, a surveyor, mapmaker, and author of a popular navigation manual, died in Bermuda in 1675, he owned a cross-staff, a quadrant, and a circumferentor.[27] While these scientific devices were not necessary for mariners negotiating coastlines (a captain's compass, log and line, and sea chart were often sufficient for this task), for the mapmaker interested in locating points on a geometric plane (or for captains sailing far from the coast), they were essential because they allowed individuals to establish latitude and longitude as best they could.

Mariners and surveyors primarily determined latitude (the angular distance north or south along the surface of the earth from the equator) and longitude (the angular distance east or west along the surface of the earth from a meridian) by observing the position of celestial bodies and comparing these readings to published charts and tables. If Herrman followed the lead of most mid-seventeenth-century geographers in calculating latitude, he would have employed a cross-staff, quadrant, or mariner's astrolabe to measure the angle between the horizon and the sun at its highest point ("merioninal altitude") or between the horizon and any of a number of stars at their zenith. Each of these instruments varied in their construction but in essence all included an eyepiece and a scale. The easiest of these to use and the most readily available was the cross-staff, a straight piece of wood about 30–36 inches long with a smaller transverse piece attached through a perforated hole at right angles to the longer piece. Bracing himself firmly, Herrman would have held the cross-staff to his eye, moving the "Transversary upon . . . [the] Staff to and fro . . . until at one and the same instant" he was able to position the "upper edge of . . . [the] Transversary" upon "halfe the body of the Sun, or Stars" and "the lower edge" so that it "touch[ed] the Horizon, at that place where it seemeth that the skie and the Seas are joined." Next, Herrman would have recorded the reading along the graduated staff to determine the angle of elevation of the celestial body, which corresponds to its altitude. After selecting the printed table appropriate for his position and performing several basic mathematical calculations,

Herrman could then have converted his reading from the staff into a precise latitude.[28]

More problematic than measuring latitude was calculating longitude. Because the earth rotates around an axis, the two poles and the equator offer fixed points of reference from which to measure latitude. In determining longitude, however, two fixed points do not exist. Eventually astronomers and geographers realized that if they could accurately determine the difference in time from their position to a common meridian (zero degrees longitude) they would be able to determine their position (each hour the earth rotates 15 degrees, meaning that each degree of longitude equaled four minutes) in reference to that meridian. The result expressed in degrees would be their longitude. In the seventeenth century, however, the development of accurate chronometers was still in the future, and navigators had to improvise to determine longitude. Most commonly, they simply did not calculate it, using knowledge of the latitudes of their origin and destination points in tandem with their course and speed (inferred from experience or measured with the log and line) to mark their progress along a sea chart. If they veered off course, they could refer to published tables that provided new bearings by which they could correct their course. During the late Renaissance geographers looking for more precision developed a variety of complex astronomical and mathematical techniques to calculate longitude, but these gave them only a rough approximation of their longitudinal position.[29]

It is possible Herrman used these advanced methods to locate selected points, but more likely the trader disregarded these laborious techniques for finding latitude and longitude and instead relied on more practical ways to accurately place features on a plane in relation to one another. One such technique, borrowed from surveying and included in some navigation manuals, was the use of triangulation. This process involves determining the precise location of a point through the principles of geometry and the use of measuring chains and a magnetic compass or, less commonly in colonial America, a circumferentor (a compass fitted with

an eye-sight) to measure angles.[30] Knowing the distance between two
fixed points and the angles from them to the third point, it is possible
to use mathematics and the principles of trigonometry to determine the
location of the third point. Surveyors calculated these distances with
the use of specially made chains, hacking paths through the wilderness
in order to measure distances. Because triangulation was not common
in surveying large areas of land until the end of the seventeenth century and was far too time consuming to be used extensively, it is highly
unlikely that Herrman surveyed the entire coastline of the Chesapeake
in this manner. It is possible, however, that he calculated the distance
between selected coastal points whose latitude he had already determined in the same manner that sailors estimated distance at sea—by
dead-reckoning. In fact, the surveyor Richard Norwood assumed that
it would be navigators, not surveyors, who would use the trigonometric
techniques he taught when he titled his surveying guide *The Sea-Man's
Practice* (1639).[31] Although these methods to compute distances would
not have given Herrman a precise latitude and longitude for each place
on his map, they would have allowed him to place nonlinear points accurately in reference to one another. Then, working from a grid of places
for which he had calculated latitude, Herrman could fashion a map useful for navigation.[32]

Making the Map

While his map was not published until 1673, Herrman had begun collecting the information on distances, bearings, depths, and the locations
of geographic features that underlay *Virginia and Maryland* almost
twenty years earlier when he began to frequent the region as a trader.
While there is no direct evidence of how Herrman worked, John Smith's
account of his production of a map of New England offers insight into
Herrman's efforts, despite the evident differences in their final images.
Over the course of several months in 1614, Smith "with eight or nine
others . . . Rang[ed] the coast [of New England] in a small boat" looking

for opportunities to trade with Native Americans. Finding few, Smith and his men nevertheless took the opportunity to chart New England's coastline as he determined that the "six or seaven . . . plots [sea charts] of those Northern parts" he owned were "so unlike each to other, and most so differing from any true proportion, or resemblance of the Country" that they did him "no good." Aiming to rectify this situation, Smith took detailed measurements as he went, drawing a "Map from Point to Point, Ile to Ile, and Harbour to Harbour" and recording "the Soundings, Sands, Rocks, & Land-marks" as he "passed close aboard the Shore."[33] Smith's process would have been familiar to many mariners and closely mirrors the instructions found in navigation manuals. Working three decades, later Herrman most likely labored in the same way, perhaps using a small boat manned by his slaves to range the waterways of the Chesapeake.

Unfortunately none of the ephemeral documents such as manuscript maps, records of soundings, or textual descriptions of the shore Herrman would have produced as he worked survive to shed light on his exact procedures for collecting information. A perspectival sketch of New Amsterdam, however, which he may have completed sometime in 1656 or 1657, suggests his constant acquisition of topographical data (Figure 2.15). Made from a boat just off the coast and perhaps sketched on one of Herrman's many trips undertaken during these years between New Amsterdam and the Chesapeake, this drawing shows the general profile of the city with a key indicating its major features. Not intended for publication, the sketch demonstrates Herrman's consistent interest in collecting and processing source material for the geography of the region.[34] In fact he may already have produced a prototype of his map of the Chesapeake by 1661, only a year after first proposing the project. It would have been impossible for Herrman to map the entire Chesapeake in this short time, and thus the prototype must have been based on earlier drawings and measurements. Governor Charles Calvert noted as much when in July 1663 he reported to his father, Lord Baltimore, that "I shall speake to Augustine as your Lordship formerly writt about

FIGURE 2.15. View of New Amsterdam (New York) made on the spot, ca. 1650, perhaps by Augustine Herrman. Courtesy of the Austrian National Library, Vienna, Picture Archive, E 23.652-C. This image is most likely one of Herrman's topographical views. Director-General Stuyvesant noted that Herrman had completed such as view in 1656 or 1657. It is perhaps the view that appears as an inset in the Jansson-Visscher map series.

a particular Mapp for St. Johns & West St. Marys [counties]." Sometime between 1661 and February 1666, Herrman must have shown either one of these drafts to an associate of Lord Baltimore because that month Lord Baltimore noted that he had been "well informed" of "a certeine Mapp or Card of our said Province & of the Limits and boundaryes of the same" that Herrman had made but he had yet to see. Herrman certainly added new data to his findings after these dates—later in life he noted that it was only in 1670 after "having his Mapp finished upon his own Cost and Charge no less then to the Valu[e] of about 200 pounds Sterling besides his own Labour" that he had it "sent into England," to be engraved—but it is unlikely he started from scratch when Lord Baltimore commissioned the map in 1660.[35]

Although Herrman claimed that his map was the product of "his own Labour" he did not work in isolation. As a merchant who traveled widely in the Chesapeake for decades, Herrman would have garnered

much geographic knowledge from conversations with mariners, planters, merchants, and perhaps Native Americans. As local experts, these
individuals would have been especially helpful to Herrman in working out the precise details of the coastline. Innumerable small bays and
creeks make up the shoreline of the Chesapeake Bay, and it was locals
who knew these best. In 1658, for example, Eastern Shore mariner Robert Burwell was carrying Herrman's tobacco to John Custis's plantation
when "Extreordinary foule wether" prevented him from navigating the
narrow "Chanell" leading to Custis's plantation. Unfamiliar with the
small waterway, Burwell "was forced to get mr Cusis him selfe to pilate"
the vessel "into the Creek." This minor incident indicates how valuable
local geographic knowledge was for commercial success in the Chesapeake. It stands to reason that Herrman would have relied on business
partners like Custis who knew local waterways intimately to help refine
his mapping.[36] No doubt Herrman consulted his friends', partners', and
acquaintances' own manuscript maps and embellishments of printed
maps as he worked, just as he had in 1659, when Philip Calvert showed
his map of the Chesapeake "in manuscript" to Herrman. It is also likely
that Herrman shared his own rough maps with others. This is probably
how Herrman's cartographic information circulated among colonists in
the late seventeenth-century Mid-Atlantic as there is no evidence that
more than one of the printed versions of *Virginia and Maryland* was
ever sent to the Chesapeake.[37] In addition to consulting with other Europeans, Herrman may also have relied upon indigenous informants.
Though no direct evidence of this collaboration exists, other colonial
mapmakers garnered geographic information from Native American
sources. Famously John Smith relied extensively on what he called "information of the Savages" when completing *Virginia Discouvered and
Discribed*.[38] As a merchant and diplomat, Herrman worked with Native
peoples and used them as guides over his long career. His map contains
detailed information about Native American settlements, most notably
the Lenape villages of Southern New Jersey and the residences of the

Susquehannanock and the Choptico in Maryland.[39] Although far from definitive, this circumstantial evidence suggests that Herrman may have incorporated Native American geographic knowledge into his map.

In addition to the information Herrman gathered from colonial and possibly Native American sources, his critique of other maps of the region at the New Netherland–Maryland border conference of 1659 points to his familiarity with contemporary manuscript and printed charts. Prior to sending his map for engraving, he almost surely supplemented or cross-checked his work with these sources. When Director General of New Netherland Petrus Stuyvesant named Herrman an official emissary for the 1659 summit, he could very well have given Herrman access to his collection of WIC maps and rutters in preparation for his mission. While not as organized or secretive as the VOC in controlling cartographic information, WIC mapmakers like Hessel Gerritszoon and Joannes Vingboons routinely interviewed captains who returned from the Americas and scrutinized their logbooks, as we have seen. They then compiled this data into collaborative charts, navigational manuals, and printed maps. When officials like Stuyvesant were deployed to overseas posts, they took copies of these materials with them. This centralized system meant that Herrman might very well have had access to Vingboons's Atlantic charts, including, for example, *Caert vande Svydt Rivier in Niew Nederland* (see Figure 2.12). Though significantly different from Herrman's map in its framing, naming of geographic features, and presentation of data, Vingboons's chart's inclusion of shoals and sandbars (as imprecise as they were) would have provided Herrman a starting point for his more complete rendition. Pulling from other similar manuscript maps (many of which probably do not survive) would have allowed Herrman to fill in missing or under-surveyed regions while simultaneously reassuring himself of the accuracy of his own work. It is also possible that Herrman had access to publicly circulating printed materials. Most important of these would have been Johannes De Laet's the *Nieuwe wereldt* (New World) published first in 1625 then updated in 1630. A director of the WIC, De Laet intended this volume as an aid to the newly formed WIC, and as such, the book contained a history of the settlement of the Americas together with detailed navigational information about the shape of coasts, the courses of rivers, and the presence of sandbars, all drawn from previously published works, manuscript journals, and notes that skippers and pilots had deposited in the WIC archives. While we cannot know if Herrman ever saw *Nieuwe wereldt,* fellow New Netherland trader Govert Loockermans was familiar enough with it to note that a copy of "the book by Jan de Laedt" would be necessary if he was to trade at "a river south of Virginia at 35 or 36 degrees" (modern day North Carolina), which Native Americans had told him about. A set of sea charts of North America that appeared in Dutch sea atlases such as Theunis Jacobszoon Lootsman's *Nieuw Water-Werelt, Ofte Zee-Atlas* (1666) could have offered Herrman an additional resource. Not as detailed as Vingboons's manuscript charts and based on decades-old data, these maps still would have been useful to Herrman.[40]

Once satisfied that he had collected enough information, Herrman transformed his data into a manuscript map. According to navigational manuals such as Cuningham's, the first step Herrman took in drawing a map was determining the extent of the area he intended to depict and dividing the paper accordingly. Drawing a meridian down the paper's center (from the published map we can deduce Herrman chose the center of the Bay itself as this line), the mapmaker divided his paper into a precisely measured grid with equally placed lines of latitude at "right Lines, or parallels," which he in turn labeled at their ends. At this point the mapmaker observed the number of degrees that the northern and southern parts of the region to be mapped deviated from the equator. Using a set of tables that Cuningham (and others like him) provided, the mapmaker then transferred the proportion of minutes and seconds equal to each degree of latitude to his chart with his compass by pricking the paper equally on each side from the meridian. Finally, the maker connected "the prickes in the hi[gh]er part of the Table, unto the Prickes in the lower part" to form the meridians. The result was a graticule—a proportional grid of latitude and longitude.[41] Using his observations of compass bearings and distances between coastal features, the precise locations of key points, the relative locations of others, sketches of the coastline, and his own experiences in moving around the Bay, Herrman laid these elements over his grid with the aid of a compass and dividers. Next, he referred to his detailed log-book entries describing the main channels along rivers and the presence of sandbars and shoals to add navigational information. The final step was to fill in the soundings he had made.

Although no copy of Herrman's manuscript map—or maps—exists, other roughly contemporary examples and several likely derivatives provide some idea of what this lost map may have looked like. One possibility is that as he worked, Herrman drew individual maps of each river in the Chesapeake and then combined these only during later stages of the work. If so, these smaller maps may have resembled Johannes Vingboons's 1639 *Caert vande Svydt Rivier in Niew Nederland* (see Figure 2.12). In producing a chart intended primarily for waterborne navigation, Vingboons left the interior of the map largely blank. Herrman did the same, placing his original work close to the Dutch tradition of navigational charts. A pair of circa 1677 manuscript maps by an unidentified maker, one of Maryland and the other of Virginia, gives us an even clearer sense of how Herrman's manuscript map may have appeared (Figure 2.16 and Figure 2.17). These 1677 manuscript maps so closely parallel the published *Virginia and Maryland* that map scholar Jeannette D. Black concluded they must be based on the data in Herrman's map. Because these charts differ from *Virginia and Maryland* in several of their toponyms, they were probably not copied from the engraved map and instead derive from of an earlier manuscript version of Herrman's map. The charts are drawn on vellum and hand colored in the style of the so-called "Thames School," a group of chart-makers living and working near one another in the maritime trade districts of London (just east of the Tower of London alongside the north bank of the Thames), who produced highly detailed sea charts for London's seafaring community. It is likely that the same maker produced two nearly identical undated

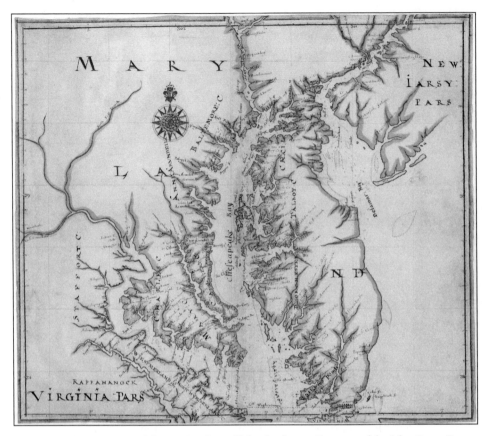

FIGURE 2.16. Manuscript chart of Maryland, 1677. Courtesy of the John Carter Brown Library at Brown University.

maps now in the British National Archives.[42] Mirroring *Virginia and Maryland* in their depiction of the rivers and coastline and the inclusion of precise navigational information, the 1677 charts differ most notably from Herrman's published map in their removal of both decoration and interior detail, elements for which navigators would have had little use. These charts evoke Herrman's manuscript map by allowing us to glimpse the manner in which he worked. Swept clean of decoration and focused directly on the water, *Virginia and Maryland* fits squarely within a long-standing Dutch nautical tradition.

FIGURE 2.17. Manuscript chart of Virginia, 1677. Courtesy of the John Carter Brown
Library at Brown University.

Dutch Ways of Seeing

The influence of Dutch mapmaking on Herrman's praxis is important beyond its implications for his immediate cartographic project because it helps to explain why Herrman pictured the Mid-Atlantic in the way he did and therefore distinguishes this colonially conceived map from its imperially designed English competitors. Central to seventeenth-century Dutch conceptions of the landscape was the accurate depiction of waterways, an element fundamental for linking the cities of the Netherlands together and for the commercial success of the republic and its empire. In New Netherland this essential structure for organizing and perceiving space was particularly vital. As described in Chapter 1, beginning in the 1610s, New Netherland's promoters conceived of the colony as a river-based territory made up of a number of trading posts, as opposed to contiguous agricultural settlements. With the Fresh River in the north, the South River to the south, and the North River in the center, New Netherland fulfilled this vision. All navigable and extending many miles inland, these rivers connected inland fur-trading settlements to the Atlantic, just as the canals and rivers of the Netherlands linked the cities of the republic together. Of course equally important to the geography of the Dutch empire were these colonial nodes' connections with the Dutch Republic—hence the proliferation of WIC charts of Atlantic sea-lanes. Residents of the Dutch Republic similarly imagined the geography of their country as being made up of a network of urban centers bound together by a series of mapped waterways, though here the country's place as a commercial entrepôt also cultivated great interest in a comprehensive understanding of the world.[43]

Unsurprisingly, early modern Dutch cartography reflects the Dutch geographic imagination and contrasts sharply with early English conceptions of space. While Dutch mapmakers certainly produced territorial maps in the sixteenth and seventeenth centuries, most of their production centered on the creation of detailed city plans and navigational charts on the one hand, and world atlases and wall maps on the other.[44]

In contrast, the English map industry began with elite Englishmen's efforts to demarcate their property with estate surveys. A distinct form of mapping that developed in England during the late sixteenth century, estate surveys differed from most other maps because they sought to represent only one individual's lands, not to systematically describe the landscape as a whole. Even those cartographers who looked to integrate these distinct renderings of property into a unified picture of the nation did so in a manner that emphasized small regions and their political borders. Christopher Saxton, for example, published a royally sponsored *Atlas of the Counties of England and Wales* in 1579. True to its title, this volume included thirty-four individual maps depicting the counties of England and Wales as well as a small overall map of the two kingdoms. Together, such estate surveys and Saxton's maps, which other mapmakers drew on into the eighteenth century, suggest that many early modern English men and women increasingly understood their country as consisting of bounded estates and counties distinct from one another. This tradition differed markedly from the Dutch, who almost completely eschewed estate surveys and instead emphasized navigational charts and world maps that celebrated fluidity and movement.[45]

The impulse to map, and thus to order and understand, the landscape also reflects seventeenth-century Dutch humanistic efforts at categorization, an inclination common to mapmakers, botanists, mathematicians, merchants, navigators, and scientists. Traders in the Dutch Republic and its colonies learned to represent the reality of their commercial worlds in neat, regularized columns of accounts, carefully noting debits and credits. As Dutch mariners and merchants plied the waters of the East and West Indies and returned to tidily pack their goods into the warehouses lining Amsterdam's canals, their ledgers gave order to an intricate web of commercial interactions. The accounts and letters Herrman sent from New Netherland to Amsterdam while working for the Gabrys served the same purpose, allowing his employers to judge how their agent was deploying their capital. Herrman's own accounts functioned similarly, enabling him to understand the range of his contacts in the Chesapeake.

Herrman transferred this desire to order his world to his cartographic work, making sense of the linked Mid-Atlantic as a Dutchman would, by mapping its waterways. The structure of the map effectively contained the natural world and harnessed it for his future use.[46]

Drawing on this Dutch empirical mode of representation, Herrman's map took possession of the Chesapeake not by marking its static borders but by furnishing the tools necessary to move through it; to navigate to and from a place was, in Herrman's understanding, to possess it. The one boundary Herrman marked distinctly—with a double line of trees—is the division between Maryland and Virginia on the Eastern Shore, a border that would have been irrelevant to most in the Chesapeake who moved by water, but one that was very important to Lord Baltimore (see Figure 2.10). Herrman's decision to enlarge the frame of the map of the Chesapeake to include the Delaware Bay, much of New Jersey, and a large portion of the Atlantic Ocean serves not only to link these colonies visually—as they were economically—but also to highlight the water's continuity through-out the Delmarva Peninsula, rendering the borders between these colo-nies irrelevant. In this way the overall visual impression and the technical elements of the map reinforce one another. Pictured precisely and marked by soundings and isobaths, the waters of the Chesapeake, Herrman in-dicated, were more knowable and useful than the land. Herrman's map eschews imperial divisions that marked territory as exclusively English in favor of offering the viewer the visual knowledge needed to take com-mercial possession of the region. Each of its features invites the viewer to envision moving along the bay and its rivers, their waters serving to knit together an otherwise isolated Atlantic community.[47]

Mapmakers in the Colonies

As important as Dutch cartographic, geographic, and visual traditions were in shaping Herrman's *Virginia and Maryland*, his status as a native cartographer with extensive local cross-border commercial experience further distinguished his work from those working in Europe. Ultimately it was Herrman's position as a resident trader that allowed him to visualize and then to map an interconnected Mid-Atlantic. As we have seen, most seventeenth-century maps of eastern North America were created by cartographers in the Netherlands or England, who worked from a combination of already extant maps, new information drawn from textual descriptions of the colonies, data collected by shipmasters and explorers, and their own imaginative blending of all of these sources. In contrast, Herrman gathered the data and drafted the manuscript copy of the map himself. *Virginia and Maryland*, though informed by metropolitan cartographic traditions, was therefore distinctly colonial.

As a first-hand observer working in North America, Herrman should be understood in relation to those mapmakers who likewise had long experience in the regions they pictured. Examining Herrman's work alongside maps made by three seventeenth-century cartographers who similarly lived and labored in British America—John Smith, Richard Norwood, and an unknown Montserrat cartographer—reveals the ways that Herrman's local experiences shaped his geographic imagination and mediated the influence of European cartographic conventions.[48] The Smith, Norwood, and the Montserrat maps all differ significantly in function: one map is most effective at communicating ethnography; another in regularizing the landscape; and the last in capturing the exotic terrain. Nevertheless, when seen in the aggregate, these maps all take their distinctive appearances from the kinds of local perceptions of the landscape available only to those who experienced each place first-hand.

Preceding Herrman to the Chesapeake by almost fifty years, Smith shared Herrman's method of local mapping and his grandest achievement, *Virginia Discouvered and Discribed*, resembles Herrman's work in its close attention to local detail and personal observation (see Figure 2.1). Though not a long-term resident of the Chesapeake like Herrman, Smith came to know the region's geography and its indigenous people well. The very crosses that mark the extent of his explorations—"what hath bin discovered" by Smith—testify to this direct experience with the landscape at the same time that they celebrate the significance of his alliances with Native peoples, which enabled him to flesh out the map's edges.[49] To Smith and Virginia's first English settlers, the most remarkable thing they discovered in Tsenacommacah was not its rivers but its indigenous inhabitants. Smith's interest in the Powhatan was not neutral, however; he hoped to seize their territory. As April Hatfield has argued, the borders of Virginia that Smith presented in his map extend not to the places Virginians actually controlled but to the larger Tsenacommacah.[50] In adopting Powhatan political geography and attempting to capture the land by renaming it Virginia and planting crosses around its borders, Smith contended that English success rested upon understanding and coopting Powhatan geography.

Surveyor Richard Norwood captured a very different but nonetheless equally locally specific geography when he completed *Mappa Aestivarum Insularum alian Bermudas dictarum* (Figure 2.18). Norwood, a mathematician who had settled in Bermuda, began working on the map in 1616, when the Somers Island Company hired him to survey the island.[51] At first glance the map's neat division of Bermuda into eight tribes (parishes) and the further subdivision of these lands into four 125-acre estates evokes the emphasis on regularity and private property seen in English estate surveys or in Saxton's county maps. A fuller understanding of Bermuda's geography, however reveals how extraordinary Norwood's decision to picture the colony as a uniform landmass was. Consisting of a series of 138 jagged volcanic islands fused by coral reefs, Bermuda is geographically fractured. Yet the colonists who lived there in the seventeenth century looked past the physical geography to see a unified community. The orderly division of the land on Norwood's map reflects this local perception of the landscape.

Perhaps the English colonial map that best reproduces a specific locally informed understanding of the land is an unsigned manuscript map of Montserrat dated to the late 1660s or early 1670s. Unusual for its presentation of a series of seven perspectival views of the coastline, *Mountserrat Island, 1673*, pictures Montserrat from the shifting

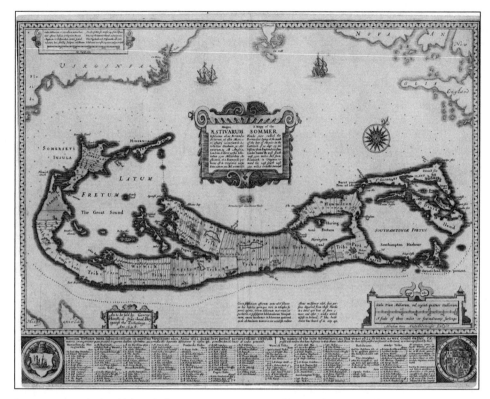

FIGURE 2.18. Richard Norwood, *Mappa Aestivarum Insularum alian Bermudas dictarum*. [London, 1626.] Courtesy of the John Carter Brown Library at Brown University.

vantage points by which most colonists experienced it (Figure 2.19). A small, rugged volcanic island located in the Lesser Antilles, Montserrat rises sharply from the sea and is characterized by steep cliffs, deep ravines, and thick vegetation. During the seventeenth century, bound laborers hacked away at the dense underbrush and built terraced tobacco and sugar fields clustered around several roadsteads at the edges of the island. It is this imposing view of Montserrat that the unnamed cartographer captured. Working in the mode of a sea captain sketching coastlines to aid navigation or an artist creating a city view, the mapmaker drew the island from each of its sides and com-

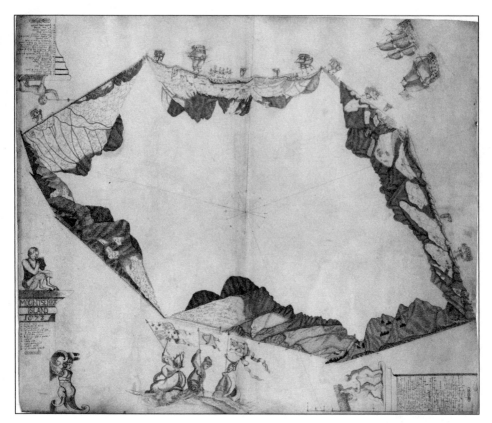

FIGURE 2.19. *Mountserrat Island, 1673.* Courtesy of the John Carter Brown Library at Brown University.

bined them to create a seven-sided polygon. Because each individual view is oriented toward the water, it is necessary to rotate the map to look at it, forcing the viewer to experience the island as an arriving visitor would have.[52]

Pictured in isolation from other colonies and in a perspective unfamiliar to most viewers, this map of Montserrat captures a highly localized understanding of the Caribbean as a place experienced from the deck of a ship. The view is not the all-encompassing aerial view from directly above (what geographers call a "planimetric view") that dominated most post-Renaissance maps, but rather that of a mariner traversing a busy Caribbean ocean passage looking for a bearing point so as to guide his vessel into port. Most other seventeenth-century cartographers had attempted to convey uneven topography on a two dimensional map by drawing in rocklike formations to indicate hills. Such a schematic solution may have been sufficient for mapmakers like Smith for depicting the transition from the tidewater to the piedmont in eastern Virginia, but this technique was clearly insufficient for capturing the dramatic cliffs and mountains of Montserrat. Instead, the unidentified cartographer employed a coastal-profile view so as to replicate the effect the view had on captains turning to the map as they approached the island or passengers emerging from their quarters to glimpse the island. The drafter of *Mountserrat Island*, in other words, designed the map to replicate the experience of those who frequented Montserrat (perhaps on the very ships pictured around its edges), more than to provide a precise geographic view of the island. This was distinctly a local understanding of the colony.

Smith, Norwood, the Montserrat cartographer, and Herrman all mapped what they knew. For Smith, the explorer, soldier, and trader, it was the Native Americans with whom he worked, traded, and clashed. For Norwood, the mathematician and surveyor, it was the regularity he saw in an otherwise geographically fractured colony. For the mariner who most likely produced *Mountserrat Island* it was the roadsteads and peaks of that island that made it so distinctive. And, for Herrman, the trader, it was the waterways that facilitated his trade. The method by which Herrman produced his map—the time spent taking meticulous soundings and recording the location of points—made it possible for those using his map to effectively enter and to master this world, something that contemporary maps like Smith's, which was largely useless for careful navigation, did not allow.

What is perhaps most extraordinary about these maps is that the makers generally succeeded in expressing their particular local experiences in a way that was appealing to both metropolitan and colonial viewers, as can be seen by the huge numbers of derivatives that preserve their individual details. The stunning array of Native American communities Smith included, for example, persist in later derivatives of his map. The same is true of those maps made after Norwood's original. The version John Ogilby included in his 1671 atlas, *America*, contains the original estate divisions that Norwood marked more than fifty years earlier. Herrman's detailed hydrography likewise persisted in subsequent adaptations. In fact, the only one of these maps not to succeed in multiple iterations was *Mountserrat Island*, which likely failed because it relied upon an idiosyncratic geography that made little attempt to adhere to dominant cartographic conventions.[53]

The success the Smith, Norwoord, and Herrman maps enjoyed and the failure *Mountserrat Island* had in shaping European perceptions of those places indicate an alternative narrative about the meanings of many early modern maps of colonies. Now almost universally seen as European instruments of conquest, these maps preserve traces of the colonial viewpoint and experience. If we ignore the role of colonial mapmakers and informants in shaping early modern maps, we lose the colonial origins and meanings of many of them. The Dutch cartographic tradition Herrman worked within and his familiarity with navigators' skills prompted him to see water as central to the Chesapeake and provided him with the tools to picture the region's commercial characteristics. Moreover, his experiences as an interimperial trader gave his map its most distinctive feature: that of an interconnected Mid-Atlantic. Republished and adapted for new uses, the original localized origins of the image nevertheless remain because they are built into the map's cartographic structure. As mariners used retracings of Herrman's map to sail the Chesapeake, they made Herrman's vision their own and re-inscribed the map with new layers of meaning.

3

The Planter

When Augustine Herrman "took Possession" of his estate on the eastern
shore of Northern Maryland, "transported his people from Manhattans . . . to seat and inhabit" the land, and began to work on his map
in 1661, he did so at a particularly fraught moment in the history of the
Mid-Atlantic.[1] During the next decade and a half Herrman witnessed a
series of political and economic convulsions that included new English
commercial regulations designed to reverse Dutch control of colonial
trade; collapsing relations with Native Americans that produced violent
conflict and disrupted trade in New Netherland, along the Delaware
River, and in Virginia and Maryland; a change in the structure of the
transatlantic tobacco market; and the English conquest of New Netherland. Each of these events threatened to undermine the cross-national
community that colonists like Herrman had worked to create in the
Mid-Atlantic since the 1640s and that Herrman's map captured.

While historians rightly point to the twin conflicts of King Philip's
War in New England and Bacon's Rebellion in the Chesapeake during
the 1670s as key to transforming Eastern North America, additional
developments in the Mid-Atlantic during the 1660s were equally mo-
mentous. Largely set in motion by the Restoration of Charles II and
Anglo-Dutch conflict in Europe, as well as a reshuffling of Native
American relations in North America, the events of this decade sent a
series of shockwaves through the settler and indigenous communities of
New Netherland, the Delaware Bay, and the Chesapeake and struck the
border-crossing inhabitants of the region particularly powerfully.[2] It was
here, along a series of waterways that connected the Chesapeake and
the Delaware Bays, that Herrman took up residence in 1661. He could
not have envisioned the changes to come in the next ten years, but his

decision to settle there in the midst of the conflicts indicates that he understood how important this region was to eastern North America. During the 1660s he and his extended cross-national network, consisting of long-term associates like Anna Varleth and Petrus Stuyvesant and recent acquaintances like Philip Calvert of Maryland and Governor William Berkeley of Virginia, worked to hold the cross-national community of the Mid-Atlantic together in the face of nationalist English efforts to seal off the empire and shore up its borders. Ultimately colonists and their Native American partners would be unsuccessful in maintaining an interimperial Mid-Atlantic, but as Herrman traversed the coastline of the Chesapeake taking measurements, making sketches, and marking soundings for his map, the importance of these local intercolonial bonds was in the forefront of his mind.

The Struggle for the Delaware River

The Swedish, Dutch, and English struggle for control of the Delaware River stretched back to the 1630s, but the late 1650s and early 1660s were years of new urgency for the parties involved. From their very beginning, the European settlements along the Delaware River were a cultural crossroads. In the late 1620s the Dutch West India Company (WIC) established a series of temporary forts along what they called the South River from which the company could manage the fur trade. Attempts to establish more permanent settlement, however, floundered. In 1631, after the WIC opened New Netherland to private investors, director Samuel Godjin established a colony called Swanendael near present-day Lewes, Delaware, from which he and his partners hoped to export grain, tobacco, and whale products. This scheme, though, came as news to the Sickoneysincks, the Lenape group who sold them the land. Living near Cape Henlopen on the west bank of the Delaware River, the Sickoneysincks were one community of a larger Lenape nation that included all of coastal Delaware and much of what is today southern and central New Jersey as well as eastern

Pennsylvania. Numbering somewhere between five thousand and ten thousand during the first half of the seventeenth century, the Lenape were an Algonquian people who lived in small towns clustered around the Delaware River and its tributaries. The Lenape began to trade beaver and otter skins to Dutch mariners for cloth and metal wares soon after the Dutch arrived in 1615. As the intensity of this trade picked up in the 1620s, the Susquehannocks (called the Minquas by the Dutch), an Iroquoian people who journeyed to the Delaware from the Susquehanna River to trade with the Dutch, began to challenge the Lenape. Increased competition meant that the Lenape were eager to accommodate Swanendael in hopes that a trading post more distant from the Susquehannocks would guarantee them a steady access to European trade. But when the Dutch settlers began to clear land, plant corn and tobacco, and raise livestock, and when it became apparent that they did not intend to offer annual gifts or regularly purchase furs, the Lenape realized that the Dutch intended a permanent settlement, not a trading station. Well aware from their neighbors in the Chesapeake that plantation agriculture was a threat to their territory, the Sickonyeysincks attacked Swanendael, killing all thirty-two inhabitants. The Lenape raid made it clear that European settlement along the Delaware could succeed only if it was compatible with their interests.[3]

After the defeat of Swanendael, the Dutch and Lenape quickly moved to patch up their differences. Trade was too important to both groups for them to forsake one another completely, and thus the Dutch quickly returned to trade on Lenape terms from a number of forts on the New Jersey riverbanks. Almost immediately, the arrival of a Swedish expedition undermined this strategy. Located on the western bank of the Minquas Kil (or Christiana River), north of the Swanendael site and thus closer to Susquehannock traders, the new Swedish settlement of Fort Christina gave the Swedes direct access to the thicker Canadian furs that European traders preferred and the Susquehannock obtained from their Huron allies north of Lake Ontario. Without a similar fort, the Dutch were at a competitive disadvantage to the Swedes. Over the next two decades the two European powers jockeyed for access to Native American commercial networks, constantly trying to outmaneuver one another in the location of their forts and their alliances with the Lenape and Susquehannock. As the Swedish and Dutch competed in the 1640s, English expeditions from Hartford and New Haven also scrambled for position along the river. The Lenape and Susquehnnock used this imperial competition to their own advantage. As one Dutch official later remembered, "both Nations . . . Sweedes as [well as] Dutch did strive on both sides to please and not to disoblige the Indians In Consideration of the trade upon which they wholly depended."[4]

Tensions between all of these groups came to a head in the 1650s. Seeking to cut off Swedish trade, in 1651 Director-General of New Netherland Stuyvesant established a new beachhead, Fort Casimir, just a few miles south of Fort Christina on the west side of the Delaware River, where New Castle, Delaware, stands today. Because New Sweden often struggled to provide them sufficient trade goods, the Susquehannock and the Lenape welcomed Stuyvesant's move, a decision that in turn provoked Swedish commander Johan Risingh to capture Fort Casimir in 1654. Stuyvesant responded with an invasion of his own, conquering New Sweden on behalf of the WIC for what would be the final time in 1655. Motivated principally by a desire to control the fur trade, the company also worried increasingly about Maryland's intentions to exercise its claim to the South River, and its leaders hoped a permanent Dutch settlement there would forestall English interference. On both counts the Dutch miscalculated. Not only would Stuyvesant's actions not keep English settlers out of the region, but also, because his removal of New Sweden deprived the Lenape and Susquehannock of a valuable trading partner, the invasion also destabilized trade in the entire region by destroying the intercolonial networks that allowed it, a development that ultimately encouraged the English to challenge for control of the river.[5]

The Delaware River Nexus

By the time the Dutch ousted the Swedish from the Delaware River
in the 1650s, the fur trade required the collaboration of a number of
different cultural groups. Understanding the interests of these communities is the key to grasping the struggle for control of the Delaware
River and to understanding Herrman's arrival there in 1661. The most
important of these groups were the Lenape and Susquehannock, who
supplied the pelts that drew Europeans to the river. The two nations
had settled their earlier conflict at the end of the 1630s and agreed to
share access to European trade. After that date the Susquehannocks
became increasingly important to European traders because of their
inland connections to more desirable Canadian pelts.[6] Swedish settlers' arrival on the Delaware River in 1638 coincided with the peace
between the Lenape and the Susquehannock, and the Swedes quickly
took advantage. Initially able to supply the European trade goods such
as metal tools, firearms, and powder that the Susquehannocks desired,
they quickly began to traffic with Susquehannock traders who reached
them along a series of navigable waterways that linked the Susquehannock fort in the Upper Chesapeake to the Delaware River. Over
time, however, the infrequent arrival of resupply ships from Sweden
and the lack of direct access to wampum, which underlay many of the
Susquehannocks' diplomatic and commercial alliances, meant that
Swedish colonists came to depend upon trade with Dutch and English
colonies to survive. Even though Swedish authorities resented them for
"oppos[ing] us on every side," Dutch and English merchants carrying
metal tools, cloth, firearms, powder, provisions, and most importantly
wampum from New Amsterdam and New England to New Sweden
enabled the colony to trade with the Susquehannock.[7] It was this trade
that first brought Herrman to the Delaware in 1649. Already spanning
the Delmarva Peninsula in their relations with the Susquehannock,
Swedish settlers hoping to diversify their exports began to buy tobacco
from Chesapeake planters who were eager for new customers. Never

the most important aspects of New Sweden's business, the colony's tobacco trade added another dimension to its complex interimperial and intercultural commercial system. Both New Sweden and the Susquehannocks—one anchored on the western bank of the Delaware River the other traveling across the Delmarva Peninsula—prospered in the 1640s by leveraging their geographic positioning into profitable commerce. In the process they made the settlements of the Delaware River into a nexus of intercolonial networks that knit together Susquehannock, Lenape, English, Dutch, and Swedish peoples.

The links that bound these European and native communities together remained fragile, however, and the WIC's conquest of New Sweden in 1655 quickly undermined productive ties and destabilized commerce. New Sweden's struggle to provide sufficient trade goods eventually frustrated the Susquehannocks and the Lenape, but these nations nevertheless had long encouraged the presence of multiple European powers so as to promote competition for their furs. As a result, they tried (unsuccessfully) to prevent the Dutch capture of New Sweden in 1655 by warning the Swedes of the imminent invasion and then by helping to convince a coalition of Munsee communities living near Manhattan to attack New Amsterdam while Stuyvesant and his troops were assaulting New Sweden. Often referred to as the "Peach War" because of an apocryphal story that it began over the theft of a peach, the Munsee assault destroyed a number of houses and other structures in New Amsterdam, led to the death and kidnapping of dozens of New Netherlanders, and spread fear through the colony. Months of diplomacy between Stuyvesant and Pennekeek (a Hackensack chief) avoided a larger conflagration, but this conflict meant that the WIC could not take advantage of its new control of the Delaware River.[8]

Burdened by debt and thus unable to provide the necessary capital to settle the colony, the WIC transferred the lands surrounding Fort Casimir to the city of Amsterdam, whose leaders hoped a new colony could provide them reliable shipments of grain and timber. In the spring of

THE PLANTER | 111

1657 roughly two hundred colonists and officials arrived in the newly christened New Amstel to begin their work. From the start the city struggled. First, New Amstel officials could not bring the Swedes and Finns who still lived in the region under their control. More pressingly, the colony could not to feed its residents, leaving them reliant on New Amsterdam for supplies. And while New Amsterdam did send additional provisions new hostilities with New Netherland's indigenous neighbors—this time with the Espous—meant that aid was not always as forthcoming as New Amstel hoped. Two brutal winters and an epidemic added to the colonists' sufferings, and by 1659, with more than one hundred of them already dead, some recent arrivals had already begun to depart and decades of fruitful economic relationships centered on the Delaware River were at risk of collapse.[9]

Sensing New Amstel's vulnerability, Maryland's leaders decided it was time to challenge the Dutch for control of the Delaware River. In the summer of 1659, acting on instructions from Lord Baltimore, Governor Josias Fendall and his council commissioned militia colonel Nathaniel Utie to inform the residents of New Amstel that "they [we]re seated within . . . [Lord Baltimore's] Province" without permission and thus they were "require[d] . . . to depart."[10] Bearing a letter to this effect, Utie set out for New Amstel with a small entourage. When he arrived at the small Dutch city in early September, the militia leader spent several days trying to intimidate the residents into fleeing by suggesting that Maryland had a force of five hundred soldiers ready to attack. Not unsurprisingly, Jacob Alrichs, the director of New Amstel and Amsterdam's chief representative in America, and Willem Beeckman, the WIC's leading official on the Delaware, rejected Utie's demand. Privately, however, both men hurriedly wrote to Stuyvesant asking for reinforcements from New Amsterdam and for advice on how to deal with the crisis.[11]

Maryland's decision to press its claim to the Delaware in 1659 was both a product of Dutch vulnerability and the result of growing colonial confidence. The confirmation of Lord Baltimore's proprietorship by the

Commonwealth government in 1657 inaugurated a period of relative stability for Maryland after decades of sectarian and factional disputes. Although there would be another short-lived coup against the proprietor's power—supported by Governor Fendall—by 1659 many Marylanders agreed that the colony's future depended on controlling access to the Delaware. This access was particularly important for Nathaniel Utie. In the late 1650s, Utie, the son of an influential Virginia councilor, acquired a number of estates in the Upper Chesapeake, including three hundred acres in January 1659 at the mouth of the Sassafras River, close to where Herrman would obtain land the next year. With Utie's landholdings being located in the northern reaches of Maryland and distant from the shipping lanes of the lower Chesapeake Bay, their value depended upon ready access to the Delaware River and the Atlantic beyond.[12]

Utie's expedition to New Amstel got Stuyvesant's attention, and the Dutch director-general responded defensively, dispatching Herrman to Maryland to counter Lord Baltimore's patent. When news that the resulting border conference failed to convince the Dutch to yield, Lord Baltimore took more decisive action. No longer content to wait for the Dutch and encouraged by rising English metropolitan hostility toward Dutch interference in the wider English Atlantic, Baltimore grasped the chance to be rid of his Dutch neighbors. First he dispatched Captain James Neale to Amsterdam to appeal directly to the directors of the WIC to abandon New Amstel and the WIC trading post on the Delaware. In turn, the WIC disputed Lord Baltimore's patent and reaffirmed its claim to the Delaware River. Echoing Herrman's belief that the border dispute must be solved in Europe, the WIC directors called upon the States General to deal directly with Charles II in settling the issue. Furious over what he saw as the obstinacy of the Dutch WIC and the City of Amsterdam, Lord Baltimore responded by instructing his half-brother, Maryland's new governor Philip Calvert, to work with Neale—who had left for Maryland after his failure in Amsterdam—to find "some speedy and effectuall waye for Reduceing the Dutch in

Delaware Baye." When Neale arrived in Maryland in July 1661, he presented the governor and his council with a commission from Baltimore authorizing a military attack. Referring to Dutch residents of New Amstel as "certaine Ennemies[,] Pyratts & Robbers" and claiming that they had "invaded and usurped a parte of . . . [the] Province of Maryland," the commission instructed Neale and Philip Calvert "to make warre against [the Dutch,] . . . to vanquish [them,] . . . And to seize to our use all or any howses and Goods of the said Ennemies . . . or their Abettors which shall be upon the Shoare within the lymitts of our said Province."[13]

Meanwhile, in Maryland two vital pieces of intelligence confirmed to Baltimore that the time was right for an invasion. First, Utie's 1659 expedition had revealed that New Amstel's defenses were in shambles and that its detachment of soldiers numbered no "more than 8 or 10." The colony's population was dwindling as well, with reports of as many as fifty families having recently fled to Maryland.[14] More importantly, however, a local crisis exposed the risks Maryland invited by having a rival empire so close to their borders. In early May 1661, a party of "River Indians," probably Lenapes, killed four Maryland colonists traveling from New Amstel to their homes in Maryland. No motive for the attack was apparent, though many believed the murder of two Lenape men and a Susquehannock by a pair of Dutch servants the year before precipitated it. When Maryland officials received word that another group of Native Americans had sold some of the men's clothes at New Amstel and that authorities there had let them depart freely, Marylanders became incensed. It was clear now to many in Maryland that their Dutch neighbors could not be trusted. These local tensions, combined with the larger imperial aggression against the Dutch that Lord Baltimore signaled, must have made many in the colony eager to strike. It surely seemed this way to Willem Beeckman, who believed that Maryland would seek revenge on the Lenape and use the action as a pretext to attack New Amstel. Writing to Stuyvesant, Beeckman reported that he lived with the constant fear of "the coming of the English" believing that "if the English make war with the Indians . . . they will lay claim to all the areas from which they expel them as being conquered from their enemies by the sword" and thus claim New Amstel in the process. As a remedy, Beeckman urged New Amstel's new leader, Alexander d'Hinoyossa, to smooth things over with his English neighbors.[15]

With momentum for war building, Philip Calvert and his council shockingly elected to set Captain Neale's commission to attack New Amstel aside and instead decided to pursue peace. There was no love lost between Maryland and Delaware at this moment of tension, and Lord Baltimore's wishes could not have been clearer, yet still Calvert and his council did not act. The key to making sense of the council's decision lies in the local strategic and economic interests of a small but powerful collection of individuals who lived in the English, Dutch, and Native American communities of the Upper Chesapeake and understood that maintaining peaceful intercolonial ties across the Delmarva Peninsula was critical to colonial and individual success. Foremost among these men was Augustine Herrman.

Spanning the Peninsula

When Herrman relocated to the Upper Chesapeake in 1661, the multiethnic relationships that had made the communities of the Delaware River successful were collapsing. He knew that his particular set of skills and interimperial connections provided him with an opportunity to prosper if he could help to hold this intercolonial region together. It was not a coincidence, then, that the four-thousand-acre estate along the Oppoquimimi River that Herrman occupied sat at the western terminus of an underdeveloped trading path that cut through the peninsula and connected the Chesapeake and Delaware Bays (see Figure 1.4). Herrman had first learned about such a route in the fall of 1659 as he traveled from New Amsterdam to St. Mary's for the border conference with Governor Fendall. Leaving New Amstel on his way to Maryland, Herrman, fellow negotiator Resolved Waldron, several WIC soldiers, and at least four

Native American guides traversed the Delmarva Peninsula along a path used by Susquehannock, Lenape, and local Dutch, Swedish, and Finnish settlers. This path took them overland, as Herrman reported, through "somewhat rolling" wooded land along several small creeks for about five miles before it reached the "first stream which the Indians said flowed into the Bay of Virginia [the Chesapeake Bay]." From there the party continued "without a path" until reaching the part of the stream "where the tide rises." There, they found a small boat "hauled on shore and completely dried out," which had been left for travelers to use. After recaulking what turned out to be a leaky vessel, the party rowed "a good mile and a half" along a small creek before reaching the eastern branch of the Elk River, which in turn joined with the Sassafras River and, farther up-stream, the Susquehanna River, where it forms the head of the Chesapeake Bay. Although Herrman did not comment on it in 1659, the Elk River also took him by the small neck of land on which he would build his estate two years later. As they traveled, the party met a number of Dutch, Swedish, and Finnish colonists, some of them runaway servants, who lived as squatters on a number of small plantations in the area. From these men and women Herrman learned about the courses of the various waterways and that large "ships should be able to sail up [from the lower Chesapeake Bay] as far as this river [the Sassafras]."[16]

Almost immediately Herrman realized the potential these lands and the small waterways that connected them had for preserving trade between New Netherland and Maryland at an important moment when war seemed imminent. If conflict between the two colonies did erupt, an out-of-the-way trading path might provide the means for commercial connections to endure. Just days later at the October 1659 summit, Herrman moved to capitalize on this possibility and position himself to benefit. He proposed a scheme to Philip Calvert to encourage "trade and commerce overland between Maryland and Delaware" along this very path. While Herrman's report does not indicate how Calvert replied, he must have been familiar with the region because just weeks before, in mid-September 1659, a survey had been recorded on Calvert's behalf for one thousand acres "on the Point between [the] Elk and Oppoqui-mcni River[s]." Two years later he would let this very land parcel "faul to Augustine Herman" as part of the mapmaker's arrangement with Lord Baltimore. Although the "private conversation" is not recorded in the accounts of Calvert and Herrman's October 1659 meeting, it is never-theless clear that at that time the men hatched a plan to connect their two colonies and enrich themselves.[17] The events of the next few years would underscore how premeditated their arrangement had been.

In early 1661 Herrman began to explore his new holdings in Mary-land, now called Bohemia Manor, and reported to WIC official Willem Beeckman that "we shall be able to go overland to the Sandhoek [New Amstel] in ½ [a] day" from Bohemia Manor along a "wagon road, be-cause the Mincquas Kill and the . . . Bohemia River come within one mile of one another." This ability to "traffic by water" between Maryland and the Delaware River would, he continued, "be of service to the in-habitants [of Maryland] and an encouragement to New Netherland."[18] Perhaps overly optimistic about the time it would take to cross the peninsula and confusing the Minquas Kill (now the Christiana River, located twenty-five miles to the north of this spot) with the Appo-quinimink River, Herrman nevertheless described what would become a critical passage across the peninsula in the years to come. Given the mapmaker's familiarity with the region, it is no surprise that Herrman depicted this portion of *Virginia and Maryland* so finely; the winding paths of the creeks and streams on both sides of the peninsula are care-fully pictured, and the larger waterways have numerous soundings. For Herrman to realize the full potential of his estate, however, he needed peace between Maryland and New Netherland. In the wake of the killing of the four Marylanders near New Amstel in May 1661, it seemed that Herrman's hope for productive trade would be lost unless he could help orchestrate a reconciliation.

That same month Maryland's governor and his council met at Na-thaniel Utie's plantation on Spesutie Island on the west side of the Upper Chesapeake Bay (in modern Harford County) just opposite the mouth of the Elk River, fortuitously providing Herrman with an opening. The council had traveled there from St. Mary's to gather information from "all persons that have suffred any dammage by the Indians or have engaged with them in an hostyle manner," and it was there that the council learned about the seeming complicity of the Dutch in the murder of the four Marylanders earlier that month. Herrman traveled to the council meeting and summarized the situation for Beeckman. Noting that Dutch "fears last winter that the South River would be invaded" by Maryland had been overblown, Herrman nonetheless explained that the recent killings had stirred up old tensions in the colony. "It would be desirable," Herrman wrote, "if Mr. d'Inyniouse [Alexander d'Hinoyossa] replied to the governor [of Maryland] and arranged matters to the satisfaction of the English because it probably depends on this whether friendship will be continued and the aforesaid trade carried out or the friendship broken off. The best advice I could give," Herrman concluded, is "that a speedy reply be transmitted, for which the governor and council are waiting. Wise counsel is needed!"[19] Herrman's letter evidently worked, because d'Hinoyossa immediately dispatched Abraham Van Nas from New Amstel to Spesutie Island. There Van Nas presented the governor with a letter from d'Hinoyossa explaining that Dutch officials had not prosecuted the Native men who had entered New Amstel because the men had "not been accessory to the Murther." D'Hinoyossa closed the appeal by explaining that above all he wanted to avoid "warres[,] [which] are prejudiciall to the Commons," at all costs and that he hoped "in tyme" to reestablish "a good traffique Betweene" the colonies.[20]

Herrman's efforts to avoid warfare faced obstacles on another front. As bright as prospects for cross-peninsula trade now looked, many Marylanders still worried that their uneasy relationship with the Lenape threatened regional trade. Here Maryland again called upon those with intercolonial ties to aid them. Maryland's most important indigenous allies in 1661 were the Susquehannock on whom Marylanders depended both for the fur trade and as a buffer between their growing settlements in the Upper Chesapeake and Dutch- and French-allied Iroquois to the interior. Since the Susquehannock were close allies of the Lenape, Maryland's dispute with that nation endangered their ties to the Susquehannock as well. Moving to rectify the situation, Maryland made a series of overtures to the Lenape that eventually resolved the dispute. Brokered by New Amstel's d'Hinoyossa and Pieter Alricks, the Passyunk Lenape leader Pinna and Governor Philip Calvert agreed to a treaty that signaled mutual support for a "perpetuall peace" in September 1661.[21]

More remarkable than the treaty itself was the other business that the parties conducted. Left unreported in the Maryland accounts of the summit with the Lenape was a commercial pact Calvert sealed with d'Hinoyossa at the same meeting. If the Dutch were willing to supply the English "with Negroes and other merchandise," the agreement stipulated, the English would "transport 2[000] or 3000 hogsheads of tobacco to" the Dutch "at Apoqienemingh [Appoquinimink]." Held at the intersection of the Appoquinimink River and "another stream which empties into the English River [the Chesapeake]" (a spot in the region of what is today Middletown and Odessa, Delaware), this meeting took place just east of Augustine Herrman's new estate and along the trading path he was striving to develop.[22] There is no record that Herrman was present at the negotiations, but there is strong circumstantial evidence that he was involved in the deal. Not only was he at Bohemia Manor—just miles away—before and after the summit, but he had also proposed such an arrangement to Calvert just two years before—an arrangement that depended upon his overland trading route. New Amstel and Maryland now had a commercial agreement to drive trade across the Delmarva Peninsula, the culmination of years of diplomacy. And it was not completed a moment too soon, for just as the English and Dutch colonists of the Upper Chesapeake and the Delaware River had begun to repair their alliance, metropolitan politics interceded to reshape local affairs and to threaten intercolonial ties.

Imperial Priorities and Local Needs

In late 1661 Charles Calvert, Philip's nephew and Lord Baltimore's eldest son, arrived in Maryland as the new governor. Calvert's appointment coincided with the Restoration of Charles II, and the new governor brought the monarch's priorities with him. Charged with increasing revenues, bringing the colony under closer proprietary control, and aligning it to the policies of the crown, Calvert moved to better regulate Maryland's trade. In January 1662 he issued "A Proclamacon for the better observacon of the Acte for Navigacon and increase of Shipping," which targeted the "Masters of small Vessells [that] doe come into this Province, and putt off Goods, and lade away tobaccoes without takeing notice of the Government here or of the Acte of Parliament for Navigacon."[23] In singling out the "Masters of small Vessells," Calvert was referring mainly to Dutch traders from the New Amsterdam; the "Act of Parliament" they violated was the 1660 Act of Trade and Navigation, which mandated that enumerated goods, such as tobacco, be sent to England in English (or colonial) vessels before they could pass to foreign places. Parliament designed this law explicitly to guarantee that the American colonies benefited the "Trade & navigation" of England and not the Dutch Republic. Or more precisely, it ensured that the colonies enriched the growing ranks of London merchants and the Stuart Crown. When Charles II regained the English throne in 1660, he was at first predisposed to look fondly on the Dutch who had helped shelter him and much of the Stuart Court after his father's execution. But what Charles II needed most in 1660 was revenue, and with the Dutch "wrongfully possess[ing] themselves of" English trade, he was eager to resume the commercial war against the Dutch that Cromwell had begun a decade earlier. That the stadtholder Willem II of Orange, Charles II's nephew, was out of power in the Dutch Republic and that public opinion in England was strongly anti-Dutch only strengthened his resolve.[24] For his part Lord Baltimore benefited from Charles II's return to the throne and thus he was eager to please the new monarch. In late 1660, Charles

II helped Lord Baltimore bring his colony fully under his command, ordering Virginia to aid Baltimore in quelling any lingering challenges to his authority. With imperial politics turning in his favor and anti-Dutch sentiments swirling, Lord Baltimore seized the opportunity to violently expel the Dutch from the Delaware River and to demonstrate his loyalty to Charles II.[25]

Maryland's new governor, Charles Calvert, was determined to enforce his father's more aggressive stance. Not only did Governor Calvert want to protect his family's close ties to the Stuarts, but since his father was again fighting to protect his charter, he also understood that the family's prospects depended upon maintaining Charles II's support. However, just ten months after issuing his "Proclamacon for the better observacon of the Acte for Navigacon," which targeted Dutch shipping, Calvert reversed course. In November 1662 the governor hastily arranged a secret meeting with Alexander d'Hinoyossa. According to New Amstel councilor Jean Willemszoon, d'Hinoyossa unexpectedly received a letter from the "governor of Maryland . . . telling him to go immediately to Augustine [Herrman]'s house where the aforesaid governor was waiting to speak to him." D'Hinoyossa wasted no time in having "the sloop made ready at once and . . . that night" he and Gerrit van Sweringen—another councilor and civic officer—secretly left for Bohemia Manor. Once there, d'Hinoyossa and Charles Calvert retreated to the "marsh," where "while speaking to one another they cast their eyes to the heavens and put their hands on their chests, together with many other strange grimaces." Although Willemszoon was worried that d'Hinoyossa was conspiring with Calvert to betray New Netherland, mentioning the possibility that "a basilisk"—a legendary vicious serpent—was "hatched out of their discussion in the marsh and intends to come here [New Netherland]," as subsequent events would bear out, it is more likely the men were agreeing to maintain the intercolonial commercial arrangement Philip Calvert and d'Hinoyossa had made the year before.[26]

A number of factors likely encouraged Governor Calvert to defy his father and Charles II in supporting Anglo-Dutch trade. First, he did not want to endanger the peace with the Lenape that the Dutch had helped broker a year earlier by reneging on the trade pact that had been sealed at the same time. He could also have wanted to honor the arrangement as an act of good faith, hoping it would engender good relations with his European neighbors. A final more significant factor, however, emerges in a letter Beeckman wrote to Stuyvesant appraising him of the secret meeting. Beeckman reported that when "Mr d'Hinojosse returned to New Amstel," Beeckman could not discover "what was achieved, except for learning . . . that he [d'Hinoyossa] was told by Governor Calvert that Manhattan would soon be called upon to surrender by those of New England."[27] There had indeed been talk in England in 1661 and 1662 of this possibility, but it is a puzzle why the governor of an English colony would warn a Dutch official (and, as he must have known, ultimately Stuyvesant as well) about a possible English invasion.[28] When placed into the context of Maryland's local situation, however, Calvert's actions begin to make more sense. From Governor Calvert's perspective the conquest of New Netherland would undermine his colony's success by limiting its commercial options. Although he had only recently arrived in the Mid-Atlantic, he had already discovered what those who lived there had known for decades: crossnational relationships were instrumental for local success. In short, the governor's warning was designed to protect the Anglo-Dutch trade that Herrman and other New Netherland merchants had helped to make possible.

Governor Calvert was not alone in bucking Parliament's efforts to halt Anglo-Dutch cross currents in the Mid-Atlantic in the early 1660s. Virginia's governor, William Berkeley, also worked to preserve his colonists' connections with New Netherland as he had done in the wake of the Commonwealth government's efforts to end Dutch trade a decade earlier. Out of power since forces loyal to Cromwell deposed him in 1652, Berkeley regained the governor's office in early 1660. Almost immediately, he resumed what had been on-again, off-again negotiations over a commercial pact between Virginia and New Netherland begun in 1647. Since at least the early 1640s, the governor had been allied politically, socially, and economically with elite Eastern Shore planters and traders such as Argoll Yeardley and John Custis, who, in turn both had connections in the Netherlands. These personal ties together with his experience during the 1640s, when Dutch traders helped the colony survive disruptions to English commerce, made Berkeley intimately aware of the importance of Dutch trade to the Chesapeake. For his part Director-General Stuyvesant sensed the opportunity to formalize his colony's intercolonial trade, and in March 1660 he authorized Nicholas Varleth and Bryan Newton to travel to Virginia to work out a formal agreement. There the two Dutch agents rendezvoused with Herrman who was already in Virginia on business. Varleth—Herrman's brother-in-law—and Newton relied upon Herrman to be a translator and advisor in the negotiations, since he was "well acquainted with the *English* tongue" and familiar with the Chesapeake trade. Within weeks the parties agreed to "Articles of Amitie & commerce" that provided for open trade (though Dutch traders would have to pay higher export duties than English traders in Virginia), mutually binding access to each others' courts to settle disputes, and a framework for the orderly return of runaways.[29]

Less than a year later, the news of the Navigation Act of 1661 scuttled Berkeley and Stuyvesant's trade deal just as it complicated Calvert and D'Hinoyossa's plans. Nevertheless, Berkeley remained convinced that preserving access to Dutch trade was best for Virginia. Named to the Council for Foreign Plantations in 1661, he decided to take his arguments for Dutch trade to London, where he found sympathy with those London merchants who saw a link between open trade and a more diversified and thus stronger Virginian economy. Essentially Berkeley argued that Virginia's success could not rest upon tobacco alone. Not only had falling prices made it an unreliable staple, but monoculture also allowed a small number of London merchants to dominate the colony's trade. Why, Berkeley asked, should "little more than forty merchants, who being the only buyers of our *Tobacco*" be enriched by Virginia's trade while "forty thousand people should be improverish'd[?]" If instead planters were to be allowed to "carry their goods to what Port they please," and thus be relived of the burdens of the Act of 1660, trade would increase, planters could afford to experiment with other crops, and investments would flow to Virginia.[30] Attentive to the Anglo-Dutch sentiment in London and unwilling to directly challenge Charles II, Berkeley did not openly celebrate the virtues of Dutch trade, choosing instead to hide behind calls for free trade more generally, but one of his key allies, London merchant John Bland, was less discriminating. "If the Hollanders must not trade to *Virginia*," and if English merchants continually failed to buy the complete stock, Bland wrote, "how shall the Planters dispose of their Tobacco? Will it not then perish on the Planters hands? . . . Debarring the Hollanders" from Virginia, he contended, "will utterly ruinate the Colonies['] Commerce and [the empire's] Customes . . . for if the Inhabitants be destroyed, of necessity the Trade there must cease."[31] As much sense as Berkeley's and Bland's arguments might make to colonial planters the men soon found that the coalition of metropolitan merchants and royal officials pursing mercantilist ends was too powerful to overcome; there no longer was room for Dutch trade in the English Empire. Berkeley's failure to obtain a modification in trade laws ultimately doomed the "Articles of Amitie & commerce" with New Netherland and meant there would be no formal protections for Dutch trade. Illicit trade nevertheless persisted, and like many colonial governors, Berkeley was willing to tolerate it.[32] Charles Calvert and Berkeley agreed about little in the 1660s as they clashed over Maryland and Virginia's borders and competed for investment, but the two men did both believe that commercial ties with New Netherland were vital for the Chesapeake's success. Resident in the Chesapeake, both governors embraced an intercolonial Mid-Atlantic even if such a position went against metropolitan wishes.

Meanwhile several interlocking changes in the structure of the tobacco market made it even more imperative that planters in the Chesapeake preserve their connections with New Netherland. In the 1640s planters in tidewater Virginia introduced a new variety of tobacco. This so-called sweet-scented tobacco became instantly popular in England and soon commanded higher prices than did the older Oronoco strain. But because many planters in Virginia and Maryland could not grow the new variety, they were left to covet Continental markets where demand and prices for Oronoco remained high. Selling their crop to New Netherland traders who could ship it directly to the Dutch Republic was therefore particularly attractive to Oronoco planters. Simultaneously elite planters in Virginia and Maryland worked (though unsuccessfully) throughout the 1660s to temporarily limit or cease tobacco production as a way to raise its price. Smuggling tobacco out of the Upper Chesapeake to Dutch New Amstel and smoothing the path of Dutch traders in Virginia provided hedges against the possible effects of production cuts.[33] With the combined burdens of low prices, falling English demand, and enhanced trade regulations, most Chesapeake planters would have agreed with Lord Baltimore's claim that "the Dutch Trade" had become "the Darling of the People of Virginia as well as this Province."[34]

Marylanders living in the Upper Chesapeake certainly agreed with Baltimore's assessment. Responding to Governor Charles Calvert's lead in protecting close ties to Dutch New Amstel, these planters had begun to move their tobacco to the Delaware River across Herrman's transpeninsular route by 1662. In August reports of this illicit trade reached the Council for Foreign Plantations in London, which complained that smugglers were carrying tobacco out of Maryland "by rolling" it "to the plantacions of the Dutch lyeing continguus to Delewar Bay."[35] In the months following Calvert and d'Hinoyossa's meeting at Herrman's plantation, the Bohemian and d'Hinoyossa drove a steady trade. D'Hinoyossa supplied Herrman with a wide variety of goods, including New Amstel's "millstones" and its "galliot" as well as musket balls, powder, and "a lot of nails belonging to the City." Herrman intended to use these items for the construction of a house at Bohemia Manor, for the building of the town he still planned, and, as far as the galliot was concerned, to aid future trade along the streams and creeks of the Delmarva Peninsula.[36] D'Hinoyossa also began to fulfill the terms of the deal he and Philip Calvert had first worked out in 1661, supplying Herrman (who as had been arranged in 1659 took the lead in the transaction) with "merchandize" including "Spanish wine, brandy, Rochelle [wine], linen, stockings, shoes, shirts, etc." In return Herrman was to furnish "2[000] or 3000 hogsheads of tobacco" of "the best quality, at two stivers a pound."[37]

Having only recently taken possession of his four thousand acres in the Upper Chesapeake, Herrman did not yet have the potential to produce this quantity of tobacco. Instead, he relied on his extended Chesapeake network. In 1660 and 1661 Herrman began dealing with a number of prominent plantation owners in the Upper Chesapeake Bay near Bohemia Manor. Among these was an interconnected group of planters centering on Nathaniel Utie and including Samuel Goldsmith, Henry Stockett, Charles James, and Richard Bennett. These men were Protestants who arrived in Maryland during the Commonwealth period and were associates of the elder and more famous Richard Bennett who had unsuccessfully challenged Lord Baltimore's patent in the 1650s. In early 1660 Utie, Goldsmith, and Stockett again defied the Calverts, allying themselves with Governor Fendall when he conspired with the assembly to seize control of the colony. Although their second attempt to overthrow him should have irreparably destroyed these men's standing, Lord Baltimore understood that he needed allies, and he ordered his brother Philip to pardon the men when he regained control of the colony several months later. Clustered in intertwined families in northern Anne Arundel County and Baltimore County—just across the bay from Bohemia Manor—the Utie circle performed an important function for Lord Baltimore, strengthening his claims to the Upper Chesapeake and populating an underdeveloped portion of his colony.[38] Not coincidently the council meeting at which Philip Calvert issued pardons to Utie, Goldsmith, and Stockett was the same meeting held at Utie's Spesutia Island at which he and d'Hinoyossa laid the groundwork for the New Amstel–Maryland commercial agreement. Present at this meeting, Herrman likely forged a partnership on this occasion with the Utie group to help supply him with the tobacco that Philip Calvert had promised to the burgomasters of Amsterdam.[39]

While Herrman worked to assemble these cargoes, he also probably used the route to supply tobacco to the prominent New Amsterdam trader Cornelius Steenwyck.[40] For his part, d'Hinoyossa began an ambitious plan to "make his residence" on a newly diked and drained piece of marshland where the Appoquinimink River emptied into the Delaware. Here, the WIC's Beeckman reported, D'Hinoyossa planned to "build his major city and establish trade with the English." Planning to locate the new settlement on the Delaware end of Herrman's trading trans-peninsula path, D'Hinoyossa may have been seeking to control this economically strategic location. Meanwhile, even with "the drought and early frost" of 1663, he was sure that he would be able to load two ships with "with tobacco, furs and grain" the next spring.[41] D'Hinoyossa was essentially betting his and New Amstel's future that the cross-national network Herrman had helped to assemble would enable them to maintain a steady trade with Maryland across the peninsula. This route would, in effect, extend the waters of the Chesapeake Bay— the multi-imperial space with which Herrman was so familiar—through the Delmarva Peninsula.

Another Imperial Interruption

October of 1664 brought further misfortune to Herrman and d'Hinoyossa when English forces under the command of Sir Robert Carr completed the Duke of York's conquest of New Netherland by capturing the Dutch settlements on the Delaware River. Advocated for by metropolitan merchants who were angered about Dutch interference in colonial trade and New Englanders (especially those from Connecticut) who hoped to eliminate Dutch competition for land and the fur trade, the conquest of New Netherland was an integral part of Charles

II's plans for consolidating his empire and enhancing colonial revenues. Petitions in favor of an invasion of New Netherland had begun to circulate in England soon after the Restoration. The most effective of these complained that the position of New Netherland "contiguous" to the English settlements of New England and the Chesapeake allowed "Masters, mariners, and traders" to "both by land and water carry and convey greate quantities of tobacco to the Dutch . . . thereby eluding the late Act of Navigation and defrauding His Matie." This trade was so significant, the petition held, that if New Netherland were removed, customs receipts would be "tenne thousand pounds per annum or upwards" higher. In the summer of 1663, Charles II made his brother James, Duke of York, the proprietor of a vast swath of territory running from what is today Maine through parts of Connecticut into New York, and what would become New Jersey, and eastern Pennsylvania and began to put plans for capturing New Netherland in motion. Badly in debt and in need of the revenue these lands could produce, James backed the effort. When his patent was made official in March 1664, he finalized plans for the reduction of the Dutch colony; a fleet of four vessels and between three hundred and four hundred men under the command of Sir Richard Nicolls were ready to depart by May. Nicolls's instructions could not have been more clear about English motives: the English commander should, Charles II explained, do what was "necessary soe . . . that the Dutch may noe longer ingrosse and exercise that trade which they have wrongfully possessed themselves of" in North America. In short, empire required sealing the borders.[42]

When the small English fleet arrived at New Amsterdam on August 18, 1664, it did not come as much of a surprise to Stuyvesant, who had been warned by correspondents in New England. Nevertheless the Dutch colony was poorly prepared. Stuyvesant had been pleading with the WIC to send him additional soldiers to supplement his 180 men for years, but his requests went unanswered. Adding to Stuyvesant's weak hand was a crumbling fort and insufficient munitions and provisions. When the militia largely refused to turn out and when New

Amsterdam's citizens petitioned to quickly accept the generous terms Nicolls offered, Stuyvesant was left with no alternative but to surrender the Dutch city to the English. Seeking to make his conquest of New Netherland complete, Nicolls dispatched troops to Fort Orange and to New Amstel.[43] Nicolls and Carr were well aware that the Duke of York's patent extended only to the Delaware River, not across it. Nevertheless their desire to uphold the spirit of their instructions, which had stipulated that they remove the Dutch commercial threat from English North America, trumped any concern they might have had over the legality of their actions. As Carr's orders noted, the Dutch settlements of the Delaware Bay drew "a great trade," and if "they be permitted to goe on, the gaining of this place [New Amsterdam] will be of [only] small advantage to His Majesty." Nicolls later elaborated on this point, explaining that the "great motive of the resolution to reduce [the Dutch settlements on the] Delaware" was that Marylanders' "affections . . . [were] much brib'd by their trade with the Dutch," making them so "overawed with so powerfull a neighbor" that they hesitated "to take it [New Amstel] from the Dutch." If the English hoped to end Dutch interference in their trade, Nicolls would have to do it. Carr's forces consisted of two armed vessels and one hundred soldiers, but Nicolls's orders were clear that Carr should seek a peaceful capitulation before using force. As had happened in New Amsterdam, the English commander successfully convinced the Dutch, Swedish, and Finnish residents to surrender, but when "Governor [d'Hinoyossa] and [the] soldiery altogether refused," Carr launched an attack that quickly subdued the less than thirty defenders. Succeeding admirably in capturing the fort without losing a man, Carr failed spectacularly in controlling the peace; his troops plundered the city seizing hundreds of head of livestock, enslaved Africans, and £400 worth of unsold merchandise. As retribution for New Amstel's leaders' resistance, Carr also confiscated their property including that owned by d'Hinoyossa and Van Sweringen.[44]

Herrman evidently interpreted the English capture of New Amstel as a signal that he no longer had to fulfill his end of the bargain with d'Hinoyossa, forcing the latter—who fled to Maryland—to petition Governor Charles Calvert to recover what Herrman and his partners owed him. D'Hinoyossa's petition put Calvert in a difficult position. On the one hand, he was obliged to help enforce the deal that he had helped to arrange with New Amstel. On the other hand, this trade was illegal. Trying to accommodate these conflicting interests, the governor both demanded Herman's presence in order to "sett forth upon Oath what Tobaccoes or Other Merchandizes he hath in his hands or doth know to be in other persons hands due or belonging to the said Burgomasters of Amsterdam" and simultaneously scolded him for violating the "Act of the High Court of Parliament for encouragement of trade." Then—and telling of his complicity in the whole affair—Calvert did not press the case. Herrman did not appear before the council in early February 1665 as instructed, and the case disappeared from Maryland's extant court records. Meanwhile, in deference to his Dutch partners' circumstances, Calvert naturalized d'Hinoyossa and his family and welcomed Van Sweringen to St. Mary's City, where he became a prominent resident.[45]

The English conquest eventually destroyed the multi-imperial nature of the Mid-Atlantic that Herrman and his Dutch and English partners constructed, but that process was not immediate, and in the meantime those with Dutch ties prospered. In the short term the capture of New Netherland actually enhanced Dutch merchants' ability to trade openly in the Chesapeake. The Articles of Capitulation to which New Amsterdam's burghers and Nicolls agreed provided denization for New Netherland residents, meaning they were now free to trade in any English possession with the rights of an Englishman. It was still illegal for them to carry English tobacco to the Dutch Republic, but with their growing ability to skirt trade laws those restrictions were rarely an obstacle. Local English authorities even encouraged the city's re-export trade to the Dutch Republic. Just months after taking control of the city now called New York, Nicolls wrote to Secretary of State Lord Arlington to explain that without a convoy of "merchants['] shipps with a great proportion of merchandize suitable to the trade with the Natives and both English[,] Dutch[,] and Sweedes inhabitants of New Yorke and Delaware Bay ... [,] His Matyes expences in reducing them [the Dutch] will not turne to any account." Dutch traders had formerly supplied New Netherland with goods, Nicolls continued, but because of New Amsterdam merchants' connections, it was the way that "many thousands of His Matyes subjectes in Virginia Maryland and New England were furnisht with necessaryes." Left unsaid was that these residents of the Chesapeake largely obtained the "necessaryes" with tobacco.[46] In the four years following the conquest, Dutch trade to and from New York City diminished only by half, with an average of about three to four vessels leaving for or arriving from the Dutch Republic as compared to the six to eight voyages that had been typical in the last years of Dutch rule. Mirroring the pattern of trade in earlier years, these ships carried manufactured goods to New York and furs and tobacco to the Netherlands.[47]

Manhattan merchants became more important to Chesapeake planters in the years just after the conquest as they were able to retain their connections to sources of capital and markets in the Dutch Republic while gaining the freedom to trade openly in English colonies. Elite traders like Jacob Leisler and Cornelius Steenwyck, who began venturing cargoes to Virginia and Maryland in 1662, built extended interimperial networks to move Chesapeake tobacco to Continental markets through New York City. Leisler was so important to Maryland that the colony turned to him to purchase supplies for its militia during their war with the Susquehannocks in 1675 and named him their official agent in New York. Herrman, too, remained active in preserving New York's Dutch trade. In the 1660s he worked with both Steenwyck and Leisler in channeling Chesapeake tobacco through Manhattan to the Dutch Republic. So successful was this trade that in 1667 Herrman partnered with Anna Varleth to commission a "sloope which shall Carry thirty five hogsheads of Tobacco to bee builded all of Barrell worke with a Sufficient Cabbin."[48] Perfectly sized to work the small waterways of the Chesapeake, this vessel facilitated his efforts to connect Chesapeake planters to Dutch markets along his overland path.

Herrman remained optimistic about this path's future after the conquest, and he continued to expand his landholdings on both sides of the Delmarva Peninsula. In 1665 he extended Bohemia Manor, purchasing land just to the south along Smith's Creek (today it is Little Bohemia Creek) and a one-hundred-acre parcel north of his original estate on a branch of the Bohemia River near a place he called "Delaware Landing." Several months later he acquired another tract in the region, which was "bound by Rivers['] Creek and Delawar highway on the heade of Bohemia River." Further to the north Herrman purchased 1,500 acres on the Back River. Having it surveyed in 1664 and patented in 1671, he called this portion of his estate Small Hopes (marked as "Small Hop" on the map) before renaming it Misfortune (and then later the Three Bohemian Sisters). What all these Maryland holdings had in common is that they bordered the system of tidal waterways that flowed from the middle of the peninsula into the Upper Chesapeake Bay, and given the names he used to refer to them—"Delaware Landing," "Delawar highway"—the tracts also connected to the Delaware.[49] Then, in April 1671 Herrman expanded his holdings eastward, securing an estate from the governor of New York for his son Ephraim in what is today Delaware. This estate, whose exact boundaries remain unclear, bordered the Delaware River to the east, a branch of the Appoquinimink to the north, and a branch of Black Bird Creek to the south. Herrman's son Casparus also received land in the same region along St. Augustine's Creek in February 1674.[50] Already in possession of the land bordering the Bohemia River and the tangle of waterways that flowed to the Chesapeake, Herrman now controlled the land bordering those creeks running toward the Delaware River that came closest to the Bohemia River near the Maryland-Delaware border. Together these holdings in Maryland and Delaware gave Herrman complete power over the trans-peninsula route that he had been developing for more than a decade and still hoped would become a central avenue of trade.

To ensure that these investments paid off, Herrman lobbied the commander of New Castle (the new English name for New Amstel) to help to clear a path between that city and his "Plantacion." In June 1671, just two months after he had received land for his son along this path, New York's council approved the measure.[51] Although no records detail the construction of the planned road, it is apparent that it was completed in some form. In 1672 Maryland authorities complained that this route was being used to skirt the colony's duty on tobacco. Several years later the famous Labadists (Protestant religious dissenters) Jasper Danckaerts and Peter Sluyter journeyed along a "cart road made from Apoquemene [Appoquinimink] . . . to Bohemia Creek or river" on their way to visit Herrman. "Upon this road," Danckaerts later remembered, "the goods which go from the South River to Maryland by land, are carried, and also those which pass inland from Maryland to the South River." Probably obtaining his information about the history of this path from Herrman, with whom the men visited for several days, Danckaerts's description of the cart path captures Herrman's lofty, if unfulfilled, goals. "When the Dutch governed the country," he continued, "digging a canal" connecting the "Apoquenmen and the Bohemia" Rivers "was then talked of . . . which would have afforded great convenience for trade on the South River." Maryland planters could have "come from Maryland [to the Delaware River] to buy all they had need of, and would have been able to transport their tobacco more easily to that river, than to the great bay of Virginia." Additionally, Danckaerts explained, "the cheap market of the Hollanders in the South [River] would have drawn more trade; and if the people of Maryland had goods to ship . . . [they] would have chosen this route, the more so because as many of their goods, perhaps, would for various reasons be shipped to Holland, as to England."[52]

Despite Herrman's inability to fully realize his vision, tobacco flowed along this route for decades. In 1697 Maryland authorities complained that "severall good Cart Roads" running between Maryland and the Delaware counties of Pennsylvania, "especially one which is between the Head of Bohemia river in this Countrey, and Opoquiraing Creek [Appoquinimink River] which runs into Delaware River a few Miles below New Castle" allowed "severall hundreds of Hogsheads [of tobacco]" to be smuggled out of Maryland each year.[53] It is uncertain how long what became known as the "Appoquominie path" lasted, but in the eighteenth century there remained a series of roads and cart paths that connected landings at the eastern and western ends of the Bohemia and Appoquinimink Rivers.[54] By the end of that century, the route was still well known enough that three Philadelphia entrepreneurs proposed a packet line connecting that city with Baltimore along it. Employing "good and stout vessels" the men planned to move "heavy articles of Merchandize" from Morris's Wharf in Philadelphia to "Appoquinomink Landing," then, using a seven-mile portage across the peninsula, to the "tide water[s] of Bohemia" and on to the county wharf in Baltimore. "The contiguous situation of the Landings, the safety of Navigation, the goodness of roads," the men wrote in the *Philadelphia Gazette & Universal Daily Advertiser* in April 1794, would "render this conveyance safe and expeditious" and would "facilitate . . . communication between Philadelphia and Baltimore."[55] Over thirty years later, in 1829, this venture was made obsolete when the Chesapeake & Delaware Canal opened, cutting through the peninsula just five miles to the north. Although the cities this new canal connected had changed and the economic interests of their residents had evolved, the route Herrman had planned more than a century before remained economically important to the communities of the Mid-Atlantic.

An Intercolonial Legacy

Herrman's move to Maryland in 1661 and the English conquest of New Netherland did not reorient the mapmaker's imagining of the larger Mid-Atlantic as an interconnected unit, nor did it hinder his border-crossing. Busy sailing the waterways of the Chesapeake, taking measurements, and sketching his map, Herrman understandably had fewer opportunities to travel to New York City but he nevertheless still owned property there until at least 1673, continued to appear in Manhattan courts, and even served on a jury in the city.[56] Simultaneously, Herrman assumed a more active role in Maryland, serving in the militia, sitting as a juror, and becoming a justice of the peace for the newly formed Cecil County. In 1666 Herrman (together with his children and George Hack and Anna Varleth) also took the rare step of being naturalized in Maryland.[57] Spending more time in Maryland, Herrman became aware of another problem that would require intercolonial cooperation to solve and from which he could benefit. When he had first traveled overland across the Delmarva Peninsula on his 1659 embassy to Maryland, he encountered a community of runaway Dutch, Swedish, and Finnish servants living as squatters in the borderlands between New Amstel and Maryland on the Delmarva Peninsula.[58] Now a planter dependent upon bound labor to prosper, Herrman realized that the same fluid borders between empires that had given him opportunity also provided a chance for servants and the enslaved to find freedom. Hoping to eliminate this opening and to profit in the process, Herrman lobbied the Maryland Assembly to select his plantation in the Upper Chesapeake as the location for a "Logg house Prison . . . for the Surety & Safe keeping of Runnawayes & fugitives," which the colony was planning to build. In 1669 the Assembly agreed. As part of a new law, "An Act for Preventing servants & Criminall persons from Running out of this Province," the General Assembly authorized Herrman to construct a "Twenty foot Square" prison to house captured runaways for which he would be compensated with ten thousand pounds of tobacco. In addition to housing the fugitives, Herrman was also charged with "Apprehending & remanding Runnawayes from deleware Bay or any other Northerne Plantacoons," a task for which his intercolonial network was well suited.[59] Whereas porous boundaries had allowed Herrman to tie New Netherland and

the English Chesapeake together, those same permeable borders eventually threatened Maryland's plantation economy when they facilitated
labor's mobility. Needing an agent with connections that spanned the
region, Maryland's government again turned to Herrman who was now
entrusted to help erase the space between colonial borders and unite a
now English Mid-Atlantic.

In the years after he completed the manuscript map for *Virginia
and Maryland* in 1670, Herrman's health began to fail and his ability
to continue to influence affairs in the Mid-Atlantic finally faded. New
migration to Maryland, the gradual diminishing of Dutch influence in
the region, and the eventual rise of Pennsylvania as Maryland's biggest
rival meant that his particular intercolonial skills became less useful
over time. In 1678 Herrman was called upon to "treate" with a group
of Lenape who had been accused of causing "great Damage and injury
[to] the Inhabitants in Baltemore and Caecill Counties" by "driving away
and killing their Stocks," but his involvement in regional affairs largely
ended after this date. In January 1680 Herrman's eldest son, Ephraim,
who divided his time between New York and New Castle, reported that
his father was ill and "extreame[ly] weakly."[60] Just one month earlier La-
badist visitors Jasper Danckaerts and Peter Sluyter found him unwell
and noted that Herrman had showed them "every kindness he could in
his condition, as he was very miserable, both in soul and body." In 1682
Lord Baltimore and William Penn both corresponded with Herrman
concerning their dispute over the border between Maryland and the
newly founded Pennsylvania, but the now aged mapmaker did not become directly involved in their dispute.[61] With its creator in poor health
and largely confined to his house, Herrman's map was left to stand for
the cross-national community that he and his fellow border-crossers
helped to create, confidently recording colonists' belief that their intercolonial world had worked. Understood within this context, Herrman's
map emerges as a local response to the Restoration government's efforts
to reshape the empire on metropolitan terms. Its depictions of orderly
plantations and towns, recordings of shoals and channels, and naming

of rivers and creeks testify to the local inhabitants whose daily endeavors fashioned communities out of land grants. The map is a claim that they—colonial planters and merchants, English and Dutch—not those in England had made this place. As powerful as this declaration was, however, Lord Baltimore had a very different goal in mind when he commissioned Herrman's map, and his efforts in London to rework the map to fit his goals would transform this local understanding of the Chesapeake into a metropolitan one, at least on paper.

4

The Patron and the Engraver

In late March 1674 the London instrument-maker, geographer, and map-seller John Seller paid ten shillings to place a small advertisement in the *London Gazette*, the crown's official paper of record. Printed in two columns front and back on a single, thin, 6 ¾ by 11 inch sheet, the semi-weekly paper contained court news, dispatches on foreign affairs from English ambassadors, notices of the arrival and departure of merchant vessels, and, beginning in 1668, advertisements. Seller's notice, which appeared in the March 30–April 2, 1674 issue, read: "There is now Extant a new Map of *Virginia* and *Mariland,* in four sheets, Describing the Counties, and the Scituation of the Plantations in the said Countreys, with the Rivers[,] Creeks, Bays, Roads, and Harbors on the Sea-Coasts. Published by His Majesties especial Licence. Sold by *John Seller*, Hydrographer to the King, at his Shops at the *Hermitage* in *Wapping*, and in *Exchange-Alley* in *Cornhil, Londen*" (Figure 4.1). Only seven lines long and tucked in the bottom right-hand corner of the verso side, Seller's advertisement was printed between the news that an audience between

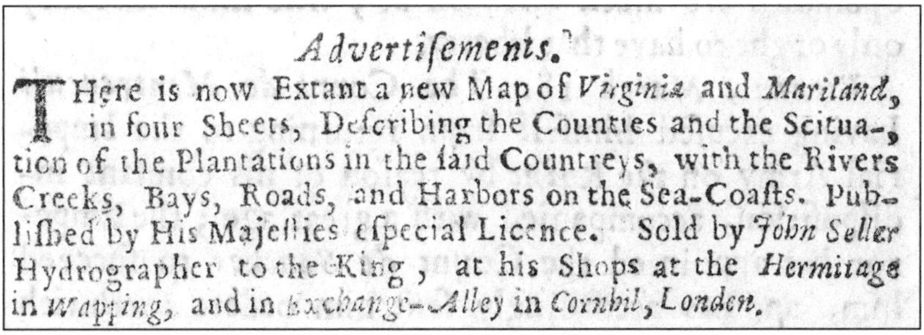
Advertiſements.

THere is now Extant a new Map of *Virginia* and *Mariland*, in four Sheets, Deſcribing the Counties and the Scitua-, tion of the Plantations in the ſaid Countreys, with the Rivers Creeks, Bays, Roads, and Harbors on the Sea-Coaſts. Publiſhed by His Majeſties eſpecial Licence. Sold by *John Seller* Hydrographer to the King, at his Shops at the *Hermitage* in *Wapping*, and in *Exchange-Alley* in *Cornhil*, *Londen*.

FIGURE 4.1. Advertisement for *Virginia and Maryland* from the *London Gazette*, March 30–April 2, 1674, verso (detail). Courtesy of the John Carter Brown Library at Brown University.

Charles II and the "Envoy Extraordinary from the Crown of *Poland*" had been conducted the day before at Whitehall "in the usual manner" and a plea for information about a runaway twelve-year-old apprentice "in a brown Searge Suit," named John Antrobus.[1] Most likely printed just weeks before, Herrman's *Virginia and Maryland* had completed its journey from manuscript to printed map.

Already a multilayered artifact that included information Herrman derived from first-hand observation, local informants, and extant maps, the map acquired still more strata of meaning in London. There, Herrman's vision of an interimperial Mid-Atlantic was surrounded and overlaid by symbols of English authority. Foremost of these emblems was the large insignia of the Royal Arms of Great Britain. Engraved deeply and thus printed darkly, the emblem sits in the top center of the map interspersed with the toponym "Virginia." Flanking this feature in the right-center are the name "Maryland" and Lord Baltimore's coat of arms. Mirroring these elements, at the bottom of the map the engraver William Faithorne added (running from left to right) a small block of text indicating the map's copyright and where it could be purchased, a large plinth serving as a cartouche that proclaims the map's title and author, a set of mariner's dividers that serve to illustrate the map's scale, and finally, an almost certainly imagined portrait miniature of Augustine Herrman. Scattered around the map's edges are a series of textual descriptions relating historical, physical, and faunal details about the region.

In order to understand the new cultural and intellectual uses to which Englishmen put *Virginia and Maryland* in London, it is necessary to analyze the process by which Herrman's manuscript became a printed map. Carefully describing these mechanical processes and unpeeling the layers of symbol and text that metropolitan actors added to the manuscript map as they transformed it into print reveal the ways this colonial object was encased in a set of imperial narratives that made the Chesapeake useful for English men and women, as well as the resulting tensions in the map that stemmed from the coexistence of these often countervailing meanings.

In the quest to understand the expanding colonial world, early modern Europeans turned to techniques of representation familiar to them to translate that world into something more comprehensible. Foremost among these was the use of print. Various kinds of printing, whether of images or text, had the effect not only of disseminating ideas more widely than was possible before but also of creating new ways of communicating knowledge. More specifically, prints, whether devotional or genre scenes, scientific illustrations, portraits, or maps, held a special place in European culture for their ability to erase distance and time and to bring life to the unfamiliar. Antwerp cartographer Abraham Ortelius captured the power of printed maps in early modern Europe in the introduction to his famous atlas, *Theatrum orbis terrarium* (Theatre of the World). When "Mappe[s]," he wrote, are "layed before our eyes" they serve as "certaine glasses" that allow us to "behold things done, or places where they were done, as if they were at this time present" and thus "will the longer be kept in memory, and make the deeper impression in us."[2] While contemporary scholars have often separated printed texts from printed images when examining early modern print culture, considering, for example, engraving and book printing as two different genres, seventeenth-century viewers did not usually make such a distinction.[3] Instead they understood this varied collection of representational devices as a whole. Maps, which made use of both printed text and engraved images, encourage us to similarly transcend such distinctions. In *Virginia and Maryland* these elements combined together to sever the map's connection to its manuscript form and to lend it new authority so it too could make a deeper impression on English viewers.

It was not just their visual impact that gave prints power; their mode of production and the range of their consumption also enhanced their authority. Early modern Europeans understood prints to be among the most civilized of objects involving, as they did, the newest technologies alongside the already revered metal and mechanical arts. The large number of individuals involved in a print's creation (artist, engraver, printer, publisher, seller), who often listed their names prominently on images, enhanced prints' power by emphasizing their authenticity. A royal or guild license to print and distribute the images reinforced the blizzard of names and reputations already listed on many engravings and lent them still greater legitimacy. Finally, the often public acts of purchasing, viewing, and displaying identical versions of the same prints created communities of viewers who invested these images with additional power.[4] In its original form, Herrman's manuscript served the interests of a narrow group of users—those traders with whom Herrman may have shared his work and Lord Baltimore who was eager to see his colony—but as a printed and public object, the map became the definitive English image of the Chesapeake, complete with a new narrative. This narrative was accomplished through the map's intertextuality, its interplay of representational media that emphasized the crown's mastery along with the details of the Chesapeake—its rivers, bays, inlets, and shoals, its counties, towns, and plantations—which together spoke to the imperial uses to which the landscape could be put.

The Publisher

The first to intercede in Herrman's interimperial vision were Lord Baltimore and his son Charles Calvert, who perceived in the Bohemian's map the potential for political advancement for themselves and for the colony they controlled. Once he finished drafting his map, Herrman most likely sent it to Lord Baltimore in England through Governor Charles Calvert. Baltimore, delighted, told Herrman that he "Received no Small Satisfaction by the Rarity of that map" and showed the manuscript to King Charles II, who "Commended the Exactness of the work—Aplauding it to be the best map, that was Ever Drawn of any Country Whatsoever." In recognition of this success, the king granted £40 to Lord Baltimore as an "award" for its "drawing, ingraveing and Printing." The timing of the king's grant to Baltimore, more than two years before the map appeared in print, suggests that this "award" was actually a subsidy to induce Baltimore to publish the map, a supposition that a letter from Governor Charles Calvert to Lord Baltimore seems to confirm. In April 1672 Charles Calvert wrote, "I am very Glad that Augustines Mapp is like to bee printed and that your Lordship has gott some Moneyes Towards itt." A decade later Lord Baltimore confirmed this chronology when he noted to secretary of the Lords of Trade, William Blathwayt, "his Majetie Had been pleas'd to allowe of, and did order some moneys for the Printing," of "Mr. Augustine Herman's Mapp."[5] When the king later issued a copyright for the map in January 1674, the proclamation confiming this grant, which suggests that the king had actively encouraged Herrman's commission, indicated that the merchant "hath by our comand been for these severall yeares last past Making A Survey of our Countryes of Virginia and Maryland, and hath made A Mapp of the same Consisting of foure Sheetes of Paper with All the Rivers, Creeks and Soundings &c."[6]

Lord Baltimore was almost certainly the map's publisher, arranging its engraving and printing. In the seventeenth century publishers played the key role in connecting the various parts of the publishing process. They were often responsible for commissioning artists, engravers, and printers and then either sold the works themselves or, as in the case of Lord Baltimore, coordinated with retailers to offer the finished works for sale. As we have already seen, the decision to commission a map in late 1660 served an immediate purpose as the Calverts clashed with officials from New Netherland over the precise northern boundary of Maryland. Particularly important in international diplomacy was the placement of the fortieth parallel of latitude, the northern extent of Baltimore's patent, which was pictured on seventeenth-century maps anywhere from the head of the Chesapeake Bay to north of the future site of Philadelphia. Establishing the location of this line of latitude, and thus Baltimore's control over what is now Delaware, was one of the chief things that he hoped Herrman's map would accomplish. While Herrman was working on the map, however, the politics of this dispute changed. The patent Charles II issued to his brother, James, the Duke of York, specified that his new province of New York stretched only to the east bank of the

Delaware River, but in 1664 Richard Nicolls's decision to oust the Dutch from their settlements on the Delaware River effectively expanded New York across the river to include the Dutch communities in Delaware. Knowing that Lord Baltimore would protest this action, Nicolls ordered Robert Carr, who captured New Amstel, to inform Governor Charles Calvert of his presence and to tell him that if "Lord Baltimore, doth pretend Right thereunto by his patent (which is a doubtfull Ca[se])," Carr was to say that he was "only Keep[ing] possession till his Majesty is informed and sattisfyed otherwise." Suddenly Lord Baltimore was forced to shore up his claim to these lands. On the ground he demanded that the mix of Swedes, Dutch, and English who lived there recognize his authority as opposed to the Duke of York's. As we have seen, when they refused, he ordered militiamen to harass the colonists by confiscating property and threatening their destruction. Maryland forces returned again when the Dutch briefly recaptured New York and the settlements on the Delaware River during the Third Anglo-Dutch War (1672–1674), taking the town of Whorekill at Cape Henlopen at the opening of Delaware Bay, burning its structures, and confiscating much of the residents' property. Meanwhile in London, Lord Baltimore hoped that publishing *Virginia and Maryland*, which clearly marked these settlements as residing within Maryland, would strengthen his position. There is no evidence that Lord Baltimore used the map to lobby Charles II directly, but the conspicuous inclusion of the settlements along the Delaware (including Whorekill and New Castle) without denoting their status as part of New York and the placement of the "N" and "D" of "Maryland" within the disputed territory suggests Baltimore at least partly intended the map to support his claim to the Delaware settlements. Ultimately his efforts failed when the same lands were transferred to William Penn in 1682.[7]

It was not only Maryland's northern border that was under threat in the 1660s and 1670s. Since Maryland's founding, the proprietor had been forced to defend his colony's borders from Virginians. In the mid-seventeenth century the flashpoint for this disagreement was at the southern tip of the Delmarva Peninsula, between the Maryland county of Somerset and the Virginia county of Accomack (which had been divided from northern Northampton County in 1663). Though marshy, this region was a productive tobacco area. This was where Herrman's sister-in-law Anna Varleth and her husband, George Hack, established their first plantation and where Herrman bought land in 1655. In the next decade the region grew quickly. The population of the Maryland and Virginia counties of the Eastern Shore rose from fewer than five hundred colonists in 1660 to more than three thousand by 1670.[8] With the population expanding, locating the border became a pressing issue as each government attempted to administer justice, certify landholding, and collect taxes. The problem was that although Maryland's charter was clear that Calvert's grant should be "divided from . . . [Virginia] by a Right Line drawn from the Promontory, or Head-Land, called Watkin's Point, situate[d] upon the Bay aforesaid, near the river Wigloo, on the West, unto the main Ocean on the East" the exact location of Watkins Point was in doubt. Virginia placed it at the Wicomico River, and Maryland believed it was farther south at the mouth of the Pokomoke Sound. This dispute explains why the border between Maryland and Virginia on the Eastern Shore is so precisely marked with a double line of trees and an explanatory note is included on *Virginia and Maryland*. In fact, one reason the Calverts accepted Herrman's offer to make a map of their province at all was to win the border dispute with Virginia. After learning that Herrman had produced a prototype of his map in February 1666, Lord Baltimore instructed his son Charles Calvert to reward Herrman for his work in mapping this boundary if he "shall finde that . . . Herman hath done us Right in stateing the said Limits and boundaryes of our said Province Justly," especially "in the True stateing of the said boundaryes and Limits in relation to Watkins Pointe and Delaware Bay."[9] The dispute with Virginia was eventually resolved through a joint agreement between Virginia's surveyor general, Edmund Scarborough, and Philip Calvert in 1668, as an inscription on the printed map indicates.[10]

Lord Baltimore's eagerness to secure Maryland's boundaries must have contributed to his decision to commission a printed copy of Herrman's map. This concern was probably not sufficient for him to undertake what was an expensive proposition, however, as manuscript maps were often sufficient legal proof in negotiations between European powers. Lord Baltimore's decision to publish the map, therefore, must have been influenced by other factors. Chief among these was his desire to advance a particular vision of his colony that aligned with a new emphasis in Restoration England on urbanization as essential to building civic community and maintaining order.[11] Since its founding, Maryland had been riven with factionalism stemming from the conflict between the colony's majority Protestant settlers and its Catholic ruling class. Lord Baltimore made religious plurality an important feature of his venture, but this did not mean that anti-Catholicism did not travel across the Atlantic with the colony's settlers. Motivated by both religion and the democratic impulses swirling through the English Atlantic during the Commonwealth period, Maryland Protestants routinely challenged the proprietor's control. In addition to being encouraged by the popish fears that surged through the English Atlantic in the mid-seventeenth century, as well as by Virginians who remained resentful that Maryland had been carved out of their colony, Protestant men and women were increasingly suspicious of the colony's Catholic ruling class, which controlled the manors where many lived as tenants and enjoyed the proprietor's favor. Twice in the colony's first two decades, Protestant rebellions briefly succeeded in undermining Lord Baltimore'scontrol of the colony, but a combination of military force and deft politicking in London preserved his proprietorship.[12]

When Lord Baltimore commissioned the map in late 1660, he had just regained Maryland from the most recent rebels only to face new economic woes as the price of Oronoco tobacco fell. In response the Calverts spent much of the decade working to improve the colony's commerce. The commissioning of Herrman's "Mapp of all the Rivers Creekes and Harbours," which Baltimore hoped would be to "the bennefitt of trade," was but one part of this effort. In addition, he planned to build a system of ports that would both encourage trade and allow him to manage commerce more efficiently. In a series of proclamations in 1668 and 1669, Lord Baltimore ordered that eleven "Certain Ports within this Province of Maryland be appointed for the Lading and unlading of Merchandize." Arguing that these commercial cities were "necessary for the good of Trade," the proprietor hoped that building them would secure him additional tax revenues.[13]

Baltimore's decision in late 1671 or 1672 to commission a printed version of Herrman's map resonated with the ways he had recently begun to reimagine his colony. Though the ports he envisioned did not yet exist, he must have hoped a new map would not only firmly display Maryland's proper boundaries but would also present an image of a commercial, urban, and, above all, orderly colony to Restoration London. This re-envisioning of Maryland, in turn, offered him the opportunity to adjust to the new political environment in Whitehall as the crown sought to make the Atlantic colonies more productive. Baltimore intended *Virginia and Maryland* to remind Charles II of Maryland's importance to the growing empire.[14] Finally, Lord Baltimore was likely inspired to fund the engraving of Herrman's map by a desire to personally connect with Maryland. An absentee proprietor who had never visited his North American colony, he must have longed to better imagine and experience his colony, and a large printed map would have provided him with exactly that opportunity.

The Engraver

The acts of engraving and printing Herrman's map in London drew a new set of metropolitan actors into the production of *Virginia and Maryland*. Before Hydrographer to the King John Seller could offer the finished map for sale in one of his two shops, at least two other skilled artisans (and their assistants) needed to transform the manuscript into copper and then back again to paper. Because producing a printed map was technically demanding and capital intensive, it was impossible for Lord Baltimore to commission a colonial printer to do the work; there were no presses capable of producing fine engraved maps in seventeenth-century British America. Instead Baltimore, and all period publishers, required the services of skilled artisans in London. These craftsmen included a skilled engraver who inscribed the map's lines in copper and a knowledgeable printer who pressed ink and paper into that plate to produce the finished map. Most European mapmakers used the intaglio process, a form of printing that German artisans pioneered in the fifteenth century. As opposed to the earlier technique of relief printing, in which unwanted material is removed from a wooden block to leave behind a raised design that is then inked and stamped onto the page, in intaglio printing, lines are incised into a metal plate with a burin. The plate is inked and wiped clean, leaving ink only in the recesses of the engraved lines. A press then exerts great pressure to push a sheet of paper laid upon the plate into the grooves where the paper absorbs the ink. The result is an image that appears slightly raised on the page, with the inked lines standing above the white, uninked surfaces. Because the intaglio process allowed engravers to make the kinds of extraordinarily precise curved lines grouped closely together that mapmaking required, this technique became the standard for cartographic printing during the sixteenth century.[15]

At first glance, Lord Baltimore's choice of William Faithorne to engrave *Virginia and Maryland* does not seem an obvious one. An engraver best known for his portrait miniatures of the Stuart court and of important English authors, artists, and scientists, Faithorne had little prior experience engraving maps. Though the craft had yet to become fully specialized in the late seventeenth century, there were nevertheless by 1670 a growing number of London engravers, many of them Dutch and French immigrants, who were vastly more experienced in producing maps. In fact Faithorne is known to have engraved only one other map in his lifetime, *An Exact Delineation of the Cities of London and Westminster and the Suburbs thereof.* Engraved in 1658 but based on a survey Richard Newcourt completed at least a decade earlier, this map is an important if rare (only two copies still exist) map of London as it looked just before the Great Fire of 1666. Printed on twelve sheets and measuring 72 ¾ inches by 39 ½ inches when assembled, it is a monumental work that resembles *Virginia and Maryland* in its large format and its topographical specificity, but as an urban bird's eye view, the image belongs to a different mapmaking tradition.[16] Without extant correspondence relating to the engraving and printing of *Virginia and Maryland*, we can only speculate as to the reasons Lord Baltimore, or perhaps his agent, chose Faithorne to engrave Herrman's work. One possible explanation is that Baltimore had seen Faithorne's London map and was convinced that he had the aptitude to engage in another large-scale detailed project. Such massive undertakings depended not only on the technical skill of the engraver, but also on the master craftsman's ability to manage a workshop of assistants and apprentices who labored on the plates. But if success in a similar endeavor was his standard for selecting Faithorne, there were other engravers with more cartographic experience whom Baltimore could have picked. A more likely explanation for his choice hinged on the engraver's biography and his social connections.

Born in about 1620 to a London metalworker who specialized in producing bits and bridles for horses, William Faithorne was apprenticed as an engraver to the printseller William Peake in 1635. Just five years later, Peake's son Robert, who took over his father's business and Faithorne's indenture upon his father's death in 1639, published Faithorne's first signed prints. Several years after that, both men's lives in London changed dramatically. Robert Peake was the grandson of one of James I's court painters, also named Robert Peake. When war broke out between the Royalists and Parliament in 1642, Peake's family connections prompted him to join the Royalist army, bringing along the twenty-two year old Faithorne as his ensign. Peake and Faithorne served together for three years until Parliamentary forces captured both in 1645. Though imprisoned, Faithorne continued to engrave, producing a number of portraits of both Royalist and Parliamentary supporters.[17]

As Royalist fortunes waned in the late 1640s, Faithorne's rose. Having somehow convinced his jailors to reduce his sentence from death to banishment from England, he moved to Paris where he worked for a variety of well-known publishers. By 1651, Faithorne was well established enough to join twenty-seven other engravers and printers in lobbying against a proposed French tax on prints. Perhaps sensing a more favorable climate in England, Faithorne returned to London in 1652 and he set up his own print shop, first in Temple Bar and then just outside of it. Capitalizing on his knowledge of Paris's print market, which was among the finest in Europe, and his connections with publishers there, Faithorne earned a reputation as London's chief importer of Continental prints. In addition to retailing others' work, Faithorne also continued to engrave and to publish his own prints, focusing primarily on engraved portraits in quarto size of leading scientific, literary, and public figures. He also experimented with portraits in colored chalks, a practice that earned him the notice of Samuel Pepys, who, in 1666, greatly admired Faithorne's depiction of "Lady Castlemayne . . . in red chalke and other colours" and tried "to buy it." Faithorne refused, however, because he still needed "it awhile to correct his Copper plate by." One month later Pepys returned to buy three copies of the completed print.[18] Possessing skill, reputation, and strong Royalist credentials, Faithorne soon earned the notice of the king and was appointed "engraver in copper to the king," upon Charles II's restoration in 1660.[19]

His ascent to the top of his trade complete, Faithorne had the time and the fame to write the most accessible English treatise on engraving in the seventeenth century. Largely a simplification and translation of an earlier French work, Faithorne's *The Art of Graveing and Etching* (1662) was nevertheless celebrated for advancing London's still nascent print trade.[20] Although Faithorne's position began to slip in the mid-1670s as new competitors from the Low Countries and France arrived in the metropole, in 1670 and 1671, however, when Lord Baltimore was looking for someone to engrave Herrman's map, Faithorne was still a prominent figure whose name added legitimacy to the endeavor. Himself a close associate of the Stuarts (Charles II's father had given him the charter for Maryland), Baltimore would surely also have been attracted to Faithorne's strong Royalist connections, making him a good choice to engrave a map that reinforced his claim to his colony and acknowledged the debt his family owed the Stuarts.

Though not an experienced mapmaker, Faithorne nevertheless possessed the necessary skills to engrave Herrman's map. As seen in Chapter 2, one of the central features of Herrman's work is the closely spaced lines indicating slight gradations in water depth along the coastline of the Chesapeake. Manuscript maps sometimes accomplished this effect through the use of color, with the darkest colors indicating the shallowest depths, so that the color grew lighter as it moved away from the coast in correspondence with increasing water depth. Alternatively, some chartmakers used different colors to highlight sandbars and shoals. Accomplishing this effect in a black and white printed image, however, required an artist to engrave closely spaced lines of different depths and thickness. The approach resulted in a print that used ink and whitespace to simulate texture. This skill, not coincidently, was exactly the one that engravers like Faithorne used to produce the visual effect of flesh when executing engraved portraits.[21] Take, for example, Faithorne's portrait of mathematician John Kersey (Figure 4.2). Published nearly simultaneously with *Virginia and Maryland* and typical of much of the engraver's work, this 10 ⅜ inch by 7 ⅛ inch print after a Gerard Soest portrait served as the frontispiece to Kersey's *The Elements of that Mathematical Art Commonly Called Algebra* (1673).[22] In order to capture the shape of Kersey's face and his long flowing hair, Faithorne engraved a dense network of closely spaced crosshatched lines that make Kersey's face appear three-dimensional. Faithorne used this same technique along the coastline of the Chesapeake in *Virginia and Maryland* by varying the thickness of his lines when necessary to

FIGURE 4.2. Frontispiece by William Faithorne, after
Gilbert Soest, to John Kersey's *The Elements of that
Mathematical Art Commonly Called Algebra*, 1673.
© National Portrait Gallery, London.

indicate specific coastal conditions, such as in the section of his map of
just south of "Pokomoack Bay." Faithorne alternated between narrow,
closely spaced grooves (as he did throughout the map) and between
smaller lines, spaced slightly farther apart and running perpendicu-
lar to the coast, to indicate shallow water (see Figure 2.10). While
Faithorne was by no means the only engraver who could have produced
this work, his technical experience merged with his royal connections
to make him an ideal choice to engrave *Virginia and Maryland*.

From Manuscript to Print

Once he received his commission and negotiated his fee, Faithorne began to work. Not yet fully specialized, engravers learned the art through a variety of apprenticeships, some to metal workers (usually silver- and goldsmiths) and some to print engravers. It is unclear who first taught Faithorne his craft, but it is possible that his father, Daniel Faithorne, was his first master. As a producer of metal bits and bridles, the elder Faithorne would have commanded some of the skills engravers utilized because these objects were often embellished with the kinds of engraved designs that were common on armor. If Faithorne did not learn his craft from his father, he likely acquired his expertise from another engraver working for the Peakes, such as the well-known John Payne.[23]

However he acquired his knowledge, we can confidently assume that Faithorne worked in the same method that he outlined in *The Art of Graveing and Etching*. Before he began to cut his plate, it was essential that he properly prepare his tools and equipment. With copper being by far the most expensive of engravers' outlays, and with most engravers working on commission and thus having to raise the capital for their supplies themselves (publishers only occasionally covered these costs), it was critical that they prepare the copper plate correctly. Among the most important of these tasks was selecting the right piece of copper. The best material was rolled copper that measured only one or two millimeters thick, had a "yellowish colour," and was "free from flaws, and not too hard." Once Faithorne picked the correct piece, he then polished the copper. Using progressively smoother grinding stones and water or oil, the engraver rubbed the plate firmly until it was impossible to "perceive any dints, or flaws, or marks of the hammer." At each stage in the process it was necessary to use smooth even strokes so as not to scratch the plate. If any "scratches" did remain, they would be smoothed using a steel burnisher. Once the plate had been washed a final time and rubbed with "stale Bread' to remove any residual grease, it was finally "fitly prepared to lay on your Varnish," the final part of the preparation process. To complete this step Faithorne would have heated the varnish, or ground, which consisted mainly of beeswax, and applied a thin layer to the plate. It was into this ground that the engraver would mark his lines with the ground helping to protect those portions of the plate that would remain smooth (Figure 4.3).[24]

Once prepared, the plate was ready to receive the image. Here Faithorne had a number of different options. The most straightforward was to begin simply by working freehand, using a readied drawing as a starting point. Because the printed image would be the inverse of whatever the engraver incised into the plate, some used a mirror to reverse the image so that they could copy the reflected image directly onto the plate. The resulting print would thus have the same orientation as the source image. Map engravers, however, did not largely work freehand. The necessity of reproducing a source map exactly meant that these kinds of images required a more precise technique for transferring the image to their plate. Ordinarily engravers took a series of tracings from the manuscript map in sections that were "of the same bignesse" as the plates to be printed. These paper tracings could then be oiled and held "by the fire" to help the oil penetrate the paper. The result was a series of translucent drawings that were then firmly attached face down to the plate. With the outlines of the map showing through the back of the now transparent paper (replicating the use of a mirror) the engraver then transferred the design to the prepared wax ground. Using a "needle or drawing-point," he either scored the lines directly into the wax or poked holes along each line, a process called "pouncing." If Faithorne used the latter of these techniques, he then dusted the entire image with fine chalk once the pouncing was completed; the dust penetrated the holes in the source map and affixed itself to the wax below. Finally, he removed the paper tracing carefully so as not to disturb the wax ground.

Once Faithorne had transferred his guidelines to the prepared plate, his next step was to engrave those lines into the copper plate so that it could be inked and printed. The tool Faithorne used to accomplish

FIGURE 4.3. The Workshop of an Engraver [*Sculptura in Aes*], plate 19, from *Nova Reperta*, workshop of Philip Gale after Jan van der Straet published by Philips Galle, ca. 1600. Courtesy of the Metropolitan Museum, Harris Brisbane Dick Fund, 1953, www. metmuseum.org.

this is called a "burin," or "graver." Essentially a square or lozenge-shaped steel shaft attached to a wooden handle, this tool was sharpened to an oblique point with an oiled whetstone so that the resulting "strokes, or hatches, show[ed] . . . life and vigour" with the application of minimal force (Figure 4.4). It was necessary for engravers to have at hand a number of different burins of varying diameters in order to make broad, deep strokes or narrow, delicate, curved ones, depending on the demands of each image. Holding the burin with the rounded handle in the palm (Faithorne advocated cutting off a portion of the knob so as to avoid scraping it against the plate), the engraver placed

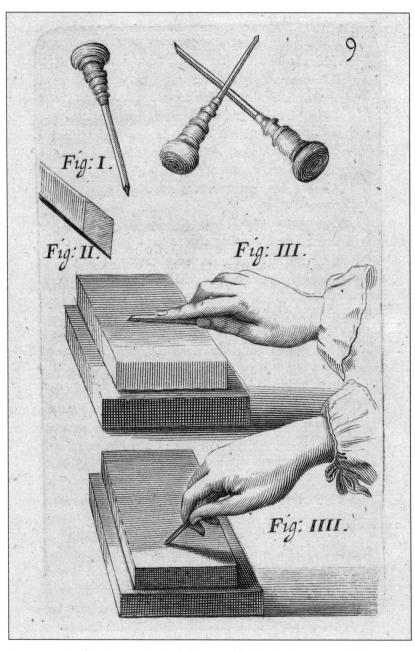

FIGURE 4.4. "Forms of graving-tools, and the manner of holding the graver," William
Faithorne (1616–1691), plate 9, from *The Art of Graveing and Etching*. London, 1662,
engraving. Courtesy of the Yale Center for British Art, Paul Mellon Collection. NE1760 E9.

his forefinger along the blade and gently pushed it along the traced lines through the wax and into the metal. Rotating the plate on a sand-filled bag so as to always be able to push the burin away from the body, he incised V-shaped grooves into the plate, scraping away the curls of copper from the sides and front of the instrument's point as he worked. Varying the pressure of the forefinger against the shaft of the burin to control the depth and width of each channel (and thus the weight of the printed line), Faithorne had to work carefully, for any mistake could only be repaired by the time consuming task of pounding out the mistake and reburnishing that section. To check his work Faithorne likely oiled the graven lines to heighten their visibility and then examined them in a mirror so as to compare them to the source image. Once he had fully incised the plate, Faithorne removed the remaining wax and tidied the engraved lines by scraping another graver across the edges of the opened lines so as to "take off the roughness of the strokes" while at the same time taking "heed of making any new scratches" in the work. Using a piece of "black Felt of Castor, liquored over a little with oyl-olive," the engraver finished his work by wiping clean the finished plate.

The Printer at Work

With the engraving completed and the plate cleaned, Faithorne's job was finished. Next, he passed the engraved plate to a printer. There is no evidence to suggest whom Lord Baltimore chose to print *Virginia and Maryland* but that person most likely would have worked for a set fee, just as Faithorne had, with some of the printer's costs possibly being paid by the £40 stipend Baltimore received from the king. As opposed to those who produced books on letter-presses, the printers who produced maps and other images were almost always specialists. Their indispensable piece of equipment was the rolling press, an expensive machine that was able to generate the tremendous amount of force needed for intaglio printing. Held firmly in a strong wooden frame, two wooden rollers, which were the most important parts of the press, were arranged horizontally, one above the other, as in a clothes wringer. While the bottom roller could turn freely, the upper roller was connected to a screw and handle that the printer turned to power the press. Usually made out of an extremely hard wood like walnut, these rollers had to be turned precisely on a lathe so that they were exactly round and as smooth as possible. To ensure their rigidity, the rollers were further reinforced with iron rings at each end. Passing between these rollers was a wooden table, also made of strong wood planed "extremely even[ly], and smooth," so that when placed between the rollers "no Light may be seen between" the parts. Finally, the table was affixed to the press's frame so that it slid between the rollers; when the artisan turned the screw and handle of the upper roller, it turned, dragging the table forward with the lower roller spinning freely in the opposite direction to allow it to move (see Figure 4.3).[25]

Before the printer could start to produce prints, he had to prepare the ink, paper, plate, and press. The ink seventeenth-century English printers most commonly employed in copperplate printing was composed of "vine black," a kind of charcoal derived from plant matter. Grinding it just before use, printers mixed the vine black with heated oil (often walnut or linseed) until it reached the consistency of a smooth syrup. While one printer mixed the ink another was probably busy preparing the paper, which in the seventeenth century was made from cloth and usually imported from France. Taking five or six sheets at a time, the printer wetted them in a large trough until they were "more or less gummed, from one side to the other very even[ly], to prevent foldings." Once the paper was wet, the printer stacked it and placed a heavy board upon the stack to "make the Water soak into the said *Paper*, and drain away what is superfluous." Taking up the engraved and smoothed plate, the printer heated it over the fire "making it pretty warm." Then, with a clean rag, he wiped it one final time to remove any stray dust that might mar the image before applying the ink. "Sliding, pressing, [and] dappling in sundry ways" with a linen ball made for the purpose, the printer applied the ink to the plate taking special care to "make the Black enter and pierce into all the [engraved] Strokes." Once he had inked the plate, the artisan then used a series of linen and muslin rags to carefully wipe off and soak up all the excess ink that did not fill the grooves, being careful neither to scratch the plate nor to remove ink from the engraved lines. Though seemingly the most straightforward step in the process, the inking of an engraved plate was itself a difficult skill; in twenty minutes even the best printers were able to ink roughly 750-square-inches of engraved plate (equivalent to only two of the four plates that produced *Virginia and Maryland*). Once he had fully inked the plate, the printer carefully lifted it and, keeping it steady and touching only the underside, carried it to the press.

While the printer was in the process of inking, one of his assistants readied the press for printing. To do this, he stacked a number of cloths neatly upon the printing table. He then slowly turned the roller so as to grip the ends of the cloths tightly and folded the uppermost cloth over the top roller to open a space between them. The printer then stacked, in order, a blank sheet of paper the same size as the one he was about to print, the inked and heated plate exactly as he wished it to be centered on the print with "the engraved side upward," "the wet sheet of Paper which he intend[ed] . . . to Print, and over that another like sheet [called the blurring paper] a little whetted with the Spunge." Repositioning the covering cloth on top of the paper he smoothed the entire stack before "turning the [press's] handle both gently and roundly" and "not by jolts and jogs" to pull the plate, paper, and cloths firmly through the press. As the stack passed between the rollers they exerted an enormous amount of pressure upon it, forcing the paper into the incised grooves where it absorbed the ink. The combination of engraved lines with the sheer force of a rolling press created the crisp precise slightly raised lines that mapmakers demanded. After the plate and paper stack passed through the press, the printer carefully removed the covering cloth and blurring paper and took up the print gently "lest the strength of the Black [ink] peel off the Paper." While one printer re-inked the plate, another hung up the printed sheet "on clean Lines" to dry overnight. When each print was dry, the printer stacked the printed pages and pressed them smoothly in a standing press, where they remained for another day. When he finished printing for the day, the printer's work was still not complete. To preserve and extend the engraved plate's life the printer needed to clean any residue ink from it with a small amount of ash mixed with water.

The entire process of transforming a manuscript into a printed map was time consuming and expensive. In order to recoup his outlay, a publisher had to sell between 110 and 220 impressions of each print; only then would he begin to turn a profit. Meanwhile the pressure the rolling press exerted on the plate required that it be reworked periodically to deepen and sharpen its engraved lines. At most a plate could produce two or three thousand images, though the number of impressions an engraved map plate could reliably generate was often lower because of the intricacy of the work and the precision of the print.[26] The entire process of having Herrman's manuscript engraved and printed would have cost Baltimore dearly.

Virginia and Maryland's New Iconography

The tasks of preparing the source image that Faithorne engraved, executing that engraving, and printing the map remade Herrman's original creation. Since Herrman's manuscript is no longer extant, it is unclear how closely the finished *Virginia and Maryland* resembled it. That much of the printed map retains precise local navigation detail suggests that Faithorne must have kept very close to Herrman's manuscript when engraving the map's cartographic features. Likewise, the printed map hews closely in its cartographic features to the only other known images that were most likely based on Herrman's original manuscript: the two 1677 Thames School maps of Virginia and Maryland and the two similar maps in the collection of the British National Archives discussed earlier (see Figure 2.16 and Figure 2.17). Because these maps isolate Virginia and Maryland from one another (though they do overlap in sections), their existence raises the possibility that Herrman produced two maps, one of each colony and that it was Faithorne who united them. This is unlikely, however, because both Herrman and the Calverts consistently referred to the map in the singular—"map"—a fact that could not have been accidental. Where Faithorne and Lord Baltimore had more freedom to shape the map was in their design of the map's ancillary decorative features and in its layout.

Although they might not have paused to enumerate them, seventeenth-century viewers of *Virginia and Maryland* would have recognized at least five different modes of representation on the print. First, of course, is the cartographic delineation of Virginia and Maryland and the bays and rivers of the Chesapeake, together with the map's related navigational components—the shoals, soundings, and isobaths—and its topographic icons marking plantations, towns, and mountains. Supporting the map's cartography is the technical information such as the latitude graduations along the map's border, the three compass roses, and the dividers and scale at the map's bottom. All of these elements were likely part of Herrman's original image in some form as they were important for making the geographic information usable.

Tying together these cartographic elements are the toponyms the makers assigned to geographic regions, rivers, bays, points and other geographic features. To be useful as a geographic device Herrman's manuscript copy must have included many place names—as many charts did—but many of these places names also served the Calverts' needs. It was probably Lord Baltimore who supplied the toponyms that are included on *Virginia and Maryland* but are missing from the 1677 pen-and-ink charts based on the Herrman manuscript. He would have enjoyed the clear demarcation of eight of the nine then-established counties of Maryland as a reminder of his proprietary power. (Oddly, Somerset County on the Eastern Shore is missing.) Since the names were located in almost exactly the same place and orientation as the county names on John Ogilby's 1671 iteration of *Nova Terra-Mariæ*, it is likely that Faithorne used this earlier map as a reference when including these county names. Their large size and the fact that each of them (except Kent County, which is set in a smaller type than the rest) is named after Lord Baltimore's family members, patrons, or, in the case of St. Mary's County, the Virgin Mary, reminded viewers of the proprietor's power and his family's Catholic identity.[27]

Along with the toponyms for riverine features and counties, the map also includes those for several Native American towns as well as English settlements, manors, and plantations. Of these manmade features, the most important, indicated by the size of their type, are major English towns, which are represented both by their names and by a symbol of a group of clustered buildings. Smaller labels mark manors, and simple icons denote the location of plantations. Absent from the manuscript charts based on Herrman's work, these icons are typical of the era and were likely Lord Baltimore's innovation. A 1672 letter from Governor Charles Calvert to Lord Baltimore reveals that the proprietor actively participated in tailoring the map's toponyms to meet his political needs. "I am very Glad that Augustines Mapp is like to bee printed," Charles Calvert wrote, "[and] I will see the names of all yor Lordshipps Manors Inserted [on it] as you direct mee, And send them by Captain Groome or Conaway."[28] Eventually delivered to Lord Baltimore in July 1672 by Captain Benjamin Cooper, Charles Calvert's letter may very well have also included a second manuscript copy of Herrman's work with Maryland's manors added to it, and it is likely that this was the image Faithorne used when engraving *Virginia and Maryland*. As this letter makes clear, it was Charles Calvert, on behalf of his father, who had these manors added; they were not present on Herrman's original.

The Second Lord Baltimore's desire that his manors be enumerated on *Virginia and Maryland* was not driven solely by a desire to reaffirm his proprietary control over the colony; rather, it was also tied to the political work he hoped his map would accomplish. The manorial system, unique in the English colonization of North America, was essential to the Calverts' plans for Maryland. George Calvert, the First Lord Baltimore and the individual who had set plans for a colony in motion, and his son Cecil both saw this feudal institution as providing the flexibility needed to establish a settlement in which Catholics and Protestants could live peacefully. As historian John Krugler has argued, the manorial system had allowed for Catholic survival in the north of England in the sixteenth early seventeenth centuries because it legally walled off Catholic worship from outside authorities' interference. Transplanted to Maryland, the same manorial system could create individual "enclaves [that] would provide the necessary privacy and safety for religious practices while at the same time offering a way to keep religious squabbles from" engulfing the community.[29] In imposing the manors on Herrman's map, Lord Baltimore must have hoped these would remind viewers of this distinctive element of his vision for a new kind of colony that embraced religious difference peacefully.

Faithorne's inclusion of the names of the towns that Lord Baltimore had only recently ordered to be constructed must have had similar political importance (see Figure 1.4). When Herrman worked on the map in the 1660s, many of these towns (including Cæciliton located in Bohemia Manor) existed only in Lord Baltimore's imagination. Nevertheless, insofar as they were key to Lord Baltimore's attempts to reshape his colony and reestablish his authority after its restoration to him in 1658, it was important that they appear on the map. It is unclear precisely who added these elements. These towns and their symbols appear on the 1677 Thames School charts based on Herrman's work but the already printed *Virginia and Maryland* could have influenced these charts as well. Regardless of when they were added, it is clear that marking each of these Maryland towns (though they existed only in theory) was in Lord Baltimore's interests, and it was his efforts to firm up political control that best explains their inclusion. Even as he celebrated Maryland's urban future, Baltimore diminished Virginia's; only icons that mark Jamestown and Governor William Berkeley's plantation of Green Spring appear in the portion of the map depicting Maryland's neighbor.

Distinct from the map's cartography, cartographic symbols, and toponyms, but nonetheless a vital aspect of the map, are a series of ornamental elements that almost certainly were not present on Herrman's manuscript and that helped to rewrite the map's political messages. Adorning the top of the map are two common heraldic symbols. Situated prominently at the top center of the map and probably among the first elements a viewer would have noticed are the Royal Arms of Great Britain. Celebrating Charles II and his control over the Chesapeake, this symbol dominates the map. Located just to the right and below the royal insignia, Lord Baltimore's coat of arms acknowledges his proprietorship of Maryland. At the map's bottom left, a decorative plinth, or column, serves as *Virginia and Maryland*'s cartouche. The central textual panels of the cartouche record the map's title, indicate that Herrman surveyed and drew the map, and explicate the map's symbols. Flanking the upper portion of column are two Native American figures, while a third coat of arms held in the mouth of a grotesque head and surrounded by fruits and vines serves as the column's pediment. Part of the cartouche, but located to its left, a brief notation indicates that the king had given the map his royal approbation and issued a copyright to Herrman and his representative Thomas Withinbrook.[30] Joining the cartouche and the mariner's compass at the bottom of the map is a portrait miniature of "Augustine Herrman Bohemian" that rests on a low pedestal. Next to the pedestal, just to the right of the shadow it casts, Faithorne signed the plate "W: Faithorne Sculp^t." Finally, ten textual blocks containing passages of varying lengths are scattered across the map. Supported by one small illustration of an "Indian canoe" at the bottom right, these texts contain physical descriptions of the land and its animals as well as historical and ethnographic information about the Chesapeake. Together, all of these elements create a symbolic assemblage that surrounds Herrman's delineation of the land and water with a new set of meanings familiar to English consumers.

Because each of the engraved map's constituent parts arose from a distinctive iconographic context, their recombination on the surface of Faithorne's print fractures the map's relation to a specific time and space. Though of course referencing a particular place (the English colonies in the Chesapeake) and specific living individuals (Augustine Herrman, Charles II, Lord Baltimore, William Faithorne, Thomas Withinbrook), the map's combination of iconographic elements detaches each place and person from their respective geographic and historic positions to create a new narrative. This narrative, unlike that of Herrman's original manuscript, was patently shaped not only by local experience and Dutch mapmaking traditions, but also by English imperial efforts to classify, and thus to claim and control, a distant colonial land. A bounded collection of metropolitan representations of the colonial world, *Virginia and Maryland* allowed its consumers to naturalize the multi-imperial colonies in a way they could comprehend.[31] At the same time it was not enough for Faithorne to use just one element—Baltimore's coat of arms, for example—to accomplish this task. Rather, the power of Herrman's distinct understanding of the Chesapeake meant that the engraver needed to overwhelm the map with a variety of metropolitan symbols in order to reclaim the image. The result is a multivalent object that speaks with dissonant voices and holds colonial as well as imperial viewpoints in tension. Unpeeling those layers that Faithorne (with the guidance and help of Lord Baltimore) added to the map in London allows us to glimpse how its engraving and printing not only remade Herrman's map physically but gave it new meanings that resonated with metropolitan consumers.

Most distinctive of the noncartographic symbols on the map is the portrait miniature of Herrman (Figure 4.5). Dominating the bottom right-center of the map and resting on a short rectangular plinth, the depiction shows Herrman in a bust-length view facing the viewer but turned slightly to his left. Herrman wears shoulder length hair, a white tie knotted at his neck, a doublet, and what is likely a cloak folded in a manner reminiscent of artists' drapery. Surrounding the portrait is an oval frame proclaiming the figure to be "Augustine Herrman Bohemian." Although scholars have assumed that Herrman played some role in drafting this portrait, it is almost certainly an imagined likeness as it closely resembles hundreds that Faithorne produced during his career.[32]

FIGURE 4.5. William Faithorne, portrait miniature of Augustine Herrman, *Virginia and Maryland* (detail).

The most common type of portrait during the later seventeenth century, engraved miniatures like this one were often used as the frontispieces to philosophical, scientific, and theological books, where they functioned to lend the text an element of authenticity and authority. Including Herrman's portrait on *Virginia and Maryland* served the same purpose for English viewers, connecting the mapmaker to a broader intellectual community. Widely popular, these small portraits affirmed the culture's growing comfort with individual accomplishment and the distinction that skill and first-hand knowledge bestowed upon those in England's rising professional classes.[33] Similarly, it was through portraiture, English men and women came to believe, that their deeds and names would endure. As the celebratory poem that the printer included in the preface to Faihorne's engraving manual claimed,

> So long as Brasse, so long as Books endure,
> So long as neat-wrought Pieces, Thour't secure
> A *Faithorne sculpsit* is a Charm can save
> From dull Oblivion and a gaping Grave.[34]

With portraiture no longer seen solely as the province of the nobility as it had been just a century before, the relatively quickly completed and inexpensive depictions that engraving allowed served to legitimize and commemorate the contributions the professional classes made to England's economic and cultural advancement in the seventeenth century. Tying Herrman to this larger collection of experts, Faithorne's inclusion of the mapmaker's portrait gave the map added legitimacy even as he contained that expertise within a metropolitan cultural ideal.

As important as ideas of authenticity and credibility were in making portraiture more popular in the second half of the seventeenth century, portraits nevertheless continued to embody two countervailing desires. Commentators and consumers remained unsure if the main function of the portrait was to represent an accurate likeness of the subject or to connote the individual's essence or interiority. While both propositions were concerned with picturing the subject, these two impulses were at odds with one another. As art historian David Piper puts it, "One tendency" of portraiture was "to particularize the subject, to distinguish him from all other men; the other to merge him" into "a type."[35] Exploiting this tension between portraits as representing either the individual or the type, Faithorne produced a portrait of Herrman that created a new fictive biography for the cartographer. Drawing on Herrman's authority as a real colonial individual to lend legitimacy and credibility to the map, the portrait's mode and style simultaneously recast him as an imperial actor complete with a life history tied to metropolitan culture and institutions. To accomplish the latter of these tasks, verisimilitude was not necessary.

Celebrated during his life as one of London's premier portrait engravers and appointed as engraver in copper to the king in 1660, Faithorne's reputation rested largely on his practice of working from his own sketches to engrave accurate likenesses of his sitters. He also endeavored to complete his portraits, almost all of which were done on commission, to the satisfaction of his customers, offering them significant freedom in shaping their own portrayal. In 1664, for example, in the midst of finishing a portrait of the scientist Robert Boyle, Faithorne contacted

Boyle through an intermediary to ask him if he "approve[d] of the dress, the frame and the bigness" of the image and if he requested a "motto or writing . . . on the pedestal" or "any books, or mathematical, or chemical instruments" surrounding him.[36] In this case, Faithorne strove for a portrayal that would allow the scientist to highlight those attributes he considered most important. In completing his portrait of Herrman, however, Faithorne, had to alter his usual methods. Because Herrman most likely never traveled to London and certainly did not do so during the 1660s or 1670s and because it is unlikely that he sent a self-portrait to London (this would have been truly remarkable as the drafting skills he learned as a mapmaker were vastly different from those portraitists acquired), Faithorne could not have based his depiction upon a life drawing. Rather, the engraver's only choice was to cast Herrman as a type.[37]

In selecting a type to use as the basis for his Herrman portrait, the engraver had a number of choices. One option was to picture Herrman as a colonial adventurer in the manner of John Smith, as Simon Passaeus did on Smith's *Map of New England*, an image that also served as the frontispiece to *The generall historie of Virginia, New England, and the Summer Isles* (1624). Placed in the upper left-hand portion of the map, Passaeus's likeness pictures Smith standing resplendent in his body armor, with a sword at his hip. Surrounding this portrait of the consummate warrior are images that remind viewers of Smith's adventures, including a globe, a ship, a knight on horseback, and a marching army. With Smith represented as looking east across New England (where the arms of Great Britain rest) and the Atlantic to London, the implication of the portrait is clear: here is a noble warrior who has crossed the Atlantic, conquered the Americas, and now has paused to gaze at the transatlantic imperial dominion he created. Faithorne's other alternative was to depict Herrman as a learned professional surrounded with the implements of his work in the style of Boyle, perhaps a compass or a theodolite, or with symbols of the Americas that elsewhere adorn the map.

Instead of adapting either of these conventions, Faithorne reimagined Herrman as a metropolitan figure. In so doing, the engraver severed Herrman from his specific multi-imperial colonial background by giving him a new imagined life history. The first element of this fictive biography was the placement of Herrman in the company of other English intellectuals and artists. Thus Herrman's portrait closely resembles those Faithorne produced for numerous men of letters and science in the 1660s and 1670s, such as John Kersey, whose portrait was published in 1673 (see Figure 4.2). But more than making Herrman simply an intellectual or artistic type, Faithorne marked him distinctly as a Bohemian, inscribing his origins alongside his portrait. While it might seem dissonant that Faithorne chose to proclaim Herrman's foreignness in an image that attempted to represent him as metropolitan, this would not have been necessarily unusual in early modern London. In fact, because of their long persecution at the hands of the Catholic Habsburgs, Protestant Bohemian exiles lived throughout Protestant Europe, including in England. The most prominent of these resident Bohemians during the 1660s and 1670s were Prince Rupert (the third son of Frederick V, elector palatine of the Rhine and king of Bohemia) and his wife Elizabeth (the so called Winter Queen). More than simply fellow Protestant allies, Rupert was Charles II's cousin, and Elizabeth was James I's eldest daughter (and thus Charles II's aunt). Rupert served as lord of the Admiralty, privy councilor, supporter of the Royal African Company, and confidant of the Duke of York. Rupert was also a patron of the arts and was a familiar, if not famous, figure in Restoration London.[38] To be Bohemian, in seventeenth-century London was to have an implied connection to the Stuarts; thus, Herrman's Bohemian portrait would have brought to mind not an exotic foreigner but the royal family itself.

Beyond evoking Prince Rupert and royalty, being marked a Bohemian also connected Herrman to a second important Londoner: the renowned Bohemian engraver Wenceslaus Hollar. Though a decade older than Herrman, Hollar shared many of the same early experiences with the mapmaker. Born in Prague, Hollar, too, fled his homeland during the 1620s. Living in a variety of German cities, Hollar, like Herrman, acquired technical skills as a young émigré, which would provide for his success as an adult. It was in Cologne, where he worked as an engraver, that Hollar's experiences diverged from Herrman's for it was in that city that he met the Earl of Arundel, one of England's most important art collectors. With Arundel's patronage, Hollar quickly earned a reputation as an accomplished artist, even serving as Prince Charles's drawing master and producing engraved portraits of the Stuarts and their circle, including one of fellow Bohemian Prince Rupert. Following a brief exile during the Civil War, Hollar returned to England even more famous than when he left, having published several impressive views and maps in Antwerp, including his famous 1647 view of London. Though he moved in elite royal circles— Charles II named him royal scenographer in 1666—Hollar preserved his Bohemian identity, signing a number of his prints "W. Hollar, Bohem."[39]

In his 1647 etched self-portrait, Hollar pictures himself in the same pose that Faithorne would later use for Herrman (Figure 4.6). Looking directly at the viewer with shoulder-length hair and turned slightly to the left, he wears a buttoned doublet with a white collar folded neatly over it. Although the pose is obviously common in engraved portrait miniatures, the similarities between the likenesses of these two Bohemian artists are nevertheless impossible to ignore. Faithorne is not likely to have known what Herrman looked like, but he was closely acquainted with his fellow Bohemian Hollar who lodged with him in the 1660s.[40] Lord Baltimore, meanwhile, was also probably familiar with Hollar, since his wife, Anne, was the Earl of Arundel's daughter. These fleeting connections between Herrman's patron, the engraver of his portrait, and the best-known Bohemian artist in London suggest that as Faithorne set about creating a likeness of a man whom he had never met, he based that depiction not on a real colonial individual who had left Europe three decades before, but instead on the thoroughly metropolitan Wenceslaus Hollar. As a whole, Faithorne's portrait of Herrman created a new narrative of the mapmaker's life for which an accurate likeness was not required. Picturing Herrman as a conventional scholar or artist and associating him with prominent individuals in the circle of the king, Faithorne's imagined portrait gave Herrman a new identity that erased his colonial experiences and reimagined him as a metropolitan type compatible with imperial ways of seeing.

FIGURE 4.6. Self-Portrait of Wenceslaus Hollar, 1647. © National
Portrait Gallery, London.

Joining with Herrman's portrait to anchor the bottom of the map is its
decorative cartouche (see Figure 4.5). The cartouche is made up of a two-
tiered column framed by acanthus leaves and resembles a seventeenth-
century monument. The focal point of the column is a textual tablet that
records the name of the map, "Virginia and Maryland," and its author:
"As it is Planted and Inhabited this present Year 1670 Surveyed and Exactly Drawne by the Only Labour & Endeavour of Augustin Herrman,

Bohemiensis." More than simply serving these basic functions, however, the title, through its style and phrasing, connects the map's cartography to an actual individual and his skill in capturing the colonies. The cartouche's text works in tandem with the portrait to reinforce the credibility and accuracy of the visual depiction. The words simultaneously celebrate the labor of a real person (Herrman's name is even engraved in a way that makes it appear as a signature) at a real moment (1670), but do so in a way that privileges the metropole. The person the text celebrates as the map's author is not any individual, but rather is it is the same fictive metropolitan Bohemian Herrman whom the idealized portrait depicts and whom the viewer cannot escape when reading the map's title.

Making this imperial narrative clear, two idealized Native American figures flank the tablet bearing the map's title and Herrman's name. Here Faithiorne chose to represent stock idealized characters, not known Native Americans. Although their faces and hair are more representative of Jacobean English men and women, both Native American carry markers of their "savageness". Wearing neither footwear nor a shirt to cover his chest, the male figure grasps a bow in his left hand and an arrow in his right while a quiver full of arrows is strung across his back. Also shoeless and bare-chested, the female figure wears a headband, necklace, bracelet, and belt, all evidently made of shells, and carries what might be a rose in her right hand. Looking to her left at Herrman's portrait, she gestures across her body with her left hand, her index finger extending toward the map's title and Herrman's name, explicitly connecting Herrman's likeness with his work. In position and posture, these Native Americans directly evoke engraver Theodor de Bry's frontispiece to the English 1590 edition of Thomas Harriot's *A brief and true report* (Figure 4.7).[41] Among the most famous European depictions of Native Americans during early modern period, De Bry's engravings, which were themselves based on John White's watercolors, circulated widely throughout Europe in the seventeenth century and were loosely copied by innumerable other engravers. Between their appearance in the late sixteenth century and the eighteenth century, these images, more than any others, shaped how

FIGURE 4.7. Theodor de Bry, title page from *A briefe and true report of the new found land of Virginia*. Frankfurt, 1590. Courtesy of the John Carter Brown Library at Brown University.

Europeans understood Native Americans.[42] The figures who dominate Smith's *Virginia*, for example, are almost direct copies of De Bry's engravings in *A brief and true report* (see Figure 2.1). Other contemporary European maps used similar figures in the same location as their cartouches as well. On *Novi Belgii Novæque Angliæ* (1655), for example, comparable Native American figures flank the map's title (see Figure 2.5).

On one level these well-known visual elements served as a generic marker of an exotic America, but more than this, the Native American figures also functioned as universal symbols that made viewers comfortable by representing unfamiliar people and places in recognizable ways. The poses and expressions of the Native couple reinforce this familiarity; each wears a welcoming smile that seems to invite the viewer to Virginia and Maryland. The only sign of potential aggression is the male figure's bow, but even though the bow is strung, the arrow he grips in his right hand is uncocked and points harmlessly away from the viewer. Moreover, though bearing markers of the exotic, these individuals signify European abstractions of the idea of native peoples as opposed to real Lenape or Susquehannock with whom Herrman interacted. Removed from their indigenous homes and posed on top of the column, naked to the viewer's leisurely examination, the Native Americans are symbols not of the actual communities and cultures of Virginia and Maryland, but instead of an abstract and universalized America. Flanking the very title of Herrman's map, these figures suggest that the waterways of the Chesapeake, as distant and complex as they may be, are now knowable and thus can be mastered. The Natives symbolize not the Americas but European expropriation and control of the Americas.

Completing the cartouche is a decorative header that rests on top of the column containing the map's title. In this ornament, a heraldic shield lies within an ornate frame that is in turn held in the mouth of a grotesque figure that may be the head of Neptune, the Roman god of the sea. Ropes of fruits and leaves broadly indicative of exotic species drape from the frame. The heraldic device at the center of this header contains two elements. The more prominent is a three-stemmed flower bearing three buds sprouting from a heart at the shield's center. Below are two crossed broad arrows. Like Herrman's portrait and the images of the Native Americans, the heraldic device is idealized, representing not any particular coat of arms or guild symbol, but rather a stock metropolitan form. Normally markers of specific families or organizations and often incorporated as decorations to portraits, coats of arms drew their authority from the elaborate royally supported and regulated system that authorized their use.[43] But since this shield is divorced from any real genealogy, it does not evoke not a specific family or individual but rather functions as a generic marker of imperial authority.

Nowhere is this imperial narrative more clear than in the heraldic symbol that dominates the top of the map. The Royal Arms of Great Britain as they existed under the Stuart monarchies were a typical feature of contemporary English maps of the Chesapeake. What distinguishes this rendition of the arms is its completeness, size, and position. Instead of limiting the coat of arms to merely the heraldic shield as on the Smith map of Virginia, Faithorne included the supporting lions, unicorn, and crowns that flank and top the shield as well as the king's motto: "Dieu et Mon Droit" (God and my Right). Although other maps place the coat of arms prominently, it is often woven into the landscape wherever convenient, as in Smith's *Virginia Discovered and Described*.[44] Instead of locating the royal arms in a less conspicuous position, Faithorne by contrast arranged the top of the map around it, forcing the label of "Virginia" to accommodate the emblem rather than the other way around. In so doing, Faithorne made it impossible to read the map without a reminder of the monarch's authority over the lands pictured below that symbol. The cartographic iteration of the royal arms that Faithorne employed in *Virginia and Maryland* most closely resembles that used by the unknown maker of *Nova Terra-Mariæ Tabula* (see Figure 2.2). The royal coat of arms dominates the right side of this map and has been placed directly over a smaller, though similarly ornate, Calvert family crest. Though designed to celebrate Lord Baltimore as the proprietor of the new colony, *Nova Terra-Mariæ Tabula* is careful to pay homage to the king whose patronage made Lord Baltimore's colony possible. Forty years later, however, Faithorne (almost certainly with the approval of Lord Baltimore) went further in aligning the colony with the larger empire: he dramatically reduced the Calvert coat of arms to only the family's shield in favor of enlarging the Royal Arms. It is unquestionably Charles II, not Calvert, whom the engraved map principally celebrates.

There are likely two reasons for Faithorne and Baltimore's decision to elevate the royal arms. One lies in Baltimore's efforts to curry favor with the king, who had helped fund the map's engraving and printing and, according to the 1674 copyright he issued for the map, who desired a map not just of Maryland but rather "A Survey of our Countryes of Virginia and Maryland." With this same copyright, the king even went out of his way to claim credit for the map, noting that "Augustine Herman hath by our comand been for these severall yeares" at work on the map. Significantly the "by our comand" was inserted into the text by virtue of a caret indicating that someone decided to more closely tie Herrman's work to the monarch after the text had already been composed.[45] The decision to sublimate his own power to that of the king indicates Lord Baltimore's acknowledgement that his proprietary authority flowed from the king. Making clear the source of his authority was particularly important in the early 1670s because Lord Baltimore's own prerogative as proprietor was under attack. The same year that he commissioned *Virginia and Maryland*, Maryland's General Assembly, following the precedent laid down by the Commonwealth Parliament, announced itself to be "a lawfull Assembly without dependence on any other Power in the Province" and thus "the highest court of Judicature." In essence, the declaration, which Governor Josiah Fendall and councilor Thomas Gerard accepted, held that the Lower House of the assembly would rule without the proprietor's appointed governor and council. An extension of the same radical ideologies that had created the Commonwealth, what became known as Fendell's Rebellion declared Lord Baltimore's authority illegitimate.[46] Although Lord Baltimore regained control of the colony just three months later and although the return of Charles II to the throne that year guaranteed the proprietor's control (for the moment), Fendall's Rebellion made Baltimore eager to articulate his authority. The pairing of two symbols of hereditary power—Lord Baltimore's coat of arms with the arms of Great Britain—at the top of *Virginia and Maryland* accomplished this goal.

While local conditions shaped Lord Baltimore's actions, his constant attention to imperial politics also played a part in his decision to celebrate the power of the king. In the years just after the Restoration, Charles II and his councilors were consumed by their desire to reassert the monarch's prerogative in the colonies just as they worked to do in England. From their perspective, the Civil War and its aftermath had allowed colonial governors, councils, and assemblies to assume greater local autonomy at the cost of the crown. This devolution of authority was most notable in New England but was true to some degree across many colonies. One of the chief goals of Restoration colonial policy was to reverse this process.[47] By so clearly indicating Charles II's ultimate authority, Lord Baltimore visually aligned Maryland with the wider Stuart political project to reinforce Charles II's power and to consolidate the English Empire. As if the royal arms were not sufficient to tie the map to Charles, the royal license (located just to the left of the cartouche) constituted a final reminder of the king's approbation of the map and of the colony it represented. Altogether, the map's noncartographic elements— the heraldic symbols, the cartouche, the portrait—literally encircle and contain the colonial Herrman and make him a client of the king. Replacing Herrman's narrative with Faithorne's and Baltimore's, these elements scripted the viewing of *Virginia and Maryland*.

If we are to understand the iconography that Faithorne and Lord Baltimore added to the map as a sustained effort to recast Herrman's role in the map's production in an imperial narrative, it is worth considering why they allowed the Bohemian's name and image to appear on the map at all. They could have followed the lead of the unknown maker of *Nova Terra-Mariæ Tabula*, who eradicated all traces of the mapmaker from his map so that it became an artifact not of the Virginia Company's colonization efforts but a wholly new effort centered on the Calverts. One reason that Baltimore and Faithorne did not follow this path was that the map's authority in accurately depicting the region rested upon the maker's local expertise. It was vitally important for the map's accuracy that Herrman, a colonist and a scientific individual, produced it on the ground.[48] At the same time, however, this dependence upon a colonist's knowledge threatened to upend the hierarchical relationship between metropole and colony that officials believed held the empire together and thus undermined metropolitan authority. The solution was to preserve Herrman's role in the map's creation but to contain Herrman and his colonial knowledge within modes of representation familiar and useful to English politicians and consumers. For in the very act of representing Herrman as the map's author, Faithorne offered viewers the chance to re-exert imperial control over Maryland and Virginia each time they read the map. The result was a complex design that coopted Herrman's colonial way of understanding and used it for imperial efforts to possess and control their distant colonies. In this way retaining Herrman's role became an act of appropriation.

When Herrman's manuscript map arrived in London it was a colonial object. By the time Faithorne engraved the map and it was printed, it had become an apparatus of empire. The complex process that transformed it from drawing to print recast the map in imperial terms. The techniques Faithorne and the other craftsmen who labored over *Virginia and Maryland* used and the iconography they deployed came from their local context and were directed to the needs of London's consumers, not those of colonial inhabitants. Still retaining Herrman's precise local navigational information and his colonial perspective, *Virginia and Maryland* accumulated new metropolitan meanings as it became a printed map. But the metropolitan actors who engraved and printed the now finished work governed its use and subsequent refashioning no better than Herrman had, and *Virginia and Maryland* continued to collect meanings as it passed into the hands of its consumers. Lord Baltimore could hope to shape viewers' ideas of the colony and his proprietorship as well as monarchical control of the empire, but he could not fully dictate viewers' responses.

5

The Consumers

It is unclear what happened to Herrman's manuscript and Faithorne's engraved plate once *Virginia and Maryland*'s unknown printer finished his work. Faithorne most likely discarded the first of these (after all, now a printed map existed) and either passed the plate to Baltimore or, more likely since there is no evidence of a second printing, hammered out the engraving he had labored over and reused the valuable copper plate. These materials' work was done; it was the printed image that now carried their combined meanings. With the image already remade once by the processes of engraving and printing, as it passed into the hands of consumers, these individuals added still more cultural and intellectual meanings. Both technical objects to be studied and ornamental items to be admired, maps like *Virginia and Maryland* sparked conversation and created wonder. Paying close attention to who bought *Virginia and Maryland*, where they purchased it, and how these consumers used it, reveals how the map functioned in London as an apparatus of empire, as an aid to polite discourse, and as a tool for self-fashioning.

Arriving in England at a critical moment when the Stuart government and mercantile interests sought to better understand and harness their growing empire, *Virginia and Maryland* joined a growing portfolio of cartographic, scientific, and statistical information that policymakers and merchants had begun to collect from overseas ventures. Derived from a multitude of local experiences, all of this empirical data was appropriated and reprocessed into familiar forms so that it could aid commerce and colony-building. At its core this reprocessing was a political act for it produced an image of an ordered and controlled empire that appealed to the imperial ambitions of the Stuarts and their commercial and political allies. Meanwhile, English gentlemen and women increasingly turned to cartography and geography as tools with which to reframe their identities as they sought to resituate themselves in relation to the expanding empire. Tracing *Virginia and Maryland*'s passage from William Faithorne's workshop into the hands of its consumers offers the opportunity to recapture the part maps played in making empire. On one level these objects were practical in that they helped merchantmen, navies, and bureaucrats to navigate and manage the colonies, but just as importantly, they allowed elite English men and women to imagine, and thus to create, an empire.

The Map-Seller

When Hydrographer to the King John Seller announced to readers of the *London Gazette* that *Virginia and Maryland* was for sale at his two shops in March 1674, he did so during a period of dramatic expansion of London's cartographic marketplace. Just four decades earlier, in the years before the English Civil War, Londoners who wished to purchase printed maps and atlases found that map-sellers largely stocked only imports from the Low Countries and France. Partly a result of underdeveloped domestic geographic and mathematical knowledge, foreign map- and atlas-makers' control over England's market was due primarily to the absence of royal or civic support for English mapmaking. Although court officials had begun to use maps to manage state affairs and landed nobles employed them for estate management, consumers tended to rely upon bespoke manuscript maps that circulated only in narrow circles. Printed maps remained rare even in cities that boasted large numbers of educated potential consumers. In Cambridge at the end of the sixteenth century, for example, one would have found relatively few printed maps and atlases beyond those in the collections of college members whose academic pursuits required them. Without a large consumer market to encourage their efforts and without a system of royal or civic grants or licenses offering financial inducements or copyright protections, English publishers were reluctant to invest the capital necessary to produce many printed maps. Those daring few entrepreneurial publishers who did so found it difficult to compete with publishers in the Low Countries who had better reputations and more experience. The result was that before the 1660s English map-sellers mostly imported the printed maps they sold from Amsterdam, Antwerp, or Paris. This was the case even for English-language atlases. Between 1620 and 1640 Low Country map publishers issued thirteen English-language atlases, while English printers published none. Even the plates for John Speed's path-breaking *A Prospect of the Most Famous Parts of the World* (1627), the first atlas authored by an Englishman, were engraved in Amsterdam.[1]

As they were for English printmaking as a whole, the decades between 1640 and 1680 were transformative for London's mapmakers. During that time, burgeoning interest in maps and geography combined with makers' growing technical proficiency to spur England's cartographic market forward. Much of English gentlemen's and women's enhanced interest in geography came from the rising importance of England's overseas trade, especially as it related to North America, the Caribbean, and Africa, and the associated rise in prosperity such trade engendered. Oliver Cromwell's and then Charles II's aggressive efforts in the 1650s and 1660s to expand the empire, coupled with new wars against the Dutch, made topographical depictions of the Atlantic necessary for ship captains sailing new routes, for merchants planning ventures, and for mercantile boosters at court eager to conceptualize an expanding empire. As the elite and ruling classes' familiarity with maps grew, many began to think geographically; they started to "use maps to analyze problems, to plan, and to display and propagate ideas that had a spatial dimension."[2]

As demand for maps rose, Englishmen continued to turn to overseas suppliers as they had in the sixteenth and early seventeenth centuries, relying most notably upon imported maps from the Low Countries. Hoping to eliminate their dependence on their Dutch commercial rivals by developing an independent English corpus of navigational knowledge that could support their new trading companies and colonies, merchants and the crown came together to promote domestic mapmaking. In 1666 the Royal Society urged mariners to "make Plots and Draughts of prospect[s] of Coasts, Promontories, Islands and Ports, marking the Bearings and Distances" as they sailed and to deposit these with the Lord High Admiral upon their return, a practice based on Dutch, Spanish, and Portuguese policies. The hope was to create a large body of geographic information that could serve as the source material for other maps. Perhaps the most important of England's domestic mapmakers in the 1660s and 1670s were the Thames School chart-makers who worked near their consumers in London's Thames-side parishes. These men specialized in portolan charts and harbor plans based on Dutch printed maps and new English surveys. Because they intended their maps to be useful to mariners as navigational aids, they drew their works on vellum and sometimes affixed them to hinged boards that would protect them at sea. Looking to expand their market, some of these men also produced similar but more ornate charts drawn on paper and intended for display. On these maps, which make up the majority of surviving Thames School examples (but probably the minority of those produced), the chart-makers sometimes included elaborate cartouches and compass roses that made them more appealing to consumers who intended to use them in their homes rather than at sea (see Figure 2.16 and Figure 2.17). The supply of these maps was necessarily limited because they were not mechanically reproducible, but they nevertheless helped spur domestic interest in geography.[3]

In the same period that the Thames School chart-makers flourished, domestically printed engraved maps also became more prevalent in London. With consumers clamoring for ever more maps, publishers became willing to invest in making them. Some of these new map publishers, like Thomas Jenner and John Ogilby, turned to maps and atlases as a supplement to their already established print businesses. Others, like Joseph Moxon and John Thornton, shifted to engraved maps from chart-making or other maritime occupations.[4] The Great Fire of 1666 further encouraged these pioneering mapmakers as the conflagration destroyed existing map collections and the stocks of sellers who clustered together in those districts the fire most heavily damaged. That so many mapmakers from divergent backgrounds rushed to meet this growing demand indicates the new importance of maps in Restoration England and the ways that mapmaking was bound up with a general English push to match Continental scientific knowledge and cultural sophistication. In order to construct the kind of expansive empire that most elite English men and women now agreed was desirable, they needed maps for the ideological work they accomplished in incorporating distant colonies into their polity, as much as the navy and mercantile fleets needed them for the practical information they offered.

One of the more prominent of London's new entrepreneurial map-makers was John Seller, the man who first advertised *Virginia and Maryland*. Like many who became mapmakers in the 1660s, John Seller had diverse interests. The son of a cordwainer, Seller apprenticed to Edward Lowe, a member of the Merchant Taylors' Company, under whom Seller apparently learned the trade of instrument making. (By the sixteenth century most of London's craft companies were no longer associated with just one craft.) Seller soon established his own shop near the Hermitage Stairs in Wapping, a London district located on the north bank of the Thames, which was home to many of London's mariners, shipbuilders, and other maritime artisans. Here Seller sold mathematical, astronomical, and nautical instruments along with en-graved maps and manuscript charts. More than simply a craftsman and retailer, Seller was also interested in helping to advance mathemati-cal and scientific knowledge. He both offered instruction in the use of instruments and published at least one short essay based on his ex-periments with the magnetic compass. In 1669 he more ambitiously authored a navigation manual, *Praxis Nautica or Practical Navigation*, which further helped to burnish his reputation as an important voice in London's growing mathematical, scientific, and maritime commu-nities.[5] A visitor to Seller's store in Wapping, surrounded by gleam-ing compasses and quadrants, numerous microscopes and telescopes, the latest celestial and terrestrial globes, and "Maps of the World in all sizes, and of any particular Country" would have witnessed first-hand the material evidence of England's explosion of interest in navigation and mapping. The visitor would also have been able to purchase one of the most ambitious English efforts to advance navigational knowledge to that point: Seller's *The English Pilot*. [6]

In 1669 Seller announced plans to produce "a Sea Waggoner for the whole World, with Charts and Draughts of particular places, and a large Description of all the Roads, Harbours, and Havens, with the Dangers, Depths and Soundings."[7] Conceiving *The English Pilot* as a multivolume sea atlas containing detailed navigation charts—as distinguished from general atlases such as Speed's *A Prospect of the Most Famous Parts of the World*—Seller hoped it would displace Dutch atlases, which dominated the English market. Perhaps published as early as 1668, but certainly in print by 1671, the first volume of Seller's atlas, *The English Pilot, Northern*, contained detailed charts covering northern European waters, including the coasts of England and Ireland. Though promoted as an English atlas, Seller's ambitions were ahead of domestic cartographers, and in order to complete the work he had to rely largely upon a set of Dutch plates that engraver Jan Jansson had worked when reproducing Willem Janszoon Blaeu's *Het Licht der Zeevaert* (1608). Seller had many of these plates retouched and added new information to others, but some contemporaries harshly disparaged his efforts. Samuel Pepys, naval administrator and long-term advocate for English mapmaking, was the atlas's most famous detractor, condemning Seller's "pretended new book" as nothing more than the product of "old worn Dutch copper plates" that the mapmaker had ordered "refreshed in several places."[8]

Pepys's critiques aside, Seller's achievement was significant enough that in 1671, just as his book was set to be printed, he received royal favor from Charles II, who declared that individuals could neither counterfeit Seller's work nor import foreign sea atlases that might compete with it. In addition to this royal privilege, the king also named Seller his royal hydrographer. The next year Seller issued the second book of his atlas, *The English Pilot, Southern*, and began work on the two remaining volumes of this magisterial project—*Oriental* and *West-India*—as well as a newly conceived of fifth book, *Mediterranean*. Aware of the criticism

THE CONSUMERS | 183

lobbed at the first volume, Seller commissioned numerous new maps and plates for these volumes. Since he continued to work on other projects that strained his finances, such as his smaller *Atlas Maritimus, or the Sea-Atlas* (1675), Seller soon enlisted additional investors, including William Fisher, John Thornton, John Colson, and James Atkinson. These men eventually took over the project after 1677, with Fisher and Thornton finishing the work on their own in 1689 when they brought out *The English Pilot, West-India.*[9]

Despite its flaws, Seller's publication indicates both how much English mapmaking had advanced since midcentury and the emerging demand for domestic cartographic knowledge. Compared to earlier ventures to collect European knowledge of the world, such as John Ogilby's seven-volume atlas of the world (each portion of which was translated from European sources), or other navigational manuals that merely copied and translated Dutch works, such as Ashley Anthony's translation of Waghenaer, *The mariner's mirrour*, Seller's work greatly advanced English cartography. Launched in the wake of one war between England and the Dutch Republic and first printed just before another, *The English Pilot* arrived on the market as many in England were eager to learn more about their Atlantic empire. Even Pepys's harsh assessment of the work indicates how profoundly interested many Englishmen were in the expanding maritime empire. English men and women were no longer content to view the world only through a Dutch lens; they wanted to see how their empire looked from London.[10]

Seller's prominent place within London's cartographic community made him a logical choice when Lord Baltimore sought a distributor for *Virginia and Maryland.* If Baltimore had stopped to look through the advertisements that the *London Gazette* printed twice weekly, he would have come across Seller's name often. Still working from his shop at "the sign of the Mariners Compass at the Hermitage Stairs in Wapping," Seller had become arguably the city's leading map-seller by the 1670s. Either alone or with a partner, he placed half of the fourteen advertisements relating to cartography, geography, and navigation published in the *Gazette* during the years 1671 and 1672. Seller was also able to appeal to a wide and diverse variety of customers. With his experience as an instrument maker, he attracted ship captains and navigators to his shop, supplying them with instruments as well as detailed charts and navigation guides. At the same time that he maintained his credibility as a skilled nautical artisan, Seller participated in London's emerging scientific community. His note on compasses in the Royal Society's *Philosophical Transactions*, for example, would have drawn the attention of elite consumers who had little interest in technical manuscript charts but who were the main market for expensive printed maps. Already hydrographer to the king, Seller gained sure public standing when he won a contract to produce compasses and optical glasses for the Royal Navy in 1672.[11] For Lord Baltimore, Seller's reputation had importance beyond just the diverse audience he could reach. In the same way that dedications and publishers listed on the title pages of books and prints increased these objects' prestige, Seller's name instantly enhanced *Virginia and Maryland*, tying its authority to Seller's stature. With increasing numbers of printed maps arriving on the market in the 1670s, such testaments of authenticity were important as consumers endeavored to choose among competing products.[12]

Exchange Alley: The Nexus of Information and Capital in Restoration London

It is telling that Seller offered *Virginia and Maryland* for sale not only in Wapping, but also in his new shop in the City of London. Hoping to reach London's mercantile elite who were less likely to make the trek east from the City to Wapping, Seller came to them, opening a shop in the spring of 1671 in Exchange Alley (known as 'Change Alley) off Cornhill. A winding alley connecting two of the City's busiest thoroughfares, Cornhill and Lombard Street, and steps away from the Royal Exchange, Exchange Alley was the heart of Restoration London's financial district (Figure 5.1). The structure that gave the alley its name stood just across Cornhill at its junction with Threadneedle Street. Since its opening in

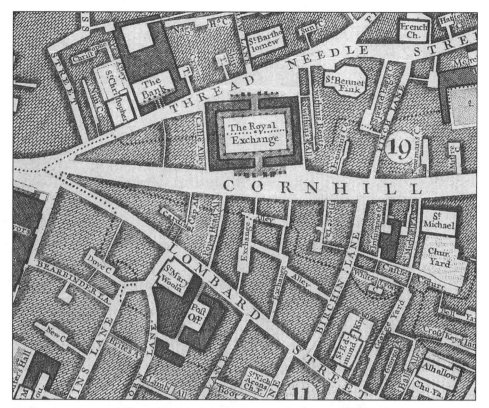

FIGURE 5.1. *A plan of the cities of London and Westminster, and borough of Southwark, with the contiguous buildings / from an actual survey, taken by John Rocque, land-surveyor, and engraved by John Pine.* London, 1746 (detail). Courtesy of the Beinecke Rare Book and Manuscript Library at Yale University. Exchange Alley connects Cornhill with Lombard Street just below the Royal Exchange.

1570, the Exchange had functioned as a gathering place for merchants of all sorts who could walk its covered walkways as they exchanged information and transacted business. The coming together of private merchants who held a variety of business concerns in places such as the Exchange allowed merchant adventurers to attract the private capital that financed their overseas colonial schemes. By the mid-seventeenth century the Exchange had also become a fashionable shopping desti-nation, with the building's shops crammed with fine and luxury goods from around the world. The City's burgeoning scientific community also frequented its stalls looking for books and scientific instruments.[13]

When the Great Fire destroyed the building in 1666, its two owners, the City of London and the Mercers Company, quickly rebuilt. So important was the Exchange to the economic and cultural life of London, that architect Christopher Wren's master plan placed it at the center of his redesign of the City. The building that eventually began to rise in 1667 on in its original location fronting Cornhill was almost as grand as Wren desired. Designed by Edward Jerman, the new Royal Exchange consisted of a rectangular courtyard enclosed by multi-storied porticoes. With a lofty archway topped with the royal arms at its center and with columns and sculptures fronting it, the three-story building presented an impressive face to the City's inhabitants. But it was the interior that contained its most important activities. Here the central feature was the Exchange's massive 144 by 117 foot paved courtyard. Surrounding this were wide two-story arcades lined with shops. Together the arcades and the courtyard provided a meeting place for traders, with individual areas, or "walks," set aside for particular trades or geographic regions. As they walked the Exchange, merchants could find potential partners, plan future endeavors, and gather information about new markets, overseas successes and failures, and international intrigues that might affect their businesses. The more than 150 shops found within the Exchange sold a wide variety of luxury goods from around the world including fine silks, jewelry, and other exotic items and made clear the connection between the empire's expanding wealth and rising domestic consumption.[14]

A center of business, the Royal Exchange, as well as the streets surrounding it, was also the place where seventeenth-century Londoners went to find and exchange political, commercial, and scientific information. Here, lining 'Change Alley, the Restoration gentleman could locate another of the City's vital institutions: several of London's most important coffeehouses. Established only two decades earlier, these coffeehouses, including the first and most famous, Garaway's Coffee House, served as meeting places for merchants, government officials, scientists, and travelers, as well as the booksellers and mapmakers who catered to these men's growing demand for empirical intelligence. In many ways coffeehouses were an extension of the Royal Exchange itself with no less than fifty of them in close proximity to it. They joined taverns, inns, and the only recently reopened theaters in creating public social spaces that stimulated discourse between strangers. Surely spaces of conviviality and leisure (some catered to gambling, others to prostitution), coffeehouses, like most inns and taverns, were distinguished mainly by the new kind of polite sociability they facilitated, which included the exchange of news, the debate of politics and science, and the pursuit of commerce. Not yet balkanized by profession or interest as they would be in the next century, seventeenth-century coffeehouses brought together the diverse men of capital and skill who were fast making London a thriving commercial metropolis.[15]

Above all, coffeehouses were places of consumption and exchange tied directly to England's rising wealth, increasing cultural sophistication, and expanding empire. Most directly, the coffee that gave these shops their name (dark and strong and sipped while still scalding from tiny cups) and the chocolate (drunk as a liquid lightly sweetened with sugar and seasoned with exotic spices) that rivaled coffee's popularity among customers were themselves products of the empire. To partake in consuming these still luxurious commodities was a political act that celebrated England's expanding trade and empire. In addition to the drinks they offered, London's coffeehouses extended patrons' opportunities to consume and trade information, placing them at the center of London's economy. Here guests could peruse manuscript newsletters; pamphlets; price currents such as Wooley's price-current, which debuted in 1671 and listed the prices of 283 commodities; the *London Gazette*; and printed newssheets that proprietors provided for their patrons. Sometimes booksellers offered their publications for sale in coffeehouses, in nearby shops, and on the streets and alleys encircling the Exchange. Even coffeehouse walls were appealing. Plastered along them were customs house returns, print and book advertisements, and cheap broadsides. Useful for the commercial and political news they contained, and intended to spur conversation, all of these printed materials brought different categories of intelligence together, uniting dispatches about commodity prices, shipping patterns, insurance rates, trading ventures, and foreign affairs with the announcement of scientific discoveries and policy recommendations. Helped along by the stimulating effects of coffee and chocolate and with ready access to the aggregated knowledge needed to asses new opportunities at hand, merchants, politicians, and other coffeehouse patrons formed partnerships, located departing vessels that might still have cargo space, found insurance, discussed the credit-worthiness of associates, and investigated the state of trade in foreign lands all while they swapped reports about the most recent developments in foreign wars and domestic political intrigues. Print culture, coffee, and sociability intersected in the interior of London's coffeehouses. So potent was the free circulation of information and opinion in them that Charles II feared that customers were using them to foment rebellion and in 1675 he briefly shuttered them.

Further cementing the connections between coffee, commerce, and inquiry, coffeehouses hosted public auctions as well as the meetings and lectures of scientific societies and clubs. Not surprisingly, maps soon appeared in coffeehouses, taking their place at the intersection between commerce and empirical study. Proprietors used maps to decorate the walls, map-sellers offered them for sale, and patrons consulted them as they talked. The connection between mapping and the educated sociability of coffeehouses is further suggested by John Ogilby's promotion of his maps in these establishments. Ogilby not only consulted with Robert Hooke, who was also the city surveyor, and the engraver Wenceslaus Hollar at the Spanish Coffee House about a planned map of London, but also sold lottery tickets to raise funds for his atlas, *Britannia*, at Garaway's. In sum, the information available to coffeehouse patrons allowed them to bring the world's knowledge under their gaze.

That Exchange Alley's coffeehouse customers would have traded political, commercial, and scientific information while casually imbibing coffee and reading the advertisements for maps that map-sellers like Seller began to place in the *London Gazette* alongside dispatches from around the world and shipping news reveals the ways that consumers connected maps to other metropolitan circuits of knowledge. As the empire expanded, gathering and processing empirical (especially mathematical and geographic) information—what William Petty called "political arithmetic"— became ever more important in helping governmental administrators and merchants increase efficiency and manage their complex affairs. For more than a century, residents of the City had been steadily developing a habit of vernacular scientific inquiry whose goal was to harness empirical knowledge for their and England's greater well-being. As early as the 1580s and 1590s, mathematicians like John Dee and Henry Billingsley worked to disseminate mathematical learning not for humanistic reasons but for its practical application in meeting the demands of navigators hoping to find ports, merchants trying to manage their accounts, and artisans hoping to improve their products. In the years after the Restoration, economic and political thinkers like Petty drew from mathematical and scientific discourse as they extolled the virtues of an accurate accounting of population, wealth, and trade in informing public policy and bettering society. Likewise, merchants increasingly depended upon managing flows of empirical information concerning geography, prices, exchange rates, and their own accounts. Linked through their desire to master information, those interested in geography, mathematics, science, and commerce all came together in the City to forge a new knowledge economy that could buttress England's expansion.[16]

Seller's decision to open a shop on Cornhill at Exchange Alley testifies to his efforts to link the dissemination of geographic knowledge to the wider information and print culture that circulated in the City as well as to the ways consumers had come to understand topographical images. Englishmen began to connect maps to other publications that attempted to rationalize and categorize and thus control England's expanding empire through the better organization and analysis of empirical data. The two additional major marketplaces for printed maps in Restoration Lon-

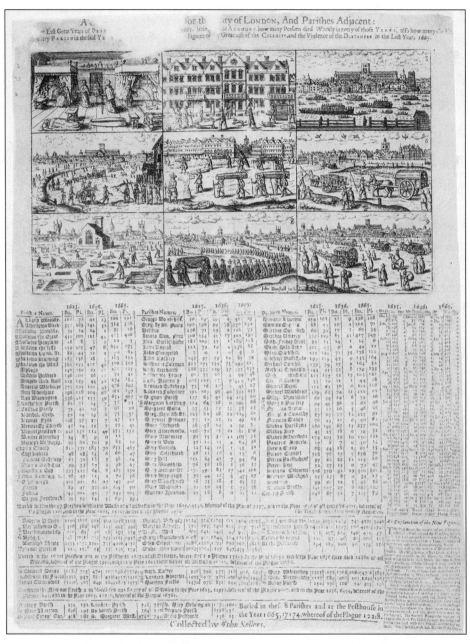

FIGURE 5.2. John Dunstall and John Sellers, *Scenes of the Plague in London with Statistical breakdown by parish for the years 1625, 1636, and 1665.* London, 1665–1666. Courtesy of the Museum of London.

don beyond 'Change Alley, the bookstalls in St. Paul's Churchyard and at Westminster Hall, further encouraged urban consumers to associate maps with the wider information economy. One extraordinary contemporary pairing of geographic representation and statistical data in the service of public policy is a broadside detailing the human cost of the plague in 1665, which Seller produced in collaboration with engraver John Dunstall. *Scenes of the Plague in London* consists of eight topographical views showing the progress of the plague through London, together with columns of numbers indicating plague deaths as compared to all other diseases delineated by parish for the years 1625, 1636, and 1665 (Figure 5.2).[17] Focused on better understanding an epidemic rather than colonial expansion, Seller's broadside nevertheless makes clear the ways Londoners integrated geographic knowledge with other forms of empirical data in their efforts to create order.

Maps and Empire

While it is possible to reconstruct the environment within which an early modern Englishman could have purchased *Virginia and Maryland*, it is impossible to be as exact about the individuals who actually did so. Of the roughly two hundred copies of the map that were likely printed only five are extant.[18] That John Seller did not advertise the map again after 1674 and that one of Herrman's acquaintances reported being unable to find a copy in London or Amsterdam in 1680 suggests that Seller eventually sold his copies but that demand was not strong enough to merit another costly printing.[19] There is clear information about the identities of two of the consumers of *Virginia and Maryland*. Sometime between September 1674 and June 1676 the Committee of the Lords of Trade and Plantations paid Seller six shillings for a "Map of Virginia &c.," a notation that almost certainly refers to Herrman's map, the newest cartographic work of the Chesapeake available at that time in London. A decade later, the Lords' copy was still in use when they commissioned cartographer and map-seller William Berry to paste "Hermans Virginia" on cloth and to color it for them. Although the copy that the Committee of the Lords of Trade and Plantations purchased is no longer extant, two manuscript maps, one of Maryland and one of Virginia, based on the Herrman image make up part of the atlas that William Blathwayt assembled while he was secretary of the Lords of Trade indicating the Lords' sustained interest in the work (see Figure 2.16 and Figure 2.17).[20] The second known owner of *Virginia and Maryland* is the ubiquitous Samuel Pepys, whose copy still resides in his library now installed at Magdalene College in Cambridge. Pepys, who served as clerk to the Navy Board for more than a decade and secretary of the Admiralty from 1673 to 1679, was, like many educated elite Englishmen in the period, immensely interested in music, science, geography, and history and was an avid consumer of sheet music, books, pamphlets, prints, and maps. Useful to him in his professional capacity, the map also would have brought Pepys pleasure through private study and display. Beyond the two consumers for whom we have definite evidence of ownership, it is likely that both Lord Baltimore and Charles II possessed copies of *Virginia and Maryland*. As the map's commissioner, it stands to reason that Lord Baltimore would have owned a copy and Charles II's decision to issue the work a copyright in 1674 indicates he received one in gratitude for this accommodation. Finally, a 1676 petition likely written in Maryland suggests that the map was visible to the public there.[21]

Examining the ways these Englishmen and colonists used *Virginia and Maryland* reveals how imperial consumers reshaped the map's meaning and pushed it further from its colonial origins. Produced at the periphery by an individual who often ignored the boundaries European states tried to place between their Atlantic territories, Herrman's manuscript represented local understandings of the multi-imperial origins of the Mid-Atlantic. To elite metropolitan English men and women, though, the map looked very different. For these individuals *Virginia and Maryland* was valuable as one part of London's developing information network, which enabled them to claim, imagine, and control a distant but now measurable and "accurately" pictured land. Metropolitan consumption of *Virginia and Maryland* located the map firmly within the discourse of colonial expansion and administration.

By the time Charles II assumed the throne in 1660, English monarchs had long been employing maps as a critical part of their efforts to chart English exploration and claim foreign territories. As European states jockeyed for position in the Americas, maps became instruments of possession and control. In this way maps served legal and imaginative purposes: they demarcated borders and marked colonies as English even as they conjured those spaces into being by naming, measuring, and describing them in English terms. Elizabeth I was perhaps the first English monarch to track exploration with a map, using one produced by mathematician and navigator John Dee. Following her lead, Francis Drake and Walter Ralegh also placed great importance in mapping, issuing strict instructions to their expeditions to keep accurate charts of their discoveries. Although the crown mandated that some details of early Atlantic expeditions remain secret—especially those that might reveal a possible northwest passage—Elizabeth recognized the importance of publishing these maps so as to claim the newly discovered lands for England, though she was not as active in commissioning and funding mapmaking as were monarchs in Spain and Portugal.[22] Maps were especially important for English colonization because they served to justify dominion over foreign lands in the absence of a higher supranational authority like the pope. The English crown ascribed to a generally accepted European doctrine that held that newly discovered lands unoccupied by any European monarch were susceptible to an act of possession. In this system of international law, discovery of new places was not enough for a nation to hold dominion over them; the kingdom also had to subsequently control that territory. Planting colonists, building structures, and fencing land was one way to possess newly found lands, but another, less costly method, was to map them. By cartographically representing new colonies, England staked a claim of possession recognizable to Europeans.[23]

As important as printed maps were for articulating control of foreign lands to other European empires, they were also fundamental for helping imperial officials to imagine their own expanding empire. The first decade of Charles II's rule was a period of tremendous growth for the English Empire as sugar imports flooded London, as traders expanded the slave trade, and as warships conquered New Netherland. By the time Charles II issued a copyright for Herrman's map in the mid-1670s, some 200,000 people populated the British American colonies.[24] Physical descriptions of territory, census records, and customs accounts gave Stuart policymakers some understanding of the scope of the these settlements, but maps, seemingly comprehensible at first glance, offered a level of verisimilitude that words and numbers could not match. The existence of so many waterways bisecting what Herrman illustrated as a largely unpopulated Chesapeake must have reassured the monarch of the land's productive possibilities and the riches the American colonies offered. Aside from the geographical information provided by map itself, the king, Lord Baltimore, and other officials would have welcomed the symbolism of the other iconographic features of the engraving, such as the prominent insignia of the Royal Arms of Britain and the large, bold place-names of "Virginia" and "Maryland" emblazoned across its top. As they viewed *Virginia and Maryland*, consuming its cartographic information alongside the imperial emblems Faithorne added, these architects of the empire would have been able to reenact England's gaining ownership of the Chesapeake.[25] Such reassurances were needed because the dramatic colonial expansion of the 1660s not only made it difficult for imperial bureaucrats to imagine the changing empire but also created significant administrative problems. Like contemporary efforts to develop tools of "political arithmetic" that could accurately reflect the national accounting and improve economic management, cartography offered state-builders a way to exert control over overseas settlements. An accurate picture of colonial lands as they were "planted and inhabited" enabled more than abstract possession; topographic depictions also allowed measurement and evaluation. Whereas beginning in the sixteenth century, maps had been used in England as a tool for proper estate superintendence and tax collection, as the empire expanded beyond the seas, they took on additional importance as administrative tools.[26]

Eager to properly manage the empire's finances, channel its shipping, and govern its colonies, Charles II and his ministers spent much of the 1670s trying to govern the empire more rationally. In keeping with other contemporary European efforts to order the world through categorization in the fields of science and political economy, English intellectuals attempted to transform the distant and unfamiliar colonies into knowable and thus governable places through universalizing modes of representation such as natural histories, paintings, censuses, customs records, and maps.[27] As the Renaissance opened up new universes, lands, and fields of inquiry, it forced many to adjust their worldviews. The uncertainties, dissonances, and anxieties that resulted from new discoveries propelled many Europeans to grasp for control. One result of these efforts, of course, was the rise of a new science that sought to understand the laws of nature by categorizing and classifying information. Another was in the development of new tools for governing.[28]

Important in spurring this desire for categorization as an aid to statecraft was the growth of the machinery of state during the English Civil War, a set of developments the Stuarts built upon after the Restoration. In the 1640s mobilization for war required an expansive government that could assess and collect taxes. By midcentury this meant both that the state claimed a larger portion of national wealth and that it deployed a larger bureaucracy to manage it. While originally developed to meet the need of massing large armies, the state's bureaucratic growth was increasingly put to use in advancing overseas expansion. As commerce and colonization rose together, the use of a powerful navy to protect shipping and a massive customs administration to collect taxes further expanded the power of the English fiscal-military state. With growing confidence in the ability of an active government to manage the empire, Cromwell and Parliament deployed the power of the state to manage colonial affairs. This approach resulted in the 1651 Act of Trade and Navigation, which relied upon governmental officials on both sides of the Atlantic to prevent colonial produce from flowing to foreign markets. Aimed explicitly at the Dutch who were besting English trade in both America and Europe, the law resulted from an alliance between the state and overseas merchants who came to see their interests as linked. The framework the Navigation Act established continued to guide imperial decision-making into the next century even though metropolitan regulatory ambitions ran ahead of their capacities to enforce the law. After the Restoration, the financially strapped Charles worked with his councilors and London's rising merchants to build on Commonwealth efforts to support shipping and enhance trade revenues. To this end Charles, Parliament, and his merchant allies passed a series of new trade laws intended to more fully capture the colonies' trade for the empire's benefit. The next decade saw them adjusting these laws and finding new ways to enforce them.[29]

As critical as regulations were in helping to harness the trade of a growing empire, a lack of proficiency in navigation and cartography continued to hamper English empire-building. Since at least midcentury, many of England's merchants, politicians, and government bureaucrats had complained that the nation's inferior technical knowledge hurt their ability to compete with the Dutch. Englishmen had just received a strong reminder of their relative maritime weakness in the Second Anglo-Dutch War (1665–1667), when Dutch ships destroyed much of what remained of the English naval fleet. When it came to considering why England lagged so far behind in maritime strength, there was plenty of blame to go around. Many commentators pointed to the Dutch Republic's potent combination of low interest rates, favorable laws and taxes that encouraged trade, and superior commercial and ship-building expertise to explain Dutch dominance.[30] Other mercantile boosters focused on England's collective lack of navigational and cartographic skill. In his position as a naval administrator Samuel Pepys observed English technical weakness first hand, and he intended to make it one of the key themes of his history of the royal navy. The notes that he prepared for the unfinished volume acerbically catalog England's failure to promote geography stretching back to the sixteenth century. "We frequently . . . [have] owned our ignorance in sea affairs," he wrote, to "our never having had any Lectures for navigation." When Francis Drake pledged "20*l.* per annum towards a Navigation Lecture," he continued, the offer was "made ineffectual for want of 20*l.* more." Even the supposed success of the first volume of Seller's *The English Pilot* was empty as, according to Pepys, this volume was "little less than transcripts of the Dutch maps, some of them even with papers pasted over and names scratched." The result was that not only did "English masters, even upon our own coasts" sail with a "Waggener printed by the Dutch" but also that "the Dutch know our coasts . . . as well as we."[31] At a moment of intense rivalry and warfare with the Dutch Republic the lack of a sufficient corpus of geographic and cartographic knowledge threatened English security and constrained mercantile expansion.

Charles II recognized this imbalance in expertise and encouraged England's maritime strength. The new monarch used his 1661 coronation as an occasion to make it clear that his empire's commercial and political success was bound up with navigation, cartography, and geography. Erected outside the Royal Exchange in Cornhill, the second of four triumphal arches designed by John Ogilby through which the Charles II processed employed an elaborate geographic iconography that captured the interplay between the king's claim to authority, the importance of the navy, and the centrality of commerce. Crowned by the figure of Atlas holding a globe on which a ship in full sail perched, the 80-foot-tall wooden and masonry arch had four niches that contained figures representing arithmetic, geometry, astronomy, and navigation (Figure 5.3). The collection of navigational and astronomical equipment that seems about to pour forth from behind the Native American figures on the right side of the printed image of this arch suggests the kinds of physical artifacts that were actually displayed on the processional arch at the coronation, recalling the swelter of similar devices for sale at Seller's shop. Painted on the face of the arch was a scene depicting a king and

FIGURE 5.3. David Loggan, *Triumphal arch; near the Royal Exchange* [second arch] in Cornhill, in John Ogilby, *The Entertainment of his Most Excellent Majestie Charles II, in his Passage through the City of London to his Coronation.* London: Thomas Roycroft, 1662. E.570-1890. © Victoria and Albert Museum.

prince (likely a young Charles II and his father) inspecting a naval vessel. Cannons, ropes, and anchors surround the picture. Finally, at the coronation living figures depicting Europe, Asia, Africa, and America stood on pedestals at the register above the arch. On a stage in front of this arch, Ogilby organized a vignette that represented the monarch's claim to power in the form of a human map. A second stage on the other side of the street was "made like the upper Deck of a Ship" with "three Sea-men" pacing its decks and singing songs proclaiming English naval might.[32] As historian Robert J. Mayhew has argued, Ogilby's use of geographic imagery in the procession was political. This vignette reinforced Charles's claim to his dominions by arguing that the unity of the state flowed through him. The figures of the continents on the arch behind the stage extended this metaphor and indicated the breadth of England's international ambitions. In short, "Charles II and Britain grounded their unity and expansionism on a solid grasp of geography."[33] At the same time, the public deployment of navigational and cartographic iconography in service of politics suggests both how useful for statecraft this imagery was and how conversant Londoners had become in the language of geography.

Building on efforts undertaken in the Commonwealth period to construct more ships—the naval and merchant fleets had doubled in size between 1649 and 1653—and to improve seamanship, Charles II further enhanced the power of the navy and the extent of overseas commerce. He named his brother James, the Duke of York, the lord high admiral to signal the navy's importance and devoted as much as 20 percent of government expenditures to the navy. In support of merchant shipping, Charles worked with Parliament to reinforce and expand the 1651 Navigation Act with new laws in 1660 and 1663, chartered the Royal African Company, and founded new American colonies.[34] To further these initiatives, the king subsidized cartographic projects and navigational literacy. His issuance of a royal license for *Virginia and Maryland* and his sponsorship of Seller's *The English Pilot* indicate his understanding that English cartography required institutional support if it was going to catch up with the Dutch. Charles II also financed a number of efforts to teach navigation to young children, including at Christ's Hospital, where he established and endowed a foundation to instruct "40 poor boys therein . . . in the Art of Navigation."[35] The king's efforts to bolster geographic education and English sea power coincided with Englishmen's adoption of maps as tools of empire to create a ready market for *Virginia and Maryland.*

The Consumers: The Lords of Trade

One of the groups most interested in acquiring maps for their administrative power in Restoration England was the Lords of Trade. Known by a variety of names and organized and reorganized numerous times, this group emerged in the 1670s as a powerful force in shaping colonial policy. The restructuring of the Lords of Trade was part of the larger series of reforms Charles II and his ministers undertook as they reshaped the imperial bureaucracy to strengthen the crown's authority and enhance administrative efficiency. Previously, Charles II had relied on various overlapping bodies to oversee colonial affairs. Frustrated with an inefficient bureaucracy incapable of making coherent policy, Charles II scrapped the existing committees and formed a new body, the Lords Committee of Trade and Plantations, to advise him on colonial policy in 1675. This new subcommittee of the Privy Council was not in and of itself a massive departure from earlier bodies, but in executing its duties the Lords of Trade would transform imperial decision-making. Key among its innovations was the more systematic gathering of colonial intelligence. As a first step the Lords began to require colonies to keep agents in London so that they could quickly acquire information about colonial affairs. Not content to use these individuals as intermediaries, the Lords of Trade also began to send regular circular letters to all royal governors ordering them to furnish detailed reports about the demographics, laws, trade, office-holders, and physical condition of their colonies. Collectively, the governors' responses to these letters offer some of the most complete descriptions of the situation of English Atlantic colonies in the seventeenth century. Barbados governor Jonathan Atkins's 1676 report, for example, spans sixteen closely written folio pages, detailing the structure of government, the island's population, its defenses, its geography, the conditions and histories of its neighbors, and much more. Lord Baltimore likewise provided a similar, if less thorough, accounting of his colony, pointing especially to its uniquely dispersed mode of settlement.[36]

With the help of Parliament, the Lords also worked to accumulate better records on shipping and trade. In 1673 Parliament revised earlier attempts to account for colonial trade with its Plantation Duty Act. The new administrative policies were intended to make sure that ships bearing enumerated goods traveled to England (not a foreign port) and paid duties on goods shipped between plantations, but the law also created new ways to track imperial shipping by mandating that colonists post bond at their colonial port of departure for the duties that would be due on their cargoes when they reached England. To make this complex bond system work, colonial customs agents and their counterparts in England diligently recorded the names, masters, owners, cargoes, and destinations of departing ships carrying enumerated goods and passed these certificates back and forth in order to discharge the bonds once the vessels arrived at their destinations. Frequent missives reminded governors of their duty to return copies of bonds "twice every yeare" and "exact Lists of Ships, once every yeare at least."[37] Though incomplete and often tardy in arriving, these shipping returns meant that by the mid-1670s Restoration administrators were for the first time systematically able to understand the empire's expanding trade, reducing the complex movement of ships around the Atlantic to neat listings of vessels, their cargoes, and their destinations.

In addition to collecting trade statistics and relying on governors to supply textual accounts of their colonies, the Lords of Trade also sought to gather better cartographic records. Many of these maps ended up in the hands of the body's secretary William Blathwayt. Referred to today as "The Blathwayt Atlas," the collection consists of thirty-five printed and thirteen manuscript maps of North America and the West Indies.[38] Blathwayt's atlas originated in 1670, when Charles II commanded the Council of Plantations to "procure exact Mapps, Platts or Charts of all and Every our said Plantations abroad, together with the Mapps and Descriptions of their respective Ports, harbours, Forst, bayes, Rivers."[39] In acquiring these cartographic materials, the Lords of Trade turned to a variety of suppliers. One of these map-sellers was John Seller, who sold them a copy of *Virginia and Maryland* sometime between December 1674 and June 1676. To supplement their printed maps, the Lords collected manuscript maps from Thames School chart-makers from whom they most likely commissioned the two manuscript copies derived from Herrman's work that were part of Blathwayt's collection.[40] Not fully satisfied with maps they could procure in Europe, the Lords of Trade also ordered colonial governors to "send home Mapps of their Plantations."[41]

For the purposes of gaining a better sense of the scope and development of the colonies and better managing those places, these maps proved critical for the Lords of Trade and soon supplanted narrative descriptions in importance for understanding borders and administering colonies. In 1678, for example, when Lord Baltimore responded to the Lords' request for a better delineation of Maryland's borders, he referred them not to the colony's charter but rather to *Virginia and Maryland*, claiming that it was more accurate than a written description. In response to the Lords' query about the colony's borders, he wrote, "I answer that the boundaries, Longitude & Latitude of this Province are well described & sett forth in a late map or chart of this Province lately made & prepared by One Augustine Herman an Inhabitant of The said Province & printed & publiquely sold in London by His Majesties licence to which I humbly refer for greater certainty and not to give their Lordships the trouble of a large tedious description here." When asked about "Rivers, Harbours & Roads" and their "depths & soundings" Baltimore again referred the Lords to the map.[42] Several years, later the Lords of Trade used Robert Morden and William Berry's *A Map of New England New Yorke New Iersey Mary-land & Virginia* (1676) to evaluate a proposal to reorganize the New England colonies—an effort that eventually resulted in the creation of the Dominion of New England. A copy of this map, now part of the Blathwayt Atlas, records the evidence of these deliberations in the colored lines that Blathwayt's clerk, John Povey, added to demarcate the extent of the new provinces they were considering.[43] By the 1670s, it was clear that English imperial officials could not contemplate managing the empire without printed maps, so much so that the first volume of the journal of the Lords of Trade and Plantations begins not with the new body's commission, but with a printed and hand colored map of the world.[44]

Acquired at a critical moment when the crown and the lords were reevaluating and reassessing colonial policy, *Virginia and Maryland* made tangible the difficulties English authorities faced in regulating the Chesapeake's trade through its detailed depiction of the Chesapeake's numerous bays, channels, and inlets. At the same time, if placed in the right hands, the map could be a vital aid to naval officers and customs officials charged with enforcing trade laws or to bureaucrats determining policy. Just as the shipping records English colonial administrators collected reduced complex colonial affairs to neat columns of digestible and seemingly straightforward numbers, the engraved version of Herrman's map, encased as it was in metropolitan symbols that reappropriated his multinational region as an imperial one, made them confident that as distant and complex as the Chesapeake's geography was, it was also firmly under their control.

The Consumers: London's Elites

As a tool to manage England's expanding empire *Virginia and Maryland* functioned for London's elite commercial and professional communities in similar ways as it did for government bureaucrats. The prices of maps varied widely in Restoration London, depending upon size, ornamentation, coloring, and whether they were mounted on rollers or not (coloring and mounting a map more than doubled the its price), but many sold for between two and ten shillings. *Virginia and Maryland*'s price of six shillings, about the cost of an unillustrated 200-page quarto book, placed it out of reach of most Londoners, but within grasp of members of London's rising professional class; elites could afford not only the map but also the extra expense to have it colored and mounted for display.[45]

Samuel Pepys, the only individual who we know for certain owned a copy of *Virginia and Maryland*, is among the best documented of this group of elite consumers. A graduate of Magdalene College at Cambridge University, Pepys was a lifelong civil servant.[46] For him and other elites, consumption of maps like *Virginia and Maryland* was often a practical matter. Merchants engaged in foreign trade used them to plan and monitor their ships' voyages as well as to conceptualize overseas ports. "It is useful for the Merchant," John Seller noted in his *Atlas maritimus*, to own maps so "That he may see . . . (at any time) the Port or Place where his Ship is, and may inform himself of the commodiousness or danger of the Harbor or place where she is, and what Wind will carry Her into port, or bring Her out."[47] The seventeenth-century treatment of maps as useful objects so infused mercantile discourse that Lewes Roberts titled his advice manual—which introduced readers to geography, commodities, exchange rates, and accounting principles—*The Merchants Mappe of Commerce* despite containing only five maps in its 365 pages.[48]

Maps served a similar functional purpose for Pepys. Although he did not direct mercantile ventures, his and his Admiralty colleagues' professional duties required deep geographic knowledge. In 1661, for instance, he remembered that he watched Sir William Penn "with Mr. Coventry teaching of him upon the map to understand Jamaica." The next year, after making an agreement with Sir John Winter to supply the navy with timber from the Forest of Dean, Pepys "turned to the Forrest of Deane, in Speede's Mapps," to see "how it lies" in order to understand "the great charge of carrying it [the timber] to Lydny" for shipping. Castigating himself for not having understood this before, Pepys remarked that "I do perceive that I am very short in my business by not knowing many times the geographical part of my business."[49] Pepys was a diligent student, and he frequented London's most important map- and chart-sellers to acquire Dutch atlases, manuscript charts, geographic treatises, and navigational globes to aid his geographic education.[50]

By the time Pepys donated his collection to Magdalene College in 1695, he owned more than 1,100 maps, charts, and plans. Pepys's collection varied widely and encompassed much of the world, though its main strengths were maps of the British Isles followed by those of France and Italy. Of particular interest to Pepys were detailed sea atlases. Among these were a number of Dutch manuscript navigational charts and Dudley's sea atlas *Dell'Arcano del Mare*, which contained his map of the Chesapeake (see Figure 2.8). His collection of maps of the Americas and West Indies was small in comparison to his European holdings but included some of the most important seventeenth century maps of English America including John Smith's *Virginia Discouvered and Discribed*, a copy of John Lederer's map of Carolina (1672), and Richard Ligon's famous map of Barbados (1657). Nestled among these maps is a bespoke bound volume entitled "A Collection of Mr Seller's Four Books of Sea=Charts & Draughts" consisting of a number of Seller charts largely drawn from his *The English Pilot* and his *The Coasting Pilot* but supplemented with several additional maps, including *Virginia and Maryland*. Pepys probably acquired *Virginia and Maryland* before 1677 and did so directly from Seller as he and Pepys had a long relationship.[51]

More than providing practical aids for their work, maps such as *Virginia and Maryland* also offered English gentlemen like Pepys a way to understand the history and affairs of the world. Beginning in the sixteenth century, geography had become a standard part of elite men's education; Oxford University began instruction in the subject in 1541 and Cambridge University in 1548. A subject matter worthy of study itself, geography was also understood to be foundational to history and public policy. As the Elizabethan mathematician and geographer John Dee wrote in 1570, maps were essential in comprehending "things past, [such] as battles fought, earthquakes, heavenly firings, and such oc-

currences, in histor[y]." When one studied world affairs, Dee continued, maps allowed one "to vewe the large dominion of the Turke: the
wide Empire of the Moschouite: and the little morsell of ground, where
Christendome (by prfession) is certainly knowen." His countrymen, Dee
concluded, should "liketh, loveth, getteth and useth, Maps, Charts, and
Geographical Globes."[52]

Understanding geography was also expected of polite gentlemen like
Pepys. As overseas trade intensified during the seventeenth century,
and the scale of public affairs expanded, elites eager to keep abreast of
economic and political news needed to improve their fluency with geography as they sought to comprehend distant places and events. As
geographer P. C. Chamberlayne explained in his introduction to the
subject intended for general readers, "*methinks he that is ignorant of it*
[geography], *(especially if a Man of parts) must needs blush every time he
reades the* [London] Gazette, *and cannot give an account in what* Country *is seated such* Place *or* Town *of note."* If, instead, a gentleman perfected the skills of geography through Chamberlayne's book, "*his skill
in* Maps" would give "*an extraordinary light to what he reads*" and ensure that he was not "*baffled in* Geography *by every ordinary* Seaman."[53]
Studying geography was also inherently political for it helped reorient
readers' perspective from the European to the global scale and thus allowed them to conceive of an overseas empire. The technical, social,
and political importance of geographic knowledge helps explain why
handbooks such as Chamberlayne's were so widely popular in the mid-
seventeenth century. It was even possible for English men and women
to find maps printed on the backs of playing cards so that "Geography
may be easily and familiarly learnt by all sorts of People" as they engaged
in polite rituals.[54] The printing of maps on playing cards points to the
fluency with maps that elite women, as well as men, possessed in Restoration England. Gender conventions precluded women from formal
roles in government and overseas trade, but nevertheless polite women,
too, consumed maps in works of history, geography, and exploration.
Elizabeth Pepys, for one, studied geography with the aid of a pair of

globes her husband Samuel purchased explicitly because she wished to understand the subject.[55]

So profound was English gentlemen and gentlewomen's confidence in the ability of maps to help them comprehend a wide variety of topics that by the mid-seventeenth century some felt compelled to create their own when no others existed. One of the more remarkable seventeenth-century maps of the Chesapeake originated in just such a moment. John Ferrar's *A mapp of Virginia discouered to ye Falls* first appeared in 1651 as an illustration in the third edition of Edward Williams's *Virgo triumphans* (see Figure 2.4). Ferrar probably completed the first draft of this map in his copy of the first edition of Williams's book. Now in the collections of the New York Public Library, Ferrar's copy of *Virgo triumphans*, includes an annotation in Ferrar's hand that scolds Williams for not including a map with the volume. Next to Williams's observation that "The situation and Climate of Virginia is the Subject of every Map, to which I shall refer the curiosity of those who desire more particular information," Ferrar scrawled, "But a map had binn to this Book For all men love to see the country as well as to heare of it and the Eye in this kind is alsoe to be satisfied as well as the Eare."[56] An extreme example of the desire to see as well as read about distant places, Ferrar's decision to rectify Williams's failure to provide readers a map by drawing his own attests to the importance of these objects. That Ferrar chose a chorographical description of Virginia in which to draw his map and proclaim its power was not a coincidence. Most of the early English cartographic depictions of the new colonies first circulated in books describing the exploration, settlement, and history of the region. Both Smith's map and *Nova Terra-Mariæ tabula* first appeared in this form before being copied and disseminated more widely. As readers consulted maps like *Virginia and Maryland*, they read them alongside descriptions of the Americas, integrating visual and textual sources together as they strove to understand England's expanding empire.

Though not part of a chorographical account, *Virginia and Maryland* included some conventions of this tradition. Most likely added by Faithorne and derived from unknown sources, these short pieces, which vary in length from one sentence to a short paragraph, intermix geographic description, natural history, and historical information. Most of the portions that reference geographic features add information that could not easily be conveyed through images. For example, in the top left-center of the map, between the York and Mattaponi Rivers, Faithorne inserted a statement that "The Heads of these two Rivers, Proceed and issue forth out of low Marshy ground, and not out of hills or Mountaines as other Rivers doe." Other similar comments indicate the geography of those portions of the Susquehanna River beyond the map's margins. The natural history annotations speculate about resources present in the region. Near the place name of "The Goulden or Brass Hill" in the left-center of the map, the textual element explains that the hill "issued forth a glisteringe Stuff Sand like unto the Fylings of Brass" and that the "ground semed to be covered over with the same Brassy stuff." Perhaps tied to the longstanding Virginia Company hope that they would establish mines in Virginia, these notations encouraged viewers of the map to connect it to other historical and promotional accounts of the region. At the left of the map, a further comment combines geography with the fantastical in stating that the "Low Suncken Swampy Land" between the James and Roanoke Rivers is almost impassible and "harbours Tygers Bears and other Devouringe Creatures." While most of the elements focus on the natural and Native American history of the region, one portion recounts the moment when Governor William Berkeley of Virginia "Conquered and tooke Prisoner the great Indian Emperour Abatschakin, after the Massacre in Virginia." Referring to a 1644 raid on Virginia led by Powhatan chief Opechancanough and Governor Berkeley's retaliatory capture of the Native leader, this story celebrates a moment of conquest that affirmed English control of Virginia.

The longest narrative block on the map blends these genres of writing—geography, natural history, and history—and reveals the ways Englishmen integrated different types of knowledge to fully comprehend the Chesapeake. It begins by offering the quasi-scientific explanation that the "mighty High and great Mountaines" to the northwest of the Chesapeake are the cause of "the fierce . . . and extreme Stormy Cold Winds that comes N. W. from thence all over this Continent and makes frost." Next, the account turns to geographic knowledge, reporting that Native Americans believe that "the [Chesapeake's] Rivers take their Originall issuing out into the West Sea" where there is "a very great River called the Black Mincquaas River," although, the text continues, those same informants do not know "whether that same River comes out into the bay of Mexico or the West Sea." Interspersed within this account of the origins of Virginia's and Maryland's rivers is a confusing short history of the friction between the Native inhabitants of the Susquehanna River Valley. Finally, the piece ends by highlighting the future riches that still remained to be discovered in the Chesapeake. "Certain it is that as the Spaniard is possessed with great Store of Minneralls at the other side of these Mountaines the same Treasure . . . may in . . . time" be found "here on this Side when Occupyed which is Recomended to Posterity to Remember."

Based partly on the actual conditions and history of the Chesapeake and intended for a metropolitan audience unfamiliar with the region, the textual portions Faithorne added to *Virginia and Maryland* transformed the map into an object of wonder not unlike the other kinds of colonial histories that English men and women read. Part history, part natural history, part political economy, and part adventure story, these books and pamphlets allowed readers to experience the colonies vicariously. Uniting text and image these works were part of what historian John Scott has called a "process of textual navigation by which English readers . . . explored and mapped their relationships to the world, in time and space."[57] Calling upon first-hand experience reinforced with imaginary portrait miniatures like that of Herrman, these books, pamphlets, and maps allowed one to virtually inhabit distant places and thus functioned as proxies for travel to distant lands. In the preface to his important navigation manual, William Cuningham heralded the principles of cosmography (understood as a blending of textual and visual geographic information and personified there as a woman) for delivering readers "from greate and continuall travailes [travels]," "For in a pleasaunte house, or warme study, she sheweth us the hole face of all th'Earthe. . . . In travailing [with maps], thou shalt not be molested with the inclemencye of th'Aere, boisterous windes, stormy shoures, haile, Ise, & snow. Coming to they lodginge, thou shalt not have a churlish & unknowne hoste, which shall minister meate twise [twice] sodden, stinking fish, or watered wine. Going to rest, thou shalt not feare lowsy beddes, or filthy sheates." So powerful were geographic depictions in allowing viewers to "beholde the diversitie of countries; natures of people, & innumerable formes of Beastes, Foules, Fishes, Trees, Fruites, Steemes, & Meatalles" that Cuningham referred to them as "precious . . . Jewell[s]."[58]

That English men and women could vicariously travel to distant places through geographical works was also important because it made exotic colonial places more fathomable by relating them to the familiar. Although these works could evoke a fearsome and dangerous land, their familiar format, common tropes (tigers and bears made frequent appearances in them), and metropolitan symbols like those Faithorne added to *Virginia and Maryland*, placed readers at ease and gave them the chance to access the unknown on their own terms. "I cannot tell what more pleasure should happen to a gentle wit," scholar and statesman Thomas Elyot wrote, "than to behold in his own house everything that within all the world is contained."[59] This idea, that by picturing the world one can grasp its complexity made it possible for the English to appropriate colonial resources, oversee business, and impose their will abroad.[60] Taking *Virginia and Maryland* in hand, readers like Pepys could visit the Chesapeake with Herrman as guide, experience the wonders of the Americas, and participate in England's glorious expansion from the comfort of their own libraries.

Used to understand geography and history as well as for entertainment, maps were also ornamental objects. During the seventeenth century elite Englishmen rushed "to beautifie their Halls, Parlers, Chambers, Galeries, Studies, or Libraries" with them.[61] While the proliferation of atlases allowed consumers without spacious rooms to own and consult small and folded maps, those with the resources and space, like Pepys, started to follow the Dutch example and embellished their homes with "great and large *Geographicall* Maps or Chartes."[62] If Pepys considered using Herrman's map as an object of display, it would have been a good candidate. Measuring roughly three feet by two and a half feet and containing numerous elements of visual interest, it would have made a significant statement. To pursue this option Pepys could have brought the map to any number of picture-sellers, who would have attached the four sections of the map to a linen backing to make it whole, and then sent it to be colored (as the Lords of Trade did with their copy of *Virginia and Maryland*), varnished, and suspended between turned wooden rods. Once fully prepared, Herrman's map would have resembled many others for sale in Seller's shop, such as the "new map of the World . . . about three foot in breadth, and two foot and a half in depth . . . which being pasted on Cloth with roale and ledge" the map-seller offered for sale in March 1673.[63] While Pepys's copy of *Virginia and Maryland* shows no sign of receiving this treatment, he certainly displayed a number of maps both in his office and house at the Navy Office complex in Seething Lane. Pepys's map collection worked alongside other prints and paintings to serve a multitude of functions. Most directly these items beautified his rooms and marked them as elite spaces that reflected the sophistication of his taste and the scope of his erudition. Intending them as objects of self-presentation, Pepys often displayed his maps and prints in the most public rooms, arranging some in his "stayres and entry" and others in his "dining room, which ma[de] it very pretty" as he reported in his diary. In his office, a place where he also received visitors, Pepys hung framed manuscript sea charts and displayed navigational globes.[64]

Designed to impress and captivate guests of all ages and genders, the placement of maps in these spaces demonstrates their power as objects of refinement and sociability in the mid-seventeenth century. Such was Pepys's belief in the importance of maps that he could not imagine a room complete without them. In April 1666, when he remodeled what he called his "new roome," in deciding on the décor Pepys remarked in his diary that he had "bespoke some maps to hang" there so that it would be "one of the handsomest and most useful roomes in my house." He likewise furnished his office at his house in Seething Lane with numerous maps, prints, and more than five hundred books, making it a place for both work and entertainment, where Pepys could read, write, and play music, as well as keep his accounts and his famous diary. Joining the maps, books, and pamphlets related to his work with the Admiralty such as handbooks on fitting out vessels, technical navigation manuals, and pilot's guides were scientific treatises, histories of the word, travel accounts, and sermons and religious tracts. Arranged in a series of book presses and impressively gilded, his books dominated the small room, which also contained "a desk, 'a fair chest of drawers', iron chests for holding money, [and] a press for papers." On the walls were "purple hangings, maps and pictures of ships." Pepys routinely invited those he sought to impress to peruse his collections as he showed them "the method of" their arrangement. Inviting others to examine his maps also sparked "manly discourse and [gave him the] opportunity of shewing [him]self, and learning from others."[65] Owning these objects was only part of their worth; the theatricality of their display and the judiciousness of their organization were equally as important in marking their owner as learned. When he eventually moved to a larger house on Buckingham Street, Pepys designed a larger library to house his growing collection of what was now more than three thousand items encompassing music, history, art, literature, and science and consisting of books, pamphlets, sheet music, prints, and over one thousand maps. This space featured large glazed book presses with dedicated spaces above and beside in which to hang his portraits, maps, and prints (Figure 5.4). Thus Pepys could easily turn to them as aids to history, memory, and geography. Pepys's placement of cartographic images beside his book collections was not accidental; together these sources offered him access to the world's knowledge. Surrounded by books that described nature, history, and geography and by maps and prints of the world as he sat in his library, Pepys imagined himself able to see the world.

FIGURE 5.4. View of Pepys's library in Buckingham Street, showing his juxtaposition of books, maps and portraits. By permission of the Pepys Library, Magdalene College, Cambridge.

Beyond the ways that they were useful for his work, for understanding geography, and for burnishing his reputation, maps' very materiality also brought Pepys enjoyment. Numerous references in his diary indicate that though he hired workmen to help him, he was often active in hanging maps himself. In the summer of 1666 Pepys spent most of one "afternoon till it was quite darke hanging things, that is my maps and pictures and draughts, and setting up my books, and as much as we could do, to my most extraordinary satisfaction; so that I think it will be as noble a closett as any man hath."[66] Pepys also painstakingly cataloged his collection. The arrangement of it was so specific that when he left it to Magdalene College, his will specified that it be kept together in "a faire Roome" and that the catalogue "forever accompany the said Library."[67] The joy Pepys took in arranging, sorting, and cataloging these works suggests how their materiality reinforced their contents; together, reading and arranging maps allowed metropolitan consumers like Pepys an opportunity to order the world.

Lord Baltimore's efforts to sponsor the engraving and printing of *Virginia and Maryland* converted it from a colonial into a metropolitan object. In the process it also became not only Herrman's creation, but the combined work of Herrman, Baltimore, Faithorne, an anonymous printer, and John Seller. Finally, in the act of consuming it additional, mostly unknown, individuals put the map to new uses and added new meanings in the process. Sold in Seller's map shop near the Royal Exchange at the center of London's information economy, discussed in the coffeehouses of Exchange Alley, employed in the committee room of the Lords of Trade, displayed in Pepys's closet or library alongside portraits of kings and views of England or stored on Pepys's book presses beside travel narratives and histories, *Virginia and Maryland* both aided and signified its consumers' achievement in helping to create a powerful trading empire. Immediately useful as a tool for navigation, claiming territory, resolving border disputes, and imagining strange lands, it had become a thoroughly imperial artifact.

Colonial Misreadings

Given how completely the engraving, printing, and consumption of *Virginia and Maryland* transformed Herrman's map into a metropolitan object, the map as such did not necessarily hold the same meanings for colonial consumers as it did for their metropolitan counterparts. There is no affirmative evidence that proves a copy of the printed *Virginia and Maryland*—as opposed to copies of Herrman's original manuscripts that likely circulated among the Bohemian's associates—ever reached Maryland but there are several tantalizing clues that indicate at least one copy did. Though Herrman never mentions seeing the engraved map himself (notwithstanding an oft-repeated 1911 claim that he did), the mapmaker described the printed map as a "Publick Mapp of Virginia & Maryland" at the end of his life.[68] Herrman's use of the phrase "Publick Mapp" is ambiguous but this description, together with a 1676 Maryland petition that refers to *Virginia and Maryland*, suggests that the map may have been openly displayed, perhaps in the Maryland Assembly building or in Charles Calvert's house, and as was common in legislative assembly halls in colonial America in the eighteenth century.[69]

If Calvert did display *Virginia and Maryland* publicly, the 1676 petition reveals the limits of metropolitan symbolic language among the complexities and passions of local politics. In it, the missive's anonymous Maryland author attacks the now Third Lord Baltimore and "the Maryland Papists" who "drive us Protestants to Purgatory within our selves in America" and imagines a Catholic conspiracy involving Charles Calvert and extending to England. Born out of the decades' long struggle between Protestants and the Calverts for control of Maryland and seventeenth-century fears of papist plots, this petition is notable in this context because the unknown author deploys *Virginia and Maryland* as evidence of the Calverts' absolutist policies. The writer's chief charge is that the Third Lord Baltimore elevated himself to the level of the king. "The proprietary with his familiars houlds forth, That Hee is an absolute prince in Maryland, with as absolute prerogative Royall Right & Power as owr [our] gratious Souveraigne in England." The problem, however, was not just that Baltimore assumed the power and authority of the king in Maryland, but that the Catholic Lord Baltimore wished to extend this power to England. Why else, the writer asked, does "Lord Baltemore put . . . himselfe in equall computation with His court of Armes, next to the Kings Majesty in the great Mapp of Virginia and Maryland," placing "himselfe distinctly in, and the Kings Majesty out of Maryland?"[70]

Bound up intimately with Maryland's fractious seventeenth-century politics, this local reading of *Virginia and Maryland* largely defies the meanings that engraver William Faithorne and others had added in London. The author reimagined the map not as an instrument of empire that appropriated the region for imperial purposes but rather as an attempt to defy the king's authority in favor of Lord Baltimore's. The

relationship between the Calverts and Charles II, the monarch's investment in the map, and the iconography of the map itself (the Royal Arms
of Great Britain dwarf Calvert's crest) belie the plausibility of this local
reading. But that at least one colonist understood Herrman's map in
this manner suggests that even though the map had been transported
to England and significantly reshaped, its colonial meanings persisted.

Just as Herrman's understanding of the interconnectedness and
multi-imperial nature of the region could never be completely oblit-
erated by metropolitan symbols and the context of its consumption,
neither could these same forces of imperial documentation and power
control colonists' use of maps on the ground. Because only the metropolitan version of Herrman's map remains, his local way of seeing
has been obscured, leaving us a distorted vision of how colonists in the
Mid-Atlantic envisioned their connections to one another. If we could
strip away Faithorne's iconographic additions, which were intended to
universalize and contain colonial space within the empire, we would be
left with a map that reflected colonists' lived experience. Resembling
the manuscript versions of Herrman's map that likely circulated in the
Mid-Atlantic, this map would emphasize fluidity, movement, and the
materiality of the waters of the Chesapeake. It would be a map that depicted how diverse peoples were connected to one another and stressed
local situations and spatial understandings not imperial ones. We still
have much to learn about how seventeenth-century Americans imagined space, but the history of *Virginia and Maryland* teaches us that a
colonial way of seeing lurks in many metropolitan maps.

Epilogue

Afterlives

With so few copies of *Virginia and Maryland* extant, it did not become part of the cartographic canon of North America in the nineteenth and twentieth centuries as did Smith's *Virginia Discouvered and Discribed.* Nevertheless the map continued to live through a number of derivatives that began to appear almost immediately on the English market and continued to do so for more than a century. Each of these subsequent maps varies in the amount of information the makers borrowed from Herrman and in their faithfulness to his work, but they are united in their erasure of him. In this guise, stripped of its association with its colonial maker, Herrman's depiction of the Chesapeake could be used by subsequent mapmakers for their own purposes, tailoring his geo-graphic information to suit their own varied political needs. Herrman's memorialization went through a similar transformation in the years after his death. After he fell into obscurity during the eighteenth century, adherents to the emerging colonial revival and the United States' large Bohemian population resuscitated the mapmaker during the nineteenth century. While each of these groups cast Herrman's significance in a dif-ferent light, they agreed that he was best understood within a nationalist framework that effaced the reality of his multi-imperial life.

Derivatives of *Virginia and Maryland*

The first printed map to borrow Herrman's depiction of the Chesapeake was John Seller's *A Mapp of New Jarsey*. He derived the southern portion of this small single sheet map from Herrman's depiction of the Delaware

Bay and Southern New Jersey. Two years later, Seller released a larger version of this map, which included Herrman's detailed soundings and data from the Delaware River and Bay. In 1676 Robert Morden and William Berry also incorporated Herrman's work in their depiction of English settlement along North America's Atlantic coast. In producing *A Map of New England New Yorke New Iersey Mary-Land & Virginia* (1676), Morden and Berry (together with engraver Gregory King) synthesized information from a variety of sources, including the Jansson-Visscher series and a new manuscript map of New England and New York. When drawing the Chesapeake, the makers based their work on *Virginia and Maryland*, shrinking and simplifying that map to fit it into the bottom left corner of theirs.[1]

Between 1678 and 1689 John Thornton, a Thames-school chartmaker who like Seller became a map-seller and publisher in the 1670s, used *Virginia and Maryland* as the basis for a number of his most important maps, selectively reproducing portions of the map. Herrman's delineation of the Delaware Bay, the Susquehanna River, and the Upper Chesapeake, for example, appear in *A Map of Some of the South and Eastbounds of Pennsylvania in America* (1681), a work that William Penn commissioned from Thornton and Seller to promote his new colony. Thornton's most complete borrowing of Herrman's work appeared in a series of maps of the Chesapeake that culminated with the map of the region that eventually appeared in *The English Pilot*. Thornton issued the first of these maps, *A Mapp of Virginia Mary-land, New-Jarsey, New-York, & New England*, in 1678 or 1679. In 1685 Thornton published another iteration, *A new map of New England, New York, New Iarsey, Pensulvania, Maryland, and Virginia*, engraved from a new larger plate; this map extended to New England and replaced the detail of New England with one of New York City's harbor, but closely resembled the earlier work in all other respects.[2] Four years later, Thornton partnered with William Fisher to produce yet another Herrman derivative for book four of the sea atlas Seller had begun but Fisher and Thornton finished, *The English Pilot, West India* (1689). Based on Thornton's 1685 map but reduced again to fit in this atlas, *Virginia, Maryland, Pennsilvania, East*

& *West Jarsey* appeared in all thirty-seven editions of the fourth book of the *Pilot* published between 1689 and 1794, thereby becoming the most important of the *Virginia and Maryland* derivatives. Even though John Mount and Thomas Page, Thornton's and Fisher's successors as publishers, had the plates re-engraved, they made few substantive changes, meaning it was Herrman's geographic information of the Chesapeake that delineated the region in the most popular and important English guide to shipboard navigation for more than a century.[3]

Significantly smaller and cropped differently, all three of these Thornton maps clearly follow Herrman in the general shape of the Chesapeake Bay and the Delmarva Peninsula. Telling signs that they were taken directly from Herrman's work are Thornton's inclusion of tree icons to mark the border between Maryland and Virginia on the Eastern Shore, similar phrasing and spelling in many place names (such as "the Great Bay of Cheseapeake"), the distinctive shape of the sandbars in the Delaware Bay, and the inclusion of Bohemia Manor, an otherwise undistinguished plantation in the Upper Chesapeake. Although they are much fewer in number, the soundings on Thornton's maps, with only a few exceptions, exactly match those included on *Virginia and Maryland*. As similar as these maps are to Herrman's work, however, their alternative framing, smaller size, and pared-down information make them altogether different images. Thornton's decision to expand the map to include New England, New York, and New Jersey alongside the Chesapeake, for example, shifts the center of the map away from the middle of the Chesapeake Bay to New York and deemphasizes the importance of the Chesapeake to North America. Meanwhile, the reduced scale of the maps and the smaller number of soundings diminish the maps' capacity to provide users with the same level of mastery over the waters of the Chesapeake that Herrman's work allowed. For example, at the western reaches of the Potomac, as the river begins its turn northward, Herrman drew the waterways that create a number of small peninsulas along the Maryland bank of the Potomac in Charles County with whitespace between them, indicating the significant width of these small creeks and thus their navigability. In contrast, the engraver of Thornton's map had the room to depict these waterways only with a deep incision in the plate, which, when printed, appears as a dark line that obscures the accessibility of these waterways. In short, Thornton's maps replicate Herrman's general depiction of the shape of the Chesapeake Bay and the course of its waterways, but in the process they lose the intimate navigational detail that Herrman's map captured.

While its derivative remained in *The English Pilot* through the 1790s, *Virginia and Maryland* had become largely obsolete as a navigational chart by the early eighteenth century. As mariners and cartographers developed new navigational devices, as estuaries filled with silt, as changing tides reshaped the coastline, and as settlement patterns shifted, Herrman's data became less and less reliable. Responding to growing demand for newer information, two experienced captains, Mark Tiddeman and William Hoxton, published new charts based on their extensive experience in the Chesapeake in 1729 and 1735, respectively. Morden and Page soon added a version of Tiddeman's chart, which covered only the lower Chesapeake, to *The English Pilot, The Fourth Book* in 1729, and Hoxton's chart, though expensive, was reproduced widely. Even as new charts replaced *Virginia and Maryland* as a navigational instrument, it continued to remain popular as an image of the Chesapeake. Influential engraver, cartographer, and publisher Herman Moll used Herrman's map as the model for his own *Virginia and Maryland*, which appeared for the first time in John Oldmixon's *British Empire in America* (1708) and then subsequently in many editions of Moll's large decorative atlas and history of British America, *Atlas Minor* (1729–1763).[4] The inclusion of Moll's version of Herrman's map in mid-eighteenth century works intended for a general audience indicates how important it had been in shaping English men and women's understanding of the Chesapeake. At the same time, however, its presence in what were decidedly metropolitan publications aimed at promoting an expanding British Empire indicates how thoroughly Herrman's map had been stripped of its local meanings and absorbed into an imperial narrative that remade it as a patriotic object.

Reimaging Herrman's Legacy

In life Augustine Herrman found his greatest success as a border-crosser. His fluency in multiple languages and skill in interimperial trade and diplomacy enabled him to tie individuals together across imperial borders and made him successful in the cross-national Mid-Atlantic. At the end of his life, however, as the English consolidated control over the region, he found fewer and fewer opportunities to shape the history of the Chesapeake and largely retreated to Bohemia Manor to shape his legacy. In his last will of September 27, 1684, he called for the erection of a "Monument Stone with ingraphen [engraved] letters of Mee, The first Author of Bohemia Mannour A° 1660" over his "Sepulchere which is to bee in my Vinyard uppon the Mannor plantation in Maryland." Noting that this land came to him "for Geographing the Publicq Mapp of Virginia & Maryland," Herrman chose to be remembered not as a mapmaker, a merchant, or a diplomat but rather as a manorial lord.[5] In making this decision he opted to memorialize himself not as an interimperial border-crosser always in motion but as a man rooted to the land. After all Herrman had operated as he had not because he defined himself as a stateless man, but because moving between empires was a route to success. By the end of his life, he had been so successful that these aspects of his past were not even worth articulating anymore.

As had been true with his map, however, Herrman did not have the opportunity to engrave his own words on his burial monument. As Faithorne did with Herrman's map, the unknown stonecutter subtly altered his work and in so doing transformed its meaning. Still located on the same property (now the site of a commercial vineyard), the mapmaker's marker reads "AVGVSTINE HER^RMEN BOHEMIAN THE FIRST FOVNDER OF BOHEMEA MANNER ANNO 1661."[6] Besides misstating the date Herrman received the grant for Bohemia Manor, the inscription highlights his Bohemian origins more forcefully than did Herrman's own words, and thus recalls Faithorne's exuberant identification of Herrman as a Bohemian. The mapmaker certainly trumpeted his own Bohemian origins, naming his plantation after his region of birth and identifying himself as from Bohemia in court records, but he did not call himself a Bohemian in 1684 just years before his death. The consequence of this misrepresentation would be far-reaching. The stone and its inscription provided at least two narratives that, once embraced by different segments of Americans in the nineteenth century, created divergent accounts of his importance, which have persisted to the present. Marylanders, particularly those living in Cecil County, eagerly embraced Herrman as an elite plantation owner and manorial lord inventing a biography that aligned him with their own imagined patrician past. Simultaneously, Bohemian immigrants gravitated to Herrman as a symbol of ethnic pride.

In the late nineteenth century a number of local historians and journalists in Maryland celebrated Herrman as a worthy forefather, casting him as a genteel southern planter with "an adventurous spirit" who built a fine "mansion" with "many old and valuable paintings" complete with a "deer-park" and a "coach driven by liveried servants."[7] The defining story these writers repeated about Herrman derived from an oral tradition that circulated in Cecil County for decades before it first appeared in print in 1852 in the *Baltimore Sun* and was then made famous by the Civil War correspondent George Alfred Townsend. Capturing the centrality of rivers and border-crossings to Herrman, the legend holds that the mapmaker returned to New Amsterdam on business just after his move to Bohemia Manor. A group of squatters living on his estate, in league with the "spiteful Stuyvesant," had Herrman arrested in the Dutch city and sentenced him to death. Before the sentence could be carried out, however, Herrman managed to trick his guards ("the rude Dutch rustics") into allowing him to ride his horse around the prison yard. Depending on the account, he was granted this request either because he feigned insanity or because it was a dying wish. Once mounted on his "charger brave," Herrman then "bolted, with his horse, through one of the large windows, leaped down," and together man and horse escaped to Bohemia Manor, swimming the Hudson and Delaware rivers along the way. Having returned its "master" to his estate, the exhausted horse collapsed and died. The grateful Herrman then buried the steed and erected a monument in its honor.[8]

The nineteenth-century legend of Herrman's heroism and gentility was part of a larger cultural movement in the decades after the Civil War, when Americans remade national traditions. Harkening back to the founding of the nation, adherents to the so-called colonial revival celebrated a romanticized mythical past characterized by patriotism, scitizenship, and local pride. The revival was a diverse movement spearheaded by local organizations. What unified these groups was their common emphasis on ancestor worship, relic collecting, pilgrimages to historic sites, and monument-making. The 1876 Philadelphia Centennial International Exposition held in honor of the one-hundredth anniversary of the signing of the Declaration of Independence galvanized many Americans' interest in the colonial revival. Intent on showcasing American progress, the exhibition featured examples of American technology—from steam engines to the typewriter to Heinz ketchup. The exhibition also honored an idealized American past, showcasing a "New England" colonial kitchen complete with costumed interpreters. Unsurprisingly George Washington was the centerpiece of the historic exhibits. Images of Washington hung in several states' pavilions, he was featured on commemorative coins, bookmarks, and busts, his carriage was exhibited, and most dramatically the exhibition featured "a nine-foot working model" of the first president "rising from his tomb at regular intervals" as if returning from the dead to lead the nation.[9]

The Mount Vernon Ladies Association's preservation of Washington's plantation, Mount Vernon, in the 1850s was another animating moment in the emerging colonial revival. The effort to preserve Mount Vernon the plantation and the MVLA's associated promotion of Washington as a southern symbol captured an idealized notion of southern aristocracy. Like many heritage builders in the South, the MVLA envisioned the southern plantation system as constitutive of national culture. Herrman's Dutch legacy posed a problem for the Anglo-American memory-makers in Maryland, who were inspired by preservation efforts in Virginia. Reflecting this concern, early tales about Herrman are peppered with anti-Dutch sentiment left over from Washington Irving's earlier nineteenth-century characterization of Dutch New Amsterdam burghers as slovenly, inebriated, and ignorant. The stories that emerged about Herrman in the 1850s, for example, juxtapose genteel Maryland and its "rich soil and genial climate" to spiteful New Amsterdam with its "barren shores." This new narrative aligned Herrman—who was even styled "Colonel Herman" in one account—with the southern aristocratic vision of the nation's origins emerging in the colonial revival. In so doing, it allowed Marylanders to promote Herrman, and thus themselves, as true symbols of the nation. Herrman's choice to live as a southern aristocrat rather than a merchant in commercial New York confirmed the truth of this perspective to its adherents in a period of sectional rivalry.[10]

A central part of the wider historical context for the colonial revival was the changing ethnic makeup of the nation. Nativists and Progressive reformers used the colonial revival's emphasis on establishing national traditions as a means to educate new immigrants about the nation's past, which was a part of their larger effort to Americanize these communities. But equally as important, immigrants actively participated in their own colonial revival to align their communities with emerging ideas of American identity. Even as the legend of the genteel Herrman gained prominence in Maryland, Baltimore's growing Bohemian community seized upon his ethnic origins to craft a very different narrative of his life. This effort began in August 1889, when the National Convention of the Bohemian Gymnastic Union of North America took a "pilgrimage" to Bohemia Manor. An American manifestation of the Czech Sokol movement, the Bohemian Gymnastic Union focused both on physical education and on maintaining Czech language and culture among immigrants. In the Austro-Hungarian Empire, similar gymnastic organizations were the centerpiece of Czech efforts to define a distinct identity. The Baltimore branch, which had been founded in 1872, was one of the nation's strongest. Drawn to Baltimore because of its port, its railroad, and low port taxes, Bohemians flocked to the city, and by 1900 the community numbered around ten thousand. In addition to the Bohemian Gymnastic Union, a Czech paper, the *Telegraf*, served as the cultural heart of the thriving community.[11]

Hoping to draw attention to Czechs' and Bohemians' growing presence in the city, the Baltimore Gymnastic Union hosted the parent organization's 1889 National Convention and publicized it widely. The highlight of the meeting was an excursion to Bohemia Manor to honor Herrman. A party of Bohemians from all over the northeast steamed from Baltimore to the former plantation site, where they gathered in front of Herrman's "sepulcher" which "had been decorated with a wreath of flowers and ivy" for the occasion. There they listened to a series of addresses that drew a parallel between the audience of Bohemian immigrants, many of whom were economic and political refugees, and "their great countryman" Herrman, who "had established" Bohemia Manor "in his exile." Emphasizing their common origins, Baltimore's Bohemian community reimagined Herrman as a fellow countryman who not only served as a symbol of pride for Bohemians, but helped them create a common Czech history despite the lack of a Czech nation.[12] At the same time, their celebration of Herrman was intended not only for Bohemian self-fashioning but for the wider city, state, and nation as well. An immigrant, a businessman, a politician, a mapmaker, and something of an adventurer, he symbolized the rugged individualism that was another hallmark of the colonial revival. Successful in all he did, Herrman was a hard-working immigrant who had made good. Herrman's early arrival in Maryland, his self-identification as a Bohemian, and his important and enduring role in the state's history allowed later Bohemian immigrants to connect their own talents with his and highlight the benefits that immigrants brought to the nation. Being able to trace their contributions to American society back to the seventeenth century gave Bohemians a direct claim to Maryland's origins and cemented their legitimacy in the community. As banker and historian Thomas Čapek put it in a speech delivered at the Bohemian Gymnastic Union's 1889 pilgrimage to Bohemia Manor, Herrman's very presence upon the land had "imprinted his Bohemian origins and nationality" on the region. Bohemian immigrants were not outsiders in Maryland because Herrman had already engraved Bohemia into the landscape.[13]

Baltimoreans were not alone in celebrating Herrman. By the turn of the twentieth century he had become a hero to Bohemians all over the United States. Capitalizing on this interest, Čapek, who would become the most important chronicler of Czech immigrants in America, began work on a biography of the mapmaker. Having emigrated to the United States from Bohemia in the 1870s as a young man, Čapek enrolled at the University of Michigan where he studied English and law. Then, after working as a lawyer in Omaha, Nebraska, and serving one term in the Nebraska State Legislature, he moved to New York City and helped found the Bank of Europe Trust and served as the company's vice president and president. All the while Čapek devoted himself to telling the story of Czech Americans. He edited the *Bohemia Voice*, a national newsletter, and published a number of books on Czech-American history, including *The Čechs (Bohemians) in America* (1920). Čapek studied Herrman's life for decades, hiring researchers in Amsterdam and Prague to examine records there and corresponding with scholars, librarians, politicians, and Herrman ancestors in North America. These efforts culminated in a 1930 biography published in Prague. Čapek's efforts to chronicle the story of Bohemian immigrants was tied to his ethnic pride as well as to international politics as these publications dovetailed with his international efforts to secure a Czech state in Europe. At the same time, Čapek also found additional motivation to champion Bohemians from the nativist backlash against his community.[14] Living in New York City, he witnessed disparagement of the roughly 27,000 Bohemian immigrants clustered in the Upper East Side. In 1896 a group of elite New Yorkers led by Mrs. Robert Abbe founded the New York City History Club to cater to the supposed needs of the immigrant community. Key among the group's mission was educating new immigrants in the city's past as a way to fight poverty and crime. According to one profile in *Harper's Bazar*, New York was inundated with "hundreds of thousands of illiterate Hungarians, Italians, Slavs, Jews, Turks, Armenians, Greeks, and Bohemians—the rag-tag and bobtail of the earth, most of whom have never heard of history, do not know what it is, and herd in the tenements like rabbits in a warren, with no clearer ideas of citizenship." Classes on local history, the New York City History Club believed, would help cure social ills by inspiring and Americanizing youth.[15]

Čapek and the Bohemian Gymnastic Union had a different answer. For them, recapturing the contributions that American Bohemians like Herrman had made to the nation would inspire young Czechs and counter the unflattering and undeserved nativist portrayal of their community. Seizing upon Herrman as a central symbol, Baltimore's Bohemian leaders doggedly worked to keep his memory alive. At the close of the 1889 national convention (which Čapek attended), they noted the "necessity of having Hermen's memory perpetuated in marble" and began a national fundraising campaign "so that a grand memorial can be put up."[16] Two years later the group returned to Bohemia Manor for their "annual pilgrimage" to honor the 230th anniversary of its founding. One orator at the festivities referred to the site of Herrman's plantation as "the Bohemian mecca of America" and called again for the construction of a "granite monument" to commemorate "the noble deeds of Augustine Hermen."[17]

During the next two decades, the Gymnastic Union returned again and again to Bohemia Manor to honor Herrman, and even when they decided to meet elsewhere, they held "exercises in honor of Augustine Hermann."[18] The leader of the Bohemian Gymnastic Union, V. J. Shimek, continued raising funds to build a monument to Herrman, now to be located in Baltimore on North Broadway, the heart of Little Bohemia. As envisioned by Shimek, this monument was to rise thirty-five feet high and consist of a "polished granite base" topped with "a life-sized figure of Herman in white marble." As of 1908, the community's many garment workers and craftsmen were able to raise only $500 of the necessary $10,000, and the monument was never erected.[19] Czech immigrants in Baltimore, however, continued to memorialize Herrman. In the midst of World War II, they advocated for a road to be named in his honor, and the Czechoslovak relief committee donated a portrait of him to the state government as a way to raise awareness of Czech suffering under Nazi occupation. More than a decade later, on the 296th anniversary of the founding of Bohemia Manor, Herrman finally received his monument when the state of Maryland renamed Route 213 in Cecil County the "Augustine Herman Highway." Three years later, in October 1959, on the occasion of the tercentenary of Herrman's first visit to Maryland the State Assembly proclaimed "Augustine Herman Day," giving him the statewide recognition for which Bohemians had been lobbying for generations.[20] In a final testament to the enduring symbol of Czech heritage that Herrman became, he is still profiled as "The First Czech Settler in America" on the website of the embassy of the Czech Republic in Washington, DC.[21]

What the colonial revival and the Bohemian version of Herrman's legacy had in common was that both stories categorized him as either a "Bohemian" or a "true American"; there was no space left for a colonial Herrman for whom these nationalist labels would have meant little. Just as *Virginia and Maryland* was wrapped in an imperial narrative that erased its local origins and its intercolonial perspective, the ways Americans memorialized Herrman obscured his understanding of the flexibility and permeability of empire. This split Anglo-Bohemian identity recalls the ways scholars have seen the larger Mid-Atlantic—as either imperial or colonial. These labels seem especially fictitious when attached to Herrman, who found his greatest success moving between empires. Contributing the ultimate symbol of the twentieth century nationalist narrative of Herrman's life, the United States Maritime Commission named one of the so-called Liberty Ships sent to ferry goods to Great Britain under the Lend-Lease Act (1941) the SS *Augustine Herman*.[22] As was true with his map, Herrman could not control the use of his memory, and ultimately his name came to stand for an America he never imagined— though perhaps he would have appreciated the irony of a ship ferrying goods between America and Great Britain bearing his name, a Bohemian surrogate connecting these two distant Atlantic places.

ACKNOWLEDGMENTS

Just as *Virginia and Maryland* was not Augustine Herrman's work alone, this book entailed the labor of many hands, all of whom made it possible. Key to my ability to complete it was the financial support offered by numerous institutions. A Jeannette D. Black Memorial Research Fellowship from the John Carter Brown Library in Providence, Rhode Island provided me with access to their amazing map collections and the time to study them carefully. An NEH Research Fellowship at the Winterthur Museum and Library in Winterthur, Delaware, gave me the opportunity to immerse myself in the print culture of the seventeenth-century British Atlantic. Finally, my home institution, Towson University, provided the funding that enabled me both to begin the research through a Towson Academy of Scholars Grant and to track down the extant copies of *Virginia and Maryland* in England and France through a Faculty Development and Research Committee Grant. Finally, a Research Grant from the College of Liberal Arts at Towson University helped defray image costs.

More important than financial assistance has been the advice and time graciously offered at these many institutions. Susan Danforth at the John Carter Brown Library shared her incredible cartographic knowledge with me, while Rosemary Krill, Catharine Dann Roeber, Emily Guthrie, and Alana Staiti facilitated access to Winterthur's book, object, and map collections. This book benefited enormously from formal comments and audience questions at a number of conferences but especially at the *William and Mary Quarterly*-Early Modern Studies Institute 2010 Workshop, "Grounded Histories: Land, Landscape, and Environment in Early North America held at the Huntington Library"; at the Washington Area Early American Seminar held at University of Maryland, College Park, Maryland in 2012; and in a number of departmental seminars at Towson University. Many colleagues and friends have read chapters, offered leads, and made suggestions, including Zara Anishanslin, Richard Bell, Holly Brewer, Martin Brückner, Kenneth Cohen, Charles Gehring, Matthew Hale, Karen Halltuen, Dennis Maika, Daniel Richter, Edward Papenfuse, Larry Peskin, Mark Thompson, and Cynthia Van Zandt. Sarah H. Meacham and two anonoymous readers for New York University Press offered close readings and valuable suggestions. A number of my colleagues at Towson University commented on drafts and provided advice and encouragement, especially Rita Costa-Gomes, Andrew Diemer, Alhena Gadotti, Kelly Gray, Michael Masatsugu, Ronn Pineo, Akim Reinhardt, and Robert Rook. Cathy Matson deserves special mention for her continued advice and support and for wading through yet another of my manuscripts. I was especially pleased that my father (and historian), Gerard M. Koot, was able to read and comment on the manuscript. Despite the best efforts of these folks I am sure that some errors remain, and these are entirely the fault of the author. My oldest friend, Paul Pietsch, gave me the chance to unspool Herrman's story for the first time as we ran the Cherry Blossom 10-miler and has kept asking questions about Herrman ever since. Thank you, Paul. It has been a pleasure to work with New York University Press again. Clara Platter showed enthusiasm for this project from the beginning, and she, Amy Klopfenstein, and Alexia Traganas and her team have deftly guided the manuscript through production.

My family has been an unending source of support (and more than a little child minding). My parents, Gerard and Sheila Koot, and brother, Michael Koot, and his family have remained interested for many years in the life of a seventeenth-century mapmaker. My in-laws, Paul and Kay Van Horn, helped me explore Herrman's Delaware and Faithorne's London. My daughter, Abigail, arrived in the midst of this project, and I have marveled at watching her grow as she has marveled with me at maps of all kinds. Thank you, Abby, for the bountiful joy you have brought to my life. My greatest debt is to my wife, Jennifer Van Horn, who helped convince me to write this book. She is my fiercest advocate, my best editor, and my greatest friend. The book's dedication in only a small way captures her contributions.

The editors of the *William and Mary Quarterly* and *De Halve Maen* have kindly allowed me to republish work that first appeared in their pages as "The Merchant, the Map, and Empire: Augustine Herrman's Chesapeake and Interimperial Trade, 1644–1673," *William and Mary Quarterly* 67, 4 (October 2010): 603–44, and "Spanning the Peninsula: Augustine Herrman, the South River, and Anglo-Dutch overland trade in the Northern Chesapeake," *De Halve Maen: Journal of the Holland Society of New York* 84 (Winter 2011): 61–68.

NOTES

ABBREVIATIONS

Arch. Md.: *Archives of Maryland*. Edited by William Browne Hand, et al. 72 vols. Baltimore: Maryland Historical Society, 1883–1972.

BL: British Library, London, UK.

BMP: Bohemia Manor, Papers, 1660–1791.

Cartography in the European Renaissance: *The History of Cartography*, vol. 3, *Cartography in the European Renaissance*. Edited by David Woodward. Chicago: University of Chicago Press, 2007.

CDM: *Calendar of Historical Manuscripts in the Office of the Secretary of State, Albany, N.Y.* Edited by E. B. O'Callaghan. Vol. 1. *Dutch Manuscripts, 1630–1664*. Albany, NY: Weed, Parsons, 1865.

Correspondence, 1647–1653: *Correspondence, 1647–1653. New Netherlands Documents.* Edited by Charles T. Gehring. Vol. 11. Syracuse, NY: Syracuse University Press, 2000.

Correspondence, 1654–1658: *Correspondence, 1654–1658. New Netherlands Documents.* Edited by Charles T. Gehring. Vol. 12. Syracuse, NY: Syracuse University Press, 2003.

CSPC: *Calendar of State Papers: Colonial Series, America and the West Indies, 1574–1738.* Edited by W. Noel Sainsbury, J. W. Fortescue, and Cecil Headlam. 44 vols. London: H. M. Stationery Office, 1860–1969.

Curaçao Papers: *Curaçao Papers, 1640–1665*. Edited by Charles T. Gehring and J. A. Schiltkamp. Interlaken, NY: Heart of Lakes Publishing, 1987.

DRCHNY: *Documents Relative to the Colonial History of the State of New York.* Edited and transcribed by E. B. O'Callaghan and Berthold Fernow. 15 vols. Albany, NY: Weed, Parsons, 1853–1887.

EAS: *Early American Studies*.

LOC: Library of Congress, Washington, DC

LV: Library of Virginia, Richmond, Virginia.

MdHM: *Maryland Historical Magazine*.

MDHS: Maryland Historical Society, Baltimore, Maryland.

NCDW, 1655–1668: Northampton County, Deeds, Wills, Etc., nos. 7–8, 1655–1668, Library of Virginia, microfilm.

NCOB, 1657–1664: Northampton County Order Book, 1657–1664, Library of Virginia, microfilm.

NNN: Narratives of New Netherland, 1609–1664. Edited by J. Franklin Jameson. New York: Charles Scribner's Sons, 1909.

NYGBR: New York Genealogical and Biographical Record.

NYHMCM, 1638–1649: New York History Manuscripts: Dutch, Volume IV Council Minutes, 1638–1649. Edited by Arnold J. F. Van Laer, Kenneth Scott, and Kenn Styker-Rodda. Baltimore: Genealogical Publishing, 1974.

NYHMCM, 1652–1654: New York Historical Manuscripts: Dutch, Volume V Council Minutes, 1652–1654. Edited by Charles T. Gehring. Baltimore: Genealogical Publishing, 1983.

NYHMDPD: Delaware Papers (Dutch Period): A Collection of Documents Pertaining to the Regulation of Affairs on the South River of New Netherland, 1648–1664. Edited by Charles T. Gehring. Baltimore: Genealogical Publishing, 2000.

NYHMDPE: Delaware Papers (English Period): A Collection of Documents Pertaining to the Regulation of Affairs on the Delaware, 1664–1682. Edited by Charles T. Gehring. Baltimore: Genealogical Publishing, 2000.

NYHMRPS, 1642–1647: New York Historical Manuscripts: Dutch, Volume II: Register of the Provincial Secretary, 1642–1647. Edited by Arnold J. F. Van Laer, Kenneth Scott, and Kenn Stryker-Rodda. Baltimore: Genealogical Publishing, 1974.

NYHMRPS, 1648–1660: New York Historical Manuscripts: Dutch, Volume III: Register of the Provincial Secretary, 1648–1660. Edited by Arnold J. F. Van Laer, Kenneth Scott, and Kenn Stryker-Rodda. Baltimore: Genealogical Publishing, 1974.

NYHS: New York Historical Society.

OIEAHC: Omohundro Institute of Early American History and Culture.

Pepys Diary: The Diary of Samuel Pepys: A New and Complete Transcription. Edited by Robert Latham and William Matthews. 11 vols. Berkeley: University of California Press, 1970.

PMHB: Pennsylvania Magazine of History and Biography.

RNA: The Records of New Amsterdam from 1653 to 1674. Edited by Berthold Fernow. 7 vols. New York: Knickerbocker Press, 1897.

TNA: The National Archives of the United Kingdom, Kew, UK.

VMHB: Virginia Magazine of History and Biography.

WMQ: William and Mary Quarterly.

INTRODUCTION

1 Robert Latham, gen. ed., *Catalogue of the Pepys Library at Magdalene College, Cambridge,* 7 vols. (Cambridge, UK: D. S. Brewer, 1978–1991); Sarah Tyacke, comp., "Maps," in *Catalogue of the Pepys Library at Magdalene College Cambridge,* vol. 4, *Music, Maps, and Calligraphy* (Cambridge: D. S. Brewer, 1989).

2 Tyacke, *Catalogue of the Pepys Library,* 4:xii, 11.

3 Benjamin Schmidt, "Mapping an Empire: Cartographic and Colonial Rivalry in Seventeenth-Century Dutch and English North America," *WMQ* 3rd ser., 54 (1997): 551–554; Cynthia J. Van Zandt, "Mapping and the European Search for

Intercultural Alliances in the Colonial World," *EAS* 1, no. 2 (2003): 75–76; Jess
Edwards, "How to Read an Early Modern Map: Between the Particular and the
General, the Material and the Abstract, Words and Mathematics," *Early Modern
Literary Studies* 9, no. 6 (May 2003): 1–58 purl.oclc.org, par. 19–20, 52–58; Lisa
Blansett, "John Smith Maps Virginia: Knowledge, Rhetoric, and Politics," in
*Envisioning an English Empire: Jamestown and the Making of the North Atlantic
World*, ed. Robert Appelbaum and John Wood Sweet (Philadelphia: University of
Pennsylvania Press, 2005), 69–70, 81–83; Martin Brückner, *The Geographic
Revolution in Early America: Maps, Literacy, and National Identity* (Chapel Hill:
University of North Carolina Press for the OIEAHC, 2006), esp. 6–12; Sabine
Klein, "'They Have Invaded the Whole River': Boundary Negotiations in
Anglo-Dutch Colonial Discourse," Special Issue: *The Worlds of Lion Gardiner, ca.
1599–1663: Crossing and Boundaries, EAS* 9, no. 2 (2011): 324–47; Ken MacMillan,
"Centers and Peripheries in English Maps of America, 1590–1685," in *Early
American Cartographies*, ed. Martin Brückner (Chapel Hill: University of North
Carolina Press for the OIEAHC, 2011), 67–92.

4 April Lee Hatfield, "Mariners, Merchants, and Colonists in Seventeenth-Century
English America," in *The Creation of the British Atlantic World*, ed. Elizabeth
Mancke and Carole Shammas (Baltimore: Johns Hopkins University Press, 2005),
139–59; April Lee Hatfield, "Dutch and New Netherland Merchants in the
Seventeenth-Century English Chesapeake," in *The Atlantic Economy during the
Seventeenth and Eighteenth Centuries: Organization, Operation, Practice, and
Personnel*, ed. Peter A. Coclanis (Columbia: University of South Carolina Press,
2005), 205–28; Claudia Schnurmann, "Atlantic Trade and American Identities:
The Correlations of Supranational Commerce, Political Opposition, and Colonial
Regionalism," in Coclanis, *Atlantic Economy during Seventeenth and Eighteenth
Centuries*, 186–204; Mark L. Thompson, *The Contest for the Delaware Valley:
Allegiance, Identity, and Empire in the Seventeenth Century* (Baton Rouge:
Louisiana State University Press, 2013). Lauren Benton has demonstrated how
geographically uneven early modern empires were, creating the space for locals to
create alternate sources of power and authority; see her *A Search of Sovereignty:
Law and Geography in European Empires, 1400–1900* (New York: Cambridge
University Press, 2010), 1–16, 32–37. See also Elizabeth Mancke, "Spaces of Power
in the Early Modern Northeast," in *New England and the Maritime Provinces:
Connections and Comparisons*, ed. Stephen J. Hornsby and John G. Reid
(Montreal: McGil -University Press, 2005), 32–39; Andrew Lipman, *The Saltwater
Frontier: Indians and the Contest for the American Coast* (New Haven, CT: Yale
University Press, 2015).

5 Alison Games, *The Web of Empire: English Cosmopolitans in an Age of Expansion,
1560–1660* (Oxford: Oxford University Press, 2008), 83 ("inanimate forces"), 7
("decentralized"), 9–11; Susannah Shaw Romney, *New Netherland Connections:
Intimate Networks and Atlantic Ties in Seventeenth-Century America* (Chapel Hill:

University of North Carolina Press for the OIEAHC, 2014), esp. 5, 18–19; David
Hancock, *Oceans of Wine: Madeira and the Emergence of American Trade and
Taste* (New Haven, CT: Yale University Press, 2009), xvi–xxv; Michael J Jarvis, *In
the Eye of All Trade: Bermuda, Bermudians, and the Maritime Atlantic World,
1680–1783* (Chapel Hill: University of North Carolina Press for the OIEAHC,
2010), esp. 180–83. On border crossers and empire, see Ann Laura Stoler, "Tense
and Tender Ties: The Politics of Comparison in North American History and
(Post) Colonial Studies," *Journal of American History* 88, no. 3 (2001): 829–65, esp.
852, 864–65; Stephen Daniels and Catherine Nash, "Lifepaths: Geography and
Biography," *Journal of Historical Geography* 30, no. 3 (2004): 449–58; David
Lambert and Alan Lester, "Introduction: Imperial Spaces, Imperial Subjects," in
*Colonial Lives across the British Empire: Imperial Careering in the Long Nineteenth
Century*, ed. David Lambert and Alan Lester (Cambridge: Cambridge University
Press, 2006), 16–21.

6 Jack P. Greene, "Transatlantic Colonization and the Redefinition of Empire in the
Early Modern Era: The British-American Experience," in *Negotiated Empires:
Centers and Peripheries in the Americas, 1500–1820*, ed. Christine Daniels and
Michael V. Kennedy (New York: Routledge, 2002), 267–82; Elizabeth Mancke,
"Negotiating an Empire: Britain and Its Overseas Peripheries, c. 1550–1780," in
Negotiated Empires, ed. Daniels and Kennedy, 236–37, 248–49; Lauren Benton,
"Legal Space of Empire: Piracy and the Origins of Ocean Regionalism,"
Comparative Studies in Society and History 47, no. 4 (2005): 700–706; Benton,
"Spatial Histories of Empire," *Itinerario* 30, no. 3 (2006): 20–22, 27.

7 Indebted to the work of earlier scholars like Charles Andrews, a number of recent
historians have called for greater attention to metropolitan politics in the
understanding of colonial America. Owen Stanwood, *Empire Reformed: English
America in the Age of the Glorious Revolution* (Philadelphia: University of
Pennsylvania Press, 2011); Steven Pincus, "Rethinking Mercantilism: Political
Economy, the British Empire, and the Atlantic World in the Seventeenth and
Eighteenth Centuries," *WMQ* 3rd ser., 69, no. 1 (2012): 3–34; William A. Pettigrew,
*Freedom's Debt: The Royal African Company and the Politics of the Atlantic Slave
Trade, 1672–1752* (Chapel Hill: University of North Carolina Press for the
OIEAHC, 2013); Antoinette Sutto, *Loyal Protestants and Dangerous Papists:
Maryland and the Politics of Religion in the English Atlantic, 1630–1690*
(Charlottesville: University of Virginia Press, 2015); Abigail Swinden, *Competing
Visions of Empire: Labor, Slavery, and the Origins of the British Atlantic Empire*
(New Haven, CT: Yale University Press, 2015).

8 Rudolph Arnheim, "The Perception of Maps," in *New Essays on the Psychology of
Art* (Berkeley: University of California Press, 1986), 195–202; J. B. Harley and Kees
Zandvliet, "Art, Science, and Power in Sixteenth-Century Dutch Cartography,"
Cartographica 29, no. 2 (1992): 10–14; J. B. Harley, "Maps, Knowledge, and Power,"
in *The Iconography of Landscape: Essays on the Symbolic Representation, Design,*

and Use of Past Environments, ed. Dennis Cosgrove and Stephen Daniels (Cambridge: Cambridge University Press, 1988), 278–84; J. Brian Harley, "Deconstructing the Map," *Cartographica* 26 (1989): 1–20; Chandra Mukerji, *From Graven Images: Patterns of Modern Materialism* (New York: Columbia University Press, 1983), 79–130; Jeremy Crampton, "Maps as Social Constructions: Power, Communication and Visualization," *Progress in Human Geography* 25 (2001): 235–52.

9 Igor Kopytoff, "The Cultural Biography of Things: Commoditization as Process," in *The Social Life of Things: Commodities in Cultural Perspective*, ed. Arjun Appadurai (Cambridge: Cambridge University Press, 1986), 66–70. Martin Brückner has called for more attention to the materiality of maps in "Beautiful Symmetry: John Melish, Material Culture, and Map Interpretation," *Portolan, Journal of the Washington Map Society* 73 (Winter 2008); 28–35. See also Martin Brückner "Introduction: The Plurality of Early American Cartography," in *Early American Cartographies*, ed. Martin Brückner (Chapel Hill: University of North Carolina Press for the OIEAHC, 2011), 1–11, 24. Neil Safier provides a model of this approach in *Measuring the New World: Enlightenment Science and South America* (Chicago: University of Chicago Press, 2008), esp. 123–65. For work that is on a different time period but is attentive to the shifting cultures of print production and consumption, see Michael Gaudio, *Engraving the Savage: The New World and Techniques of Civilization* (Minneapolis: University of Minnesota Press, 2008).

10 The view that maps were multiple objects is increasingly appreciated but deserves more attention. Mary Sponberg Pedley, *The Commerce of Cartigraphy: Making and Marketing Maps in Eighteenth-Century France and England* (Chicago: University of Chicago Press, 2005), 14–15, 198–99; Catherine Delano-Smith, "The Map as Commodity," in *Plantejaments I Objectius D'Una Història Universal de la Cartografia*, ed. David Woodward, Catherine Delano-Smith, and Cordell D. K. Yee (Barcelona: El Institut, 2001), 91–92; Ricardo Padrón, *The Spacious Word: Cartography, Literature, and Empire in Early Modern Spain* (Chicago: University of Chicago Press, 2004), 8–9; Matthew H. Edney, "John Mitchell's Map of North America (1755): A Study of the Use and Publication of Official Maps in Eighteenth-Century Britain," *Imago Mundi* 60 (2008): 63–64; Matthew H. Edney, "The Irony of Imperial Mapping," in *The Imperial Map: Cartography and the Mastery of Empire*, ed. James R. Akerman (Chicago: University of Chicago Press, 2009), 13, 18–19, 31. On underlying colonial meanings in European maps, see Robert Paulett, *An Empire of Small Places: Mapping the Southeastern Anglo-Indian Trade, 1732–1795* (Athens: University of Georgia Press, 2012), 2–3, 8, 12–13, 21–23, 31–32.

11 Historians of cartography have paid abundant attention to both the mechanics of map construction and the ways that states mobilized maps and geographic knowledge to construct and imagine empires. Most often, though, cartographic

imperialism and map production are covered in different studies and are not in conversation with one another. Scholars of cartography and geography who have been most attentive to how the acquisition and transmission of geographic knowledge in the Americas shaped the process of empire-building include Safier, *Measuring the New World*; Padrón, *The Spacious Word*; D. Graham Burnett, *Masters of All They Surveyed: Exploration, Geography, and a British El Dorado* (Chicago: University of Chicago Press, 2000). Though about the British Empire in India, Matthew Edney's *Mapping an Empire: The Geographical Construction of British India, 1765–1843* (Chicago: University of Chicago Press, 1999) offers an impressive model of this scholarship. Historians of science in the Atlantic world (some of whom also study maps and navigation) have done perhaps the most to demonstrate the connection between technologies of knowledge transfer and the building of empire. Crucially many of these scholars have emphasized the role of local informants (both indigenous and European) and colonial networks in gathering, interpreting, and disseminating information. Safier, *Measuring the New World*; Susan Scott Parrish, *American Curiosity: Cultures of Natural History in the Colonial British Atlantic World* (Chapel Hill: University of North Carolina Press for OIEAHC, 2006); Antonio Barrera, "Empire and Knowledge: Reporting from the New World," *Colonial American Review* 15 (2006): 39–54; James Delbourgo and Nicholas Dew, ed., *Science and Empire in the Atlantic World* (New York: Routledge, 2008), esp. James Deloburgo and Nicholas Dew, "Introduction: The Far Side of the Ocean," 1–28; Molly A. Warsh, "A Political Ecology in the Early Spanish Caribbean," *WMQ* 3rd ser., 71, no. 4 (2014): 519–20, 532–35, 545–46. Ian K. Steele is a notable exception among historians of the Atlantic in his attention to the transatlantic movement of information, *The English Atlantic, 1675–1740: An Exploration of Communication and Community* (New York: Oxford University Press, 1986). More recently April Lee Hatfield, *Atlantic Virginia: Intercolonial Relations in the Seventeenth Century* (Philadelphia: University of Pennsylvania Press, 2004), has detailed intercolonial communication in early Virginia, while Katherine Grandjean has focused on the centrality of local communication networks in the history of early New England in *American Passage: The Communications Frontier in Early New England* (Cambridge, MA: Harvard University Press, 2015). Maritime historians have also given added emphasis to the technologies of communication' see Jarvis, *In the Eye of All Trade*.

12 Susan Stewart, *On Longing: Narratives of the Miniature, the Gigantic, the Souvenir, the Collection* (Durham, NC: Duke University Press, 1993), 151–53; Beth Fowkes Tobin, *Picturing Imperial Power: Colonial Subjects in Eighteenth-Century British Painting* (Durham, NC: Duke University Press, 1999), 2, 6, 25, 202, 213–25; Bruno Latour, *Science in Action: How to Follow Scientists and Engineers through Society* (Cambridge, MA: Harvard University Press, 1987), 108.

CHAPTER 1. THE MERCHANT

1 "Commission of Augustine Heermans and Resolved Waldron to meet with the Governor of Maryland," September 23, 1659, *NYHMDPD*, 160–61. For the basis of Lord Baltimore's claims, see *The Charter of Maryland, June 20, 1632*, Maryland State Archives 350th Anniversary Document Series (Annapolis, 1982), 10–11. For Dutch claims, see "Declaration and Manifest delivered by way of a Speech to the Honorable Governor and Council of the Province of Maryland, Chesapeake bay, from the Honorable Governor-General and Council of the Province of New Netherland," October 6, 1659, *DRCHNY*, 2:80–84.

2 "Augustine Herrman's Journal of the Dutch Embassy to Maryland," October 12/2, 1659, *NYHMDPD*, 217, 218, 220, 222 (quotations); *DRCHNY*, 2:80–84, 85–86; *Arch. Md.*, 3:366–69, 375–77.

3 "Augustine Herrman's Journal," 220, 222.

4 Cynthia J. Van Zandt, "The Dutch Connection: Isaac Allerton and the Dynamics of English Cultural Anxiety in the *Gouden Eeuw*," in *Connecting Cultures: The Netherlands in Five Centuries of Transatlantic Exchange*, ed. Rosemarijn Hoefte and Johanna C. Kardux (Amsterdam: Vrije Universiteit Amsterdam Press, 1994), 51–76; April Lee Hatfield, "Mariners, Merchants, and Colonists in Seventeenth-Century English America," in *The Creation of the British Atlantic World*, ed. Elizabeth Mancke and Carole Shammas (Baltimore: Johns Hopkins University Press, 2005), 139–59; April Lee Hatfield, "Dutch and New Netherland Merchants in the Seventeenth-Century English Chesapeake," in *The Atlantic Economy during the Seventeenth and Eighteenth Centuries: Organization, Operation, Practice, and Personnel*, ed. Peter A. Coclanis (Columbia: University of South Carolina Press, 2005), 205–28; Cynthia J. Van Zandt, *Brothers among Nations: The Pursuit of Intercultural Alliances in Early America, 1580–1660* (Oxford: Oxford University Press, 2008), esp. 95–118; Mark L. Thompson, *The Contest for the Delaware Valley: Allegiance, Identity, and Empire in the Seventeenth Century* (Baton Rouge: Louisiana State University Press, 2013), 77–138, 160–77.

5 There has been much dispute about many of the facts of Herrman's early life, including his birth date and the date of first arrival in New Netherland. The balance of sources points to 1621 or 1622 as his birth year and 1644 as the year he first arrived in New Netherland. In 1667 the clerk of the Accomack County, Virginia, court noted his age as "abot 44 yeares," placing his birth date in 1622 or 1623. See "The Deposition of Augustine Herman," May 27, 1667, Accomack County Order Book, 1666–70, LV, microfilm reel no. 78, fol. 30. His will of September 27, 1684, notes his age as "63," placing his birth in 1621. Gilbert Cope and Augustine Herrman, "Copy of the Will of Augustine Herrman, of Bohemia Manor," *PMHB* 15, no. 3 (1891): 321–26. See also *DRCHNY* 1:431, 588, 593; Thomas Čapek, *Augustine Herrman of Bohemia Manor* (Prague: State Printing Office, 1930), 9–11; Paul G. Burton, "The Age of Augustine Herrman," *NYGBR* 78, no. 3 (1947): 130–31; Edwin R. Purple, "Contributions to the History of the Ancient

Families of New York," *NYGBR* 9, no. 1 (1878): 57–59; Earle L. W. Heck, *Augustine Herrman, Beginner of the Virginia Tobacco Trade, Merchant of New Netherland, and First Lord of Bohemia Manor in Maryland* (Richmond, VA.: William Byrd Press, 1941), 14–19; Hatfield, "Dutch and New Netherland Merchants," 213–16, 224–26. On Bohemia, se R. J. W. Evans, *The Making of the Habsburg Monarchy, 1550–1700: An Interpretation* (Oxford, Clarendon Press, 1979), 9–14, 26–27, 39, 41–48, 63–70; Jaroslav Pánek, "The Czech Estates in the Habsburg Monarchy (1526–1620)," and Jiří Mikulec, "Baroque Absolutism (1620–1740)," both in *A History of the Czech Lands*, ed. Jaroslav Pánek and Oldřich Tůma (Prague: Karolinum Press, 2009), 194–204, 213–15, 233–37.

6 *NYHMRPS, 1642–1647*, 225–26; *NNN*, 375. For the Gabry's, see *DRCHNY* 1:436–37. While Herrman and the Gabry's were tied together until at least 1661, there is no evidence of Herrman's continued work for Coymans (who may have been related to the important Amsterdam merchant Balthasar Coymans) though Coymans may have continued as a silent investor with the Gabry's. Katrina V. H. Taylor, "A Note on the Identity of a Member of the Coymans Family by Frans Hals," *Report and Studies in the History Af art, 1969* (1970): 106–8.

7 "Certified copy of a receipt for sundry goods delivered by Govr Printz to Augustyn Heermans' Agents," December 14, 1650, *DRCHNY*, 12:70–71 (quotation); *CDM*, 46, 95, 375; *NYHMCM, 1638–1649*, 354; *NYHMDPD*, 22–34, esp. 29, *NYHMRPS, 1648–1660*, 238; *NYHMRPS, 1642–1647*, 373, 412–13; *Connecticut (Colony), The Public Records of the Colony of Connecticut*, ed. J. Hammond Trumbull (Hartford, CT: Brown & Parsons, 1850), 218–19; I. N. Phelps Stokes, *The Iconography of Manhattan Island, 1498–1909* ... (New York: Robert H. Dodd, 1915), 1:139.

8 *DRCHNY*, 1:11; Jaap Jacobs, *The Colony of New Netherland: A Dutch Settlement in Seventeenth-Century America* (Ithaca, NY: Cornell University Press, 2009), 19–27; Donna Merwick, *Stuyvesant Bound: An Essay on Loss across Time* (Philadelphia: University of Pennsylvania Press, 2013), 33.

9 For this and the following paragraph, see Cornelis Charles Goslinga, *The Dutch in the Caribbean and on the Wild Coast, 1580–1680* (Gainesville: University of Florida Press, 1971), chaps. 1–3, 116–38; as well as Victor Enthoven, "Early Dutch Expansion in the Atlantic Region, 1585–1621," 18–47, Christopher Ebert, "Dutch Trade with Brazil before the Dutch West India Company, 1587–1621," 49–75, and Wim Klooster, "Curaçao and the Caribbean Transit Trade," 203–6, all in *Riches from Atlantic Commerce Dutch Transatlantic Trade and Shipping, 1585–1817*, ed. Johannes Postma and Victor Enthoven (Leiden: Brill, 2003); Jacobs, *The Colony of New Netherland*, 28–31; Linda M. Rupert, *Creolization and Contraband: Curaçao in the Early Modern Atlantic World* (Athens: University of Georgia Press, 2012), 34–41, 68–71.

10 "Journal of New Netherland, 1647, described in the Years 1641, 1642, 1643, 1644, 1645 and 1646," in *NNN*, 270 ("wide and deep"); "From the 'Historisch Verhael' by

Nicolaes van Wassenaer, 1624–1630," in *NNN*, 77 ("very pleasant"); Donna
Merwick, *The Shame and the Sorrow: Dutch-Amerindian Encounters in New
Netherland* (Philadelphia: University of Pennsylvania Press, 2006), 8 ("alongshore"), 14–23, 35–44; Jacobs, *The Colony of New Netherland*, 2–6, 30–32, 69–70,
118; Henk Den Heijer, "The Dutch West India Company, 1621–1791," in *Riches
from Atlantic Commerce Dutch Transatlantic Trade and Shipping, 1585–1817*, ed.
Johannes Postma and Victor Enthoven (Leiden: Brill, 2003), 92–94.

11 The Eight Men to the Amsterdam Chamber of the West India Company, October
28, 1644, *DRCHNY*, 1:209–13 (quotation); "Novum Belgium, by Father Isaac
Jogues," 1646 in *NNN*, 259.

12 *DRCHNY*, 1:119–23; Van Cleaf Bachman, *Peltries or Plantations: The Economic
Policies of the Dutch West India Company in New Netherland, 1623–1639*
(Baltimore, MD: Johns Hopkins University Press, 1969), chap. 7; Cathy Matson,
Merchants and Empire: Trading in Colonial New York (Baltimore, MD: Johns
Hopkins University Press, 1998), 16–19; Oliver Rink, *Holland on the Hudson: An
Economic and Social History of Dutch New York* (Ithaca, NY: Cornell University
Press, 1986), 117–38; Jacobs, *The Colony of New Netherland*, 45–46; Simon
Middleton, "'How It Came that the Bakers Bake No Bread': A Struggle for Trade
Privileges in Seventeenth-Century New Amsterdam," *WMQ* 3rd ser. 58, no. 2
(2001), 361–66; Pieter C. Emmer and Wim Klooster, "The Dutch Atlantic,
1600–1800: Expansion without Empire," *Itinerario* 23, no. 2 (1999): 57–58; Joyce D.
Goodfriend, *Before the Melting Pot: Society and Culture in Colonial New York City,
1664–1730* (Princeton, NJ: Princeton University Press, 1992), 13–16.

13 Andrew Lipman, *The Saltwater Frontier: Indians and the Contest for the American
Coast* (New Haven, CT: Yale University Press, 2015), 142–71; Evan Haefeli, "Kieft's
War and the Cultures of Violence in Colonial America," in *Lethal Imagination:
Violence and Brutality in American History*, ed. Michael A. Bellesiles (New York:
New York University Press, 1999), 17–42; Merwick, *The Shame and the Sorrow*,
137–50.

14 *NYHMCM, 1638–1649*, 438–42; Simon Middleton, *From Privileges to Rights: Work
and Politics in Colonial New York City* (Philadelphia: University of Pennsylvania
Press, 2006), 31–37; Simon Middleton, "Order and Authority in New Netherland:
The 1653 Remonstrance and Early Settlement Politics," *WMQ* 3rd ser. 68, no. 1
(2010): 147–53; Jacobs, *The Colony of New Netherland*, 78–83; Merwick, *Stuyvesant
Bound*, ix–xx, 10–13, 20–32, 136–66. Herrman probably first bought land in New
Amsterdam in 1647, purchasing a lot near the fort and the WIC warehouses.
CDM, 375.

15 *DRCHNY*, 1:259–61, 262–70, 271–318 (quotation 268); Middleton, *From Privileges
to Rights*, 37–52; Jacobs, *The Colony of New Netherland*, 81–87; Merwick,
Stuyvesant Bound, 24–28.

16 "Freedoms and Exceptions," July 19, 1640, *DRCHNY*, 1:121.

17 WIC Directors to Stuyvesant, April 26, 1651, *DRCHNY*, 14:138–39.

18 *Bradford's History of Plymouth Plantation, 1606-1646, Original Narratives of Early
American History*, ed. William T. Davis (New York: Scribner's Sons, 1920), 223
(first quotation), 224–27, 233–34 (second quotation), 235–55; Charlotte Wilcoxen,
"Dutch Trade with New England," in *"A Beautiful and Fruitful Place": Selected
Rensselaerswijk Seminar Papers*, ed. Nancy Anne McClure Zeller (Albany, NY:
New Netherland Publications, 1991), 235–41; Kim Todt, "Trading between New
Netherland and New England, 1624–1664," Special Issue: *The Worlds of Lion
Gardiner, ca. 1599-1663: Crossing and Boundaries, Early American Studies* 9, no. 2
(2011): 349–53, 363–63, 377–78; Cynthia Van Zandt, "The Dutch Connection,"
52–55, 67–76; Lynn Ceci, "The First Fiscal Crisis in New York," *Economic
Development and Cultural Change* 28 (1980): 839–44; Daniel K. Richter, *Trade,
Land, Power: The Struggle for Eastern North America* (Philadelphia: University of
Pennsylvania Press, 2013), 100–101.

19 Stuyvesant to Governors Eaton, Endecott, and Bradford, May 24, 1647,
Correspondence, 1647-1653, 48–51 (quotation, 48); Ronald Cohen, "The Hartford
Treaty of 1650: Anglo-Dutch Cooperation in the Seventeenth Century," *New York
Historical Society Quarterly* 53 (1969): 311–20; Middleton, "Order and Authority in
New Netherland," 36–41; Todt, "Trading between New Netherland and New
England," 367–68.

20 Stuyvesant to John Winthrop, Jr. (copy), March 6, 1653, NYC, Misc. MSS, Box 1,
#1, NYHS (quotation); John Winthrop, Jr., to Peter Stuyvesant, March 28, 1653,
Collections of the Massachusetts Historical Society, 4th ser. 6 (1863): 523; Cohen,
"The Hartford Treaty of 1650," 324–29.

21 Stuyvesant to the Commissioners of the United Colonies, May 26, 1653, in *Records
of the Colony of New Plymouth in New England: Acts of the Commissioners of the
United Colonies of New England*, ed. David Pulsipher, vol. 2, *1653-1679* (Boston:
William White, 1859), 2:59–65 (quotations 63, 64); Katheribe Grandjean, *American
Passage: The Communications Frontier in Early New England* (Cambridge, MA:
Harvard University Press, 2015), 77–78, 82–93, 103–9; Julie A. Fisher and David J.
Silverman, *Ninigret, Sachem of the Niantics and Narragansetts: Diplomacy, War,
and the Balance of Power in Seventeenth-Century New England and Indian
Country* (Ithaca, NY: Cornell University Press, 2014), 73–79.

22 "Petition of certain Dutch Merchants to the States General," August 19, 1651,
DRCHNY, 1:436–37 (quotation); *Correspondence, 1654-1658*, 92–93; Lionel Gatford,
Publick good without private interest . . . (London, 1657), 13–14; Victor Enthoven and
Wim Klooster, "The Rise and Fall of the Virginia-Dutch Connection in the
Seventeenth Century," in *Early Modern Virginia: Reconsidering the Old Dominion*,
ed. Douglas Bradburn and John C. Coombs (Charlottesville: University of Virginia
Press, 2011), 95–98; Charlotte Wilcoxen, *Dutch Trade and Ceramics in America in
the Seventeenth Century* (Albany, NY: Albany Institute of History and Art, 1987),
20–21. On Dutch commercial advantages, see Violet Barbour, "Dutch and English
Merchant Shipping in the Seventeenth Century," *Economic History Review*, 2nd ser.

2 (1930): 261–90; Jonathan I. Israel, *Dutch Primacy in World Trade, 1585–1740* (New York: Oxford University Press, 1989), chaps. 1–5.

23 "Richard Ingle in Maryland," *MdHM* 1, 2 (1906): 131–33; David Pietersz de Vries, *Voyages from Holland to America: 1632–1644*, trans. Henry C. Murphy (New York, 1853), 107–13; Enthoven and Klooster, "The Rise and Fall of the Virginia-Dutch Connection," 97–98; John R. Pagan, "Dutch Maritime and Commercial Activity in Mid-Seventeenth-Century Virginia," *VMHB* 90 (1982): 485–87.

24 Enthoven and Klooster, "The Rise and Fall of the Virginia-Dutch Connection," 99–105 (quotation 105); Pagan, "Dutch Maritime and Commercial Activity," 486–91; Hatfield, "Dutch and New Netherland Merchants," 210–17; David M. Riker, "Govert Loockermans: Free Merchant of New Amsterdam," *De Halve Maen* 54 (1981): 4–10; Rink, *Holland on the Hudson*, 177–80.

25 Stuyvesant to Governor William Berkeley, November 24, 1647, *CDM*, 270 (quotation); *Correspondence, 1647–1653*, 26. On Berkeley's actions, see Act XXVIII, March 1642/43 in *The Statutes at Large: Being a collection of all the laws of Virginia*, ed. William Waller Hening (New York: R.W. & G. Bartow, 1823), 1:258; Warren M. Billings, *Sir William Berkeley and the Forging of Colonial Virginia* (Baton Rouge: Louisiana State University Press, 2004), 77–78, 101–2; Susie M. Ames, *Studies of The Virginia Eastern Shore in the Seventeenth Century* (New York: Russell & Russell, 1973), 45; Pagan, "Dutch Maritime and Commercial Activity," 491–92.

26 *Arch. Md.*, 3:232, 302–3; Timothy B. Riordian, *The Plundering Time: Maryland and the English Civil War, 1645–1646* (Baltimore: Maryland Historical Society, 2004), 269.

27 Govert Loockermans to Gillis Verbrugge and Associates, May 27, 1648, letter 15 (F3-F), and "List of sale of goods in New Netherland," 1648, letter 15 (F3-Q), Stuyvesant-Rutherford Papers, Box 23, NYHS, in Wim Vanraes, trans. and ed., "Goovert Loockermans: Correspondence and Papers" (Albany, NY: New Netherland Institute, 2014), 32 (quotations), 42.

28 Loockermans to Verbrugge and Associates, May 27, 1648, letter 15 (F3-F), Stuyvesant-Rutherford Papers, Box 23, NYHS in ibid., 32.

29 Seth Verbrugge to Loockermans, March 16, 1648, letter 11 (F3-B), Stuyvesant-Rutherford Papers, Box 23, NYHS in ibid., 25–26.

30 *CDM*, 229, 276; *NYHMRPS, 1648–1660*, 286–87; Edmund Mathew, Deposition of John Custis, March 5, 1654/5, recorded September 20, 1655, NCDW, 1655–68, fol. 13v; "Agreement between Allard Anthony and Augustyn Herrman," May 8, 1653, *NYHMRPS, 1648–1660*, 351–52 (first quotation), 352–53; "Resolution of the States General on a Petition of Messrs. Gabry," April 22, 1652, *DRCHNY*, 1:469 (second quotation); *DRCHNY*, 14:205; *NYHMCM, 1652–1654*, 71.

31 *NYHMRPS, 1642–1647*, 373; *NYHMCM, 1638–1649*, 603–5; Dennis J. Maika, "Commerce and Community: Manhattan Merchants in the Seventeenth Century" (Ph.D. diss., New York University, 1995), 47–49.

32 "A General Court of Election at Hartford," May 15, 1651, in *The Public Records of the Colony of Connecticut*, ed. J. Hammond Trumbull (Hartford, CT: Brown & Parsons, 1850), 218–20.

33 Proclamation, March 3, 1654, *NYHMCM, 1652–1654*, 122 (quotation); Samuel Smith Purple, *Index to the marriage records from 1639–1801 of the Reformed Dutch church in New Amsterdam and New York* (New York, 1890), 17; Hatfield, "Dutch and New Netherland Merchants," 211–17; Ames, *Studies of the Virginia Eastern Shore*, 47; Purple, "Contributions to the History of the Ancient Families of New York," 57–62; Susanah Shaw Romney, *New Netherland Connections: Intimate Networks and Atlantic Ties in Seventeenth-Century America* (Chapel Hill: University of North Carolina Press for OIEAHC, 2014), 5, 18–19, 103–10.

34 "Petition of Augustyn Heerman . . . ," December 24, 1658, *CDM*, 204 (quotation); *NYHMCM, 1652–1654*, 45, 50; Hatfield, "Dutch and New Netherland Merchants," 213–14.

35 Ames, *Studies of the Virginia Eastern Shore*, 66–67.

36 Lawrence A. Harper, *The English Navigation Laws: A Seventeenth-Century Experiment in Social Engineering* (New York: Octagon Books, 1964), 38–49; Charles H. Wilson, *Profit and Power: A Study of England and the Dutch Wars* (New York: Longmans and Green, 1957), 48–77; Michael J. Braddick, "The English Government, War, Trade, and Settlement, 1625–1688," in *The Origins of Empire*, ed. Nicholas Canny, vol. 1, *The Oxford History of the British Empire*, ed. Wm Roger Lewis (Oxford: Oxford University Press, 1998), 292–96.

37 "Speech of Gov. Berkeley," March 17, 1650/51, *Journals of the House of Burgesses, 1619–1658/59*, ed. H. R. Mcllwaine, (Richmond, VA.: Colonial Press, 1915), 76 (first quotation); Billings, *Sir William Berkeley*, 107–09; "Petition of certain Dutch Merchants to the States General," August 19, 1651, *DRCHNY*, 1:436–37 (second quotation).

38 Wilson, *Profit and Power*, 49–77; J. R. Jones, *The Anglo-Dutch Wars of the Seventeenth Century* (New York: Longman, 1996), 8–14.

39 *A Collection of the State Papers of John Thurloe*, ed. Thomas Birch (London, 1742), 5:80–81; Enthoven and Klooster, "The Rise and Fall of the Virginia-Dutch Connection," 106–15; Billings, *Sir William Berkeley*, 114–15; Russell R. Menard, "Plantation Empire: How Sugar and Tobacco Planters Built Their Industries and Raised an Empire," *Agricultural History* 81, no. 3 (2007): 317–21.

40 Ames, *Studies of the Virginia Eastern Shore*, 1–8; James R. Perry, *The Formation of a Society on Virginia's Eastern Shore, 1615–1655* (Chapel Hill: University of North Carolina Press, 1990), 8–9, 30, 36–43.

41 Perry, *The Formation of a Society*, 139–40, 144–49; Ames, *Studies of the Virginia Eastern Shore*, 43–50.

42 Perry, *The Formation of a Society*, 150–59; Billings, *Sir William Berkeley*, 95–97, Ralph T. Whitelaw, *Virginia's Eastern Shore: A History of Northampton and

Accomack Counties, (Richmond: Virginia Historical Society, 1951), 108–9, 397, 405, 410; Ames, *Studies of the Virginia Eastern Shore*, 48–49.

43   Deposition of John Custis, NCDW, 1655–68, fol. 13v; *RNA*, 1:379, 385; *RNA*, 2:68, 70, 73–74, 119, 167, 380; *CDM*, 168, 226; "Testimony of Augustine Harmen," May 28, 1657, NCOB, 1657–1664, fols. 42r–43r (mispaginated); "Bill of Sale, John Billingsly of Nansemond County, Virginia to A. Herrman," September 1, 1657, Deed Book, 1654–58, photostat at Historic Hudson Valley, Tarrytown, NY; "Depositions of John Royne and Thomas Teackle," January 29, 1657/58, in NCOB, 1657–1664, fols. 6r–7v (mispaginated); *Arch. Md.*, 41:353; *Herman v. Overzee*, January 7, 1660/1, *Arch. Md.*, 41:389–92 ("fifteen thowsand pounds"), 403–4, 440–41 ("firme Coepartnership"); 516.

44   Depositions of John Royne, Thomas Teackle, Lovinge Denwood, January 29, 1657/8 and Robert Burwell, April 19, 1658, NCOB, 1657–1664, fols. 5r–7v, 14, (mispaginated; third quotation from Denwood, all other quotations from Teackle deposition); Ames, *Studies of the Virginia Eastern Shore*, 66–67; Hatfield, "Dutch and New Netherland Merchants," 213–14.

45   Bond, John Stringer, August 4, 1656, recorded May 22, 1657, NCOB, 1657–1664, fols. 42–43 ("Seaven Thousand"); *RNA*, 2:68, 70, 73–74, 380; "Articles of Agreement between James Fookes and Ann Hack," May 6, 1665, and "Deposition of Augustine Herman," May 27, 1667, both in Accomack County Order Book, 1666–70, microfilm reel no. 78, fol. 30 ("sloop which shall"); Dennis J. Maika, "Jacob Leisler's Chesapeake Trade," *De Halve Maen* 68 (1994): 9.

46   *NYHMDPD*, 20.

47   "Certified copy of a receipt for sundry goods delivered by Govr Printz to Augustyn Heermans' Agents," December 14, 1650, *DRCHNY*, 12:70–71.

48   *Curaçao Papers*, 120–21, 122–24 (first quotation), 125, 136–37, 137–39 (second quotation); *DRCHNY*, 14:121.

49   *RNA*, 1:385; Martha Dickinson Shattuck, "Women and Trade in New Netherland," *Itinerario* 18, no. 2 (1994): 44–47; Romney, *New Netherland Connections*, 5, 18–19, 90–91, 94–97, 118–19.

50   *Arch. Md.*, 41:355; *RNA*, 2:428; *DRCHNY*, 1:497–98.

51   D. C. Crass, "The Clay Pipes from Green Spring Plantation (44JC9), Virginia," *Historical Archaeology* 22, no. 1 (1988): 83–97; James G. Gibb and Wesley J. Balla, "Dutch Pots in Maryland Middens: Or, What Light From Yonder Pot Breaks?" *Journal of Middle Atlantic Archaeology* 9 (1993): 67–85; Julia A. King and Henry M. Miller, "The View from the Midden: An Analysis of Midden Distribution and Composition at the van Sweringen Site, St. Mary's City, Maryland," *Historical Archaeology* 21, no. 2 (1987): 37–59; Al Luckenbach, *Providence 1649: The History and Archaeology of Anne Arundel County Maryland's First European Settlement* (Annapolis: Maryland State Archives, 1995), 11–23; Alain Charles Outlaw, *Governor's Land: Archaeology of Early Seventeenth-Century Virginia Settlements*

(Charlottesville: University of Virginia Press for the Department of Historic Resources, 1990), 51–53. On tin-glazed earthenwares, often called Defltware, see Ivor Noël Hume, *Early English Delftware from London and Virginia, Colonial Williamsburg Occasional Papers in Archaeology II* (Williamsburg, VA: Colonial Williamsburg Foundation, 1977), 2–18.

52 Robert A. Leath; "Dutch Trade and Its Influence on Seventeenth-Century Chesapeake Furniture," in *American Furniture*, ed. Luke Beckerdite (Milwaukee, WI: Chipstone Foundation, 1997), 21–46; Object Report and File, 1957.0087.001, Henry Francis du Pont Winterthur Museum and Library; Peter M. Kenny, Frances Gruber Safford, and Gilbert T. Vincent, *American Kasten: The Dutch-Style Cupboards of New York and New Jersey, 1650–1800* (New York: Metropolitan Museum of Art, 1991), 1–14, 38–39; Roderic H. Blackburn and Ruth Piwonka, *Rememberance of Patria: Dutch Arts and Culture in Colonial America, 1609–1776* (Albany, NY: Albany Institute of History and Art, 1988), 257–60; T. H. Lunsingh Scheurleer, "The Dutch and Their Homes in the Seventeenth Century," in *Arts of the Anglo-American Community in the Seventeenth Century*, ed. Ian M.G. Quimby (Charlottesville: University of Virginia Press for the Henry Francis du Pont Winterthur Museum, 1975), 17–24.

53 Leath, "Dutch Trade and Its Influence," 29–33.

54 Whitelaw, *Virginia's Eastern Shore*, 668. For the contract, see Bond of John Rickards to Anne Boote, June 6, 1668, Accomack County, Va., Orders, Wills &c., 1671–1673, folio 231, cited in Leath, "Dutch Trade and Its Influence," 36.

55 "Inventory of Captain William Moseley," October 16, 1671, Norfolk County, Va., Wills, Deeds, &c., bk. E, 1666–1675, folios 105–7, reprinted in ibid., Appendix A, 41–43, 25 (quotation), 29 (number of pieces with Dutch influence); Gary Wheeler Stone, "St. John's: Archaeological Questions and Answers," *MdHM* 69, no. 2 (1974): 157–58.

56 Herrman and Waldron to Stuyvesant, October 21/11, 1659, *DRCHNY*, 2:99–100.

57 Augustine Herrman, "Memorandum or Journall of the first foundation and seating of Bohemia Manor and Bohemia River Middle next, Adjacent & Apendant," BMP, Ms. 1556, MdHS. This document is a ca. 1783 manuscript copy of a now missing document.

58 "Denization of Augustine Herrman," January 28, 1660/61, in *Arch. Md.*, 3:398–99. On denization, see William Blackstone, *Commentaries on the Laws of England (Oxford, 1765)*, bk. 1, chap. 10, avalon.law.yale.edu.

59 For Herrman's relocation to Maryland, see Herrman, "Memorandum or Journall," June 13, 1681, BMP, Ms. 1556, p. 1, MdHS.

CHAPTER 2. THE MAPMAKER

1 The scholarship on maps as tools of state expansion and empire-building is long. Begin with Rudolf Arnheim, "The Perception of Maps," in Rudolf Arnheim, *New Essays on the Psychology of Art* (Berkeley: University of California Press, 1986),

194–202; J. B. Harley, "Maps, Knowledge, and Power," in *The Iconography of Landscape: Essays on the Symbolic Representation, Design and Use of Past Environments*, ed. Denis Cosgrove and Stephen Daniels (Cambridge: Cambridge University Press, 1988), 277–312; Chandra Mukerji, *From Graven Images: Patterns of Modern Materialism* (New York: Columbia University Press, 1983), 117–30; Richard L. Kagan and Benjamin Schmidt, "Maps and the Early Modern State: Official Cartography," in *Cartography in the European Renaissance*, 661–79. In North America, see Benjamin Schmidt, "Mapping an Empire: Cartographic and Colonial Rivalry in Seventeenth-Century Dutch and English North America," *WMQ* 3rd ser., 54, 3(1997): 551–54; Ken MacMillan, "Centers and Peripheries in English Maps of America, 1590–1685," in *Early American Cartographies*, ed. Martin Brückner (Chapel Hill: University of North Carolina Press for the OIEAHC, 2011), 67–92; Matthew H. Edney, "The Irony of Imperial Mapping," in *The Imperial Map: Cartography and the Mastery of Empire*, ed. James A. Akerman (Chicago: University of Chicago Press, 2009), 3, 31–32, 37–38.

2 Benjamin Schmidt, *Inventing Exoticism: Geography, Globalism, and Europe's Early Modern World* (Philadelphia: University of Pennsylvania Press, 2014), 25–81, 339–340fn38. On praxis, see Bruno Latour, *Science in Action: How to Follow Scientists and Engineers through Society* (Cambridge, MA: Harvard University Press, 1987).

3 John R. Hébert, "The Westward Vision: Seventeenth-Century Virginia," in *Virginia in Maps: Four Centuries of Settlement, Growth, and Development*, ed. Richard Stephenson and Marianne McKee (Richmond: Library of Virginia, 2000), 10; Laura Benton, *A Search for Sovereignty: Law and Geography in European Empires, 1400–1900* (New York: Cambridge University Press, 2010), 49–53, 56–58, 100fn166.

4 Coolie Verner, "Smith's *Virginia* and Its Derivatives: A Carto-Bibliographic Study of the Diffusion of Geographical Knowledge," in *The Mapping of America*, ed. R. V. Tooley (London: Holland Press, 1980), 141 (quotations), 143; Hébert, "The Westward Vision," 11.

5 Cynthia J. Van Zandt, "Mapping and the European Search for Intercultural Alliances in the Colonial World," *EAS* 1, no. 2 (2003): 96–97; Lisa Blansett, "John Smith Maps Virginia: Knowledge, Rhetoric, and Politics," in *Envisioning an English Empire: Jamestown and the Making of the North Atlantic World*, ed. Robert Appelbaum and John Wood Sweet (Philadelphia: University of Pennsylvania Press, 2005), 77–83; MacMillan, "Centers and Peripheries," 77–81; Jess Edwards, "A Compass to Steer By: John Locke, Carolina, and the Politics of Restoration Geography," in *Early American Cartographies*, ed. Martin Brückner (Chapel Hill: University of North Carolina Press for the OIEAHC, 2011), 101–02, 109–10; April Lee Hatfield, "Spanish Colonization Literature, Powhatan Geographies, and English Perceptions of Tsenacommacah/Virginia," *Journal of Southern History* 69, no. 2 (2003): 263–65.

6 Coolie Verner, "The First Maps of Virginia, 1590–1673," *VMHB* 58, no. 1(1950): 3–15; Verner, "Smith's *Virginia* and Its Derivatives," 161, 165, 171, plates 69–70.

7 The map is located between pages 12 and 13 in the copy of *Relations of Maryland* at the John Carter Brown Library. Margaret Beck Pritchard, "A Selection of Maps from the Colonial Williamsburg Collection," in Pritchard and Henry G. Taliaferro, *Degrees of Latitude: Mapping Colonial America* (Williamsburg, VA: Colonial Williamsburg Foundation, 2002), 90–91; Pritchard, "Claiming the Land," in ibid., 4; David A. Cobb and Robert W. Shoeberlein, ed., *Mapping of Maryland: The Willard Hackerman Collection* (Baltimore: Maryland Historical Society, 1998), 5–6.

8 Hébert, "The Westward Vision," 14.

9 William Paterson Cummings, *The Southeast in Early Maps* (Chapel Hill: University of North Carolina Press, 1962), 148–51.

10 I. N. Phelps Stokes, *The Iconography of Manhattan Island, 1498–1909 . . .* (New York: Robert H. Dodd, 1915), 1:143–48; Jeannette D. Black, *The Blathwayt Atlas*, vol. 2 *Commentary* (Providence, RI: Brown University Press, 1975), 73; Tony Campbell, "The Jansson-Visscher Maps of New England," in *The Mapping of America*, ed. R. V. Tooley (London: Holland Press, 1980), 283–84.

11 Richard Blome, *A description of the island of Jamaica . . .* (London, 1672).

12 Herrman and Waldron to Stuyvesant, Oct. 21/11, 1659, *DRCHNY*, 2:99–100; *Arch. Md.*, 5:265.

13 Edward B. Mathews, "The Maps and Map-Makers of Maryland," *Maryland Geological Survey* (Baltimore, MD: Johns Hopkins University Press, 1898), 2:380–86; Philip Lee Philips, *The Rare Map of Virginia and Maryland by Augustine Herrman* (Washington, DC: W. H. Lowdermilk, 1911); Karel Kansky, "Augustine Herrman: The Leading Cartographer of the Seventeenth Century," *MdHM* 73, no. 4 (1978): 355–57; Russell Morrison and Robert Hansen, *Charting the Chesapeake*, ed. Edward C. Papenfuse and Ann Hofstra Grogg (Annapolis: Maryland State Archives, 1990), 13–21. For keys relating Herrman's place names with current ones, see J. Louis Kuethe, "A Gazeteer of Maryland, A.D. 1673," *MdHM* 30, no. 4 (1935): 310–25; Louis Dow Scisco, "Notes on Augustine Herman's Map," *MdHM* 33, no. 4 (1938): 343–51.

14 Thomas R. Smith, "Manuscript and Printed Sea Charts in Seventeenth-Century London: The Case of the Thames School," in *The Compleat Plattmaker: Essays on Chart, Map, and Globe Making in England in the Seventeenth and Eighteenth Centuries*, ed. Norman J. W. Thrower (Berkeley: University of California Press, 1978), 45–100, esp. 46.

15 Lucas Janszoon Waghenaer, *The mariners mirrour . . .* (London, 1588); Günter Schilder, "The Netherland Nautical Cartography from 1550 to 1650," *Revista da Universidade de Coimbra* 32 (1985): 99–101; Günter Schilder and Marco van Egmond, "Maritime Cartography in the Low Countries during the Renaissance," in *Cartography in the European Renaissance*, 1384–99; Günter Schilder, "Lucs Janszoon Waghenaer's Nautical Altases and Pilot Books," in *Images of the World:*

The Atlas Through History, ed. John A. Wolter and Ronald E. Grim (Washington, DC: LOC, 1997), 135–39, 145; Kees Zandvliet, *Mapping for Money: Maps, Plans and Topographic Paintings and Their Role in Dutch Overseas Expansion during the 16th and 17th Centuries* (Amsterdam: Batavian Lion International, 1998), 34–37. On dead reckoning and the limitations of unprojected charts, see Tony Campbell, "Portolan Charts from the Late Thirteenth Century to 1500," in *The History of Cartography*, vol. 1 of *Cartography in Prehistoric, Ancient, and Medieval Europe and the Mediterranean*, ed. J. B. Harley and David Woodward (Chicago: University of Chicago Press, 1987), 385–86; Eric H. Ash, *Power, Knowledge, and Expertise in Elizabethan England* (Baltimore, MD: Johns Hopkins University, 2004), 93–94.

16 For this and the following two paragraphs, Peter van der Krogt, "Commercial Cartography and Map Production in the Low Countries, 1500–ca. 1672," in *Cartography in the European Renaissance*, 1305–18; Schilder, "The Netherland Nautical Cartography," 106–8, 111–12; Crone, *Maps and Their Makers*, 68–70; J. B. Harley and Kees Zandvliet, "Art, Science, and Power in Sixteenth-Century Dutch Cartography," *Cartographica* 29, no. 2 (1992): 11–12, 15; John P. Snyder, "Map Projections in the Renaissance," in *Cartography in the European Renaissance*, 376–78; David Woodward, "Starting with the Map: The Rosselli Map of the World, ca. 1508," in *Plantejaments I Objectius D'Una Història Universal de la Cartografia*, ed. David Woodward, Catherine Delano-Smith, and Cordell D. K. Yee (Barcelona: El Institut, 2001), 88–89; Zandvliet, *Mapping for Money*, 37–49, 164–86.

17 Kees Zandvliet, "Mapping the Dutch Overseas World in the Seventeenth Century," in *Cartography in the European Renaissance*, 1452–53.

18 Zandvliet, *Mapping for Money*, 45, 165–71; Michael Jarvis and Jeroen van Driel, "The Vingboons Chart of the James River, circa 1617," *WMQ* 3rd ser., 54, no. 2 (1997): 378; Smith, "Manuscript and Printed Sea Charts," 89–90; Helen M. Wallis, "Geographie Is Better than Divinitie: Maps, Globes, and Geography in the Days of Smauel Pepys," and David A. Woodward, "English Cartography, 1650–1750: A Summary," both in *The Compleat Plattmaker: Essays on Chart, Map, and Globe Making in England in the Seventeenth and Eighteenth Centuries*, ed. Norman J. W. Thrower (Berkeley: University of California Press, 1978), 31–32, 160–61; Ash, *Power, Knowledge, and Expertise in Elizabethan England*, 117.

19 *Arch. Md.*, 3:464; *NYHMDPE*, 113. Augustine Herrman, "Memorandum or Journall of the first foundation and seating of Bohemia Manor and Bohemia River Middle next, Adjacent & Apendant," BMP, Ms. 1556, p. 6, MdHS. Most scholars follow Thomas Čapek in assuming Herrman was a surveyor; see his *Augustine Herrman of Bohemia Manor* (Prague: State Printing Office, 1930), 11–13. On making maps from the sea, see Mary Sponberg Pedley, *The Commerce of Cartography: Making and Marketing Maps in Eighteenth-Century France and England* (Chicago: University of Chicago Press, 2005), 123, 168.

20 Samuel Smith, *The History of the Colony of Nova-Caesaroa or New-Jewsey* (Burlington, 1765), 186, quoted in Jeannetter D. Black, "Mapping the English Colonies in North America: The Beginnings," in *The Compleat Plattmaker: Essays on Chart, Map, and Globe Making in England in the Seventeenth and Eighteenth Centuries*, ed. Norman J. W. Thrower (Berkeley: University of California Press, 1978), 122–23.

21 Reid's *map of the Rariton River* has a scale of 1.25 English per inch. John P. Snyder, *The Mapping of New Jersey: The Men and the Art* (New Brunswick, NJ: Rutgers University Press, 1973), 24. For surveying in the colonial Chesapeake, see Sarah S. Hughes, *Surveyors and Statesmen: Land Measuring in Colonial Virginia* (Richmond: Virginia Surveyors Foundation, Virginia Association of Surveyors, 1979).

22 No inventory for Herrman's estate exists. "Inventory of the estate of the late Jonas Bronck," May 6, 1643, *NYHMRPS, 1642–1647*, 121–23; Ruth Piwonka, "'I Could Not Guess What She Intended to Do with It': Colonial American-Dutch Material Culture," in *Dutch New York: The Roots of Hudson Valley Culture*, ed. Roger Panetta (New York: Fordham University Press for the Hudson River Museum, 2009), 161–65. On navigation manuals, see Eric H. Ash, "Navigation Techniques and Practice in the Renaissance," in *Cartography in the European Renaissance*, 424–26. On the connection between mathematics and navigation, see Deborah E. Harkness, *The Jewel House: Elizabethan London and the Scientific Revolution* (New Haven, CT: Yale University Press, 2007), 122–24.

23 Quotations from Waghenaer's *Die Speitghel de Zeevaert* from Anthony Ashley's translation, *The mariners mirrour* (London, 1588), A2r. Also see William Bourne, *A regiment for the sea . . .* (London, 1577), 40–42v; John Seller, *Practical navigation; or, An introduction to the whole art* (London, 1680), 34. Sarah Tyacke, "Chartmaking in England and Its Context, 1500–1660," in *Cartography in the European Renaissance*, 1736; Schilder and Van Egmond, "Maritime Cartography in the Low Countries," 1385, 1393; Susan Rose, "Mathematics and the Art of Navigation: The Advance of Scientific Seamanship in Elizabethan England," *Transactions of the Royal Historical Society* 6th ser., 14 (2004): 178–79.

24 Lord Baltimore to the Lords Committee of Trade and Plantations, March 26, 1678, *Arch. Md.*, 5:265.

25 John Davis, *The Seamans Secret* (London, 1633), B1v; Richard Norwood, *The sea-man's practice* (London, 1697), 34–35; D. W. Waters, *The Art of Navigation in England and Elizabethan and Early Stuart Times* (New Haven, CT: Yale University Press, 1958), 41–52.

26 John Smith, *The generall historie of Virginia, New-England, and the Summer Isles . . .* (London, 1624), 47, 184; William C. Wooldridge, *Mapping Virginia: From the Age of Exploration to the Civil War* (Charlottesville: University of Virginia Press for the Library at the Mariners' Museum, 2012), 33.

27 "Inventory of the Estate of Richard Norwood, Bermuda," February 4, 1675/6, in Richard Norwood, *The Journal of Richard Norwood. Surveyor of Bermuda* (New

York: Published for Bermuda Historical Monuments Trust by Scholars' Facsimiles & Reprints, 1945), 136–41.

28 Davis, *The Seamans Secret*, D2v (quotation)–d3v; Seller, *Practical Navigation*, 152–57; E. G. R Taylor and M. W. Richey, *The Geometrical Seaman: A Book of Early Nautical Instruments* (London: Hollis and Carter for the Institute of Navigation, 1962), 37–40.

29 Davis, *The Seamans Secret*, G4r; Bourne, *A regiment for the sea*, 42v–45v; William Cuningham, *The cosmographical glasse* (London, 1559), 108; Ash, "Navigation Techniques and Practice," 513–19; Waters, *The Art of Navigation*, 58–62; E. G. R. Taylor, *The Haven-Finding Art: A History of Navigation from Odysseus to Captain Cook* (New York: Abelard-Schuman, 1957), 151–52, 225–32.

30 Though not as widely available in colonial America as in England, Maryland's 1674 decision to offer surveyors double the normal payment for their surveys if they used a "Chaine [and] Circumferenter with Sights" indicates that this instrument would have been available to Herrman. "An Act for the surveyor Generalls fees with addicon of fees upon Resurveys and for Leavying the same," April 13, 1674 in *Arch. Md.*, 2:393.

31 Both Norwood's *The Sea-Man's Practice* (London, 1639) and his later *Epitome, Being the Application of the Doctrine of Triangles* (London, 1659) were available in Virginia. Hughes, *Surveyors and Statesmen*, 33–35.

32 Bourne, *A regiment for the sea*40–42v; Taylor, *The Haven-Finding Art*, 237.

33 Smith, *A description of New England . . .* (London, 1616), 4–5.

34 Zandvliet, *Mapping for Money*, 237. In October 1660, Stuyvesant mentioned this sketch to the Directors of the WIC, noting that "we thought it advisable, to send you also a small sketch of the city, drawn in perspective by Sieur *Augustine Heermans* three or four years ago" (October 6, 1660, *DRCHNY*, 14:486). For the debate about this image, see Stokes, *Iconography of Manhattan Island*, 1:121, 142–54; Joep M. J. de Koning, "Dating the Visscher, or Prototype, View of New Amsterdam," *De Halve Maen* 72, no. 3 (1999): 47–51.

35 Governor Charles Calvert to Cecilius, Lord Baltimore, April 27, 1664, *Calvert Papers, Number One*, Maryland Historical Society, Fund Publication No. 28 (Baltimore: Maryland Historical Society, 1889), 236 (first quotation); Lord Baltimore to Governor Charles Calvert, February 16, 1665/6, *Arch. Md.*, 15:18 (second quotation); Augustine Herrman, "Memorandum or Journall," June 13, 1681, BMP, Ms. 1556, p. 3, MdHS (final quotation). The best evidence for the existence of a manuscript version of his map in 1661 comes from Herrman's denization, which refers to a map that Herrman "hath drawn." "Denization of Augustine Herrman," January 28, 1660/1, in *Arch. Md.*, 3:398–99. See also "Money Warrant for 40l. to Cecil Lord Baltimore," December 12, 1671, T 51/19, p. 27, TNA; Black, *Blathwayt Atlas*, 2:113–14.

36 Deposition of Robert Burwell, April 19, 1658, NCOB, 1657–1664, fol. 14.

37 "Augustine Herrman's Journal of the Dutch Embassy to Maryland," October 12/2, 1659, *NYHMDPD*, 217.

38 Gavin Hollis, "The Wrong Side of the Map? The Cartographic Encounters of John Lederer," in *Early American Cartographies*, ed. Martin Brückner (Chapel Hill: University of North Carolina Press for the OIEAHC, 2011), 145–53 (Smith quotation 149); Gregory A. Waselkov, "Indian Maps of the Colonial Southeast: Archaeological Implications and Prospects," in *Cartographic Encounters: Perspectives on Native American Mapmaking and Map Use*, ed. G. Malcolm Lewis (Chicago: University of Chicago Press, 1998), 205–21; Robert C.D. Baldwin, "Colonial Cartography under the Tudor and Early Stuart Monarchies, ca. 1480–ca. 1640," in *Cartography in the European Renaissance*, 1772.

39 *The Public Records of the Colony of Connecticut*, ed. J. Hammond Trumbull (Hartford, CT: Brown & Parsons, 1850), 218–20; *Arch. Md.*, 15:175; *NYHMDPD*, 211–13.

40 Johannes de Laet, *Nieuwe wereldt ofte Beschrijvinghe van West-Indien* (Leiden, 1625); Loockermans to Gillis Verbrugge and Assoc., May 27, 1648, letter 15 (F3-F), in Stuyvesant-Rutherford Papers, Box 23, NYHS, in Wim Vanraes, trans. and ed., "Goovert Loockermans: Correspondence and Papers," (Albany, NY: New Netherland Institute, 2014), 32; Zandvliet, "Mapping the Dutch Overseas World in the Seventeenth Century," in *Cartography in the European Renaissance*, 1450–53; Wooldridge, *Mapping Virginia*, 60–61, 66–67.

41 Cuningham, *The cosmographical glasse*, 115–18.

42 Black, *The Blathwayt Atlas*, 2: maps 16 and 17, 109–15; "Maryland," CO 700/MARYLAND/1, TNA, and "Virginia," MPG 1/375, TNA; Smith, "Manuscript and Printed Sea Charts," 46–93.

43 Donna Merwick, *Possessing Albany, 1630–1710: The Dutch and English Experiences* (New York: Cambridge University Press, 1990), 3–5; Svetlana Alpers, *The Art of Describing: Dutch Art in the Seventeenth Century* (Chicago: University of Chicago Press, 1983), 142–49.

44 Schmidt, "Inventing Exoticism: The Project of Dutch Geography and the Marketing of the World, circa 1700," in *Merchants & Marvels: Commerce, Science, and Art in Early Modern Europe*, ed. Pamela H. Smith and Paula Findlen (New York: Routledge, 2002), 356–59.

45 Alpers, "The Mapping Impulse in Dutch Art," in *Art and Cartography: Six Historical Essays*, ed. David Woodward (Chicago: University of Chicago Press, 1987), 55–57, 62–67, 69–72, 76–78, 84–88. On English estate mapping, see David Buisseret, *The Mapmakers' Quest: Depicting New Worlds in Renaissance Europe* (New York: Oxford University Press, 2003), 64–67, 152–58; P. D. A. Harvey, "English Estate Maps: Their Early History and Their Use as Historical Evidence," in *Rural Images: Estate Maps in the Old and New Worlds*, ed. David Buisseret (Chicago: University of Chicago Press, 1996), 27–30, 31–32; Richard Helgerson,

"The Land Speaks: Cartography, Chorography, and Subversion in Renaissance England," *Representations* 16 (Autumn 1986): 51–53, 64–66.

46 Alpers, *The Art of Describing*, 148–59; Donna Merwick, "A Genre of Their Own: Kiliaen van Rensselaer as Guide to the Reading and Writing Practices of Early Modern Businessmen," *WMQ* 65, no. 4 (2008): 694–702. English merchants had a similar outlook. See Deborah E. Harkness, "Accounting for Science: How a Merchant Kept His Books in Elizabethan London," in *The Self-Perception of Early Modern Capitalists*, ed. Margaret C. Jacob and Catherine Secretan (New York: Palgrave MacMillan, 2008), 206–08, 210.

47 Alpers, The *Art of Describing*, 133–60.

48 For an alternate view see MacMillan, "Centers and Peripheries," 67–92. Scholars who endeavor to uncover the influence of Native American informants on European and American maps have much more consistently found that their influence was not erased in printed maps. Ropbert Paulett, *An Empire of Small Places: Mapping the Southeastern Anglo-Indian Trade, 1732–1795* (Athens: University of Georgia Press, 2012), 12–13, 21–23, 31–32, 39–40; Hollis, "The Wrong Side of the Map?," 145–68.

49 Black, "Mapping the English Colonies in North America," 106–8; J. B. Harley, "New England Cartography and the Native Americans," in *American Beginnings: Exploration, Culture and Cartography in the Land of Norumbega*, ed. Emerson W. Baker, Edwin A. Churchill, Richard S. D'Abate, Kristine L. Jones, Victor A. Konrad, and Harald E. L. Prins (Lincoln: University of Nebraska Press, 1994), 290–92.

50 Hatfield, "Spanish Colonization Literature," 262–65.

51 On Norwood and his surveying, see Introduction to *The Journal of Richard Norwood: Surveyor of Bermuda* (New York: Published for the Bermuda Historical Monuments Trust by Scholars Facsimilies & Reprints, 1945), xxvii–xxviii, xxxvii–xxxviii, 53; Black, "Mapping the English Colonies," 120–21. Though the original map on which the later examples were based is no longer extant, the inventory of Norwood's estate indicates that he possessed "The Mape of ye Survay of Bermoodas" (Book of Wills, No. 1, pp. 219–20, 221 in *The Journal of Richard Norwood* 141). On early Bermuda, see Michael J. Jarvis, *In the Eye of All Trade: Bermuda, Bermudians, and the Maritime Atlantic World, 1680–1783*, (Chapel Hill: University of North Carolina Press for OIEAHC, 2010), 16–23, 34–35.

52 Lydia Mihelic Pulsipher, "The Cultural Landscape of Montserrat, West Indies, in the Seventeenth Century: Early Environmental Consequences of British Colonial Development" (Ph.D. diss., Southern Illinois University, 1977), 15–18; Lydia Mihelic Pulsipher, "Assessing the Usefulness of a Cartographic Curiosity: The 1673 Map of a Sugar Island," *Annals of the Association of American Geographers* 77, no. 3 (1987): 409, 412–14; Black, *The Blathwayt Atlas*, 2: 175–79; Richard Dunn, *Sugar and Slaves: The Rise of the Planter Class in the English West Indies, 1624–1713* (Chapel Hill: University of North Carolina Press, 1972), 34–35.

53 Black, *The Blathwayt Atlas*, 2:175–76; Pulsipher, "Assessing the Usefulness of a Cartographic Curiosity," 413–14.

CHAPTER 3. THE PLANTER

1 Herrman, "Memorandum or Journall," June 13, 1681, BMP, Ms 1556, p. 1, MdHS.

2 Two recent narrative accounts of these wars advance this perspective even while doing much to bring out new dimensions of the conflicts: David R. Mandell, *King Philip's War: Colonial Expansion, Native Resistance, and the End of Indian Sovereignty* (Baltimore, MD: Johns Hopkins University Press, 2010); James D. Rice, *Tales from a Revolution: Bacon's Rebellion and the Transformation of Early America* (New York: Oxford University Press, 2012). Meanwhile historians of the Delaware River Valley have placed that region at the center of Eastern North American transformations. See Daniel K. Richter, *Trade, Land, Power: The Struggle for Eastern North America* (Philadelphia: University of Pennsylvania Press, 2013), 97–112; Mark L. Thompson, *The Contest for the Delaware Valley: Allegiance, Identity, and Empire in the Seventeenth Century* (Baton Rouge: Louisiana State University Press, 2013), 148–190; Jean R. Soderlund, *Lenape Country: Delaware Valley Society before William Penn* (Philadelphia: University of Pennsylvania Press, 2015), 86–131.

3 C. A. Weslager, *Dutch Explorers, Traders and Settlers in the Delaware Valley* (Philadelphia: University of Pennsylvania Press, 1961), 25–104; Charles T. Gehring, "*Hodie Mihi, Cras Tibi*: Swedish-Dutch Relations in the Delaware Valley," in *New Sweden in America*, ed. Carol E. Hoffecker, Richard Waldron, Lorraine E. Williams, and Barbara E. Benson (Newark, DE: University of Delaware Press, 1995), 70–72; Soderlund, *Lenape Country*, 6–7, 13–18, 28–48, 53.

4 "[Gerrit] Van Sweeringen's Relation Touching the seating of the Delaware River," August 12, 1684, *Arch. Md.*, 5:413.

5 Weslager, *Dutch Explorers, Traders and Settlers*, 126–27, 135–37, 140–57; Gehring, "*Hodie Mihi, Cras Tibi*," 72–79; Karen Kupperman, "Scandinavian Colonists Confront the New World," in *New Sweden in America*, Carol E. Hoffecker, Richard Waldron, Lorraine E. Williams, and Barbara E. Benson (Newark, DE: University of Delaware Press, 1995), 92–93, 101–3; Soderlund, *Lenape Country*, 30–34, 55–58, 61–62, 70–85, 87–88; Thompson, *The Contest for the Delaware Valley*, 74–101, 152–54, 165–66.

6 Francis Jennings, "Glory, Death, and Transfiguration: The Susquehannock Indians in the Seventeenth Century," *Proceedings of the American Philosophical Society* 112, no. 1 (1968): 16–19; Thompson, *The Contest for the Delaware Valley*, 129–39.

7 "Report of Governor Johan Printz," 1647, in *Narratives of Early Pennsylvania, West New Jersey, and Delaware, 1630–1707*, ed. J. Franklin Jameson, (New York: Charles Scribner's Sons, 1912), 123, 127.

8 Soderlund, *Lenape Country*, 84–85, 91–97, 225fn16; Thompson, *The Contest for the Delaware Valley*, 91–101; Donna Merwick, *The Shame and the Sorrow:*

Dutch-Amerindian Encounters in New Netherland (Philadelphia: University of Pennsylvania Press, 2006), 219–27.

9 Thompson, *The Contest for the Delaware Valley*, 165–67; Jaap Jacobs, *The Colony of New Netherland: A Dutch Settlement in Seventeenth-Century America* (Ithaca, NY: Cornell University Press, 2009), 74–76; Merwick, *The Shame and the Sorrow*, 239–51; Sonderlund, *Lenape Country*, 103–06.

10 "At a council held at Ann Arundell, August 3, 1659," *Arch. Md.*, 3:365.

11 *NYHMDPD*, 152–55; C. A. Weslager, *The English on the Delaware: 1610–1682* (New Brunswick, NJ: Rutgers University Press, 1967), 158–61.

12 John D. Krugler, *English & Catholic: The Lords Baltimore in the Seventeenth Century* (Baltimore: Johns Hopkins University Press, 2004), 193–220; Thompson, *The Contest for the Delaware Valley*, 165–69; "Captain John Utie, of Utimaria, Esq.," *WMQ* 4, no. 1 (1895): 52–54.

13 Lord Baltimore (Cecilus Calvert) to Philip Calvert, December 14, 1660, read at Maryland Council, July 1, 1661, *Arch. Md.*, 3:426–28 (quotations); *Arch. Md.*, 5:414; Weslager, *The English on the Delaware*, 170–75.

14 "Extract from a Letter of Stuyvesant to the Directors in Holland," September 17, 1659, *DRCHNY*, 12:254 (quotation); Weslager, *The English on the Delaware*, 160–62.

15 Beeckman to Stuyvesant, May 27, 1661, *NYHMDPD*, 232–33 (quotations), 233–34; *Arch. Md.*, 3:412–16, 425–36; Weslager, *The English on the Delaware*, 174–75.

16 "Augustine Herrman's Journal of the Dutch Embassy to Maryland," October 12/2, 1659, *NYHMDPD*, 211–13.

17 Ibid., 220, 222; Herrman, "Memorandum or Journall," June 13, 1681, BMP, Ms 1556, p. 1, MdHS.

18 Herrman to Beeckman, May 1661, *NYHMDPD*, 231.

19 Ibid., 232.

20 Alexander d'Hinoyossa to Governor of Maryland, May 20, 1661, *Arch. Md.*, 3:425–26 (quotation); *NYHMDPD*, 232–33.

21 "Articles of peace and amity," September 19, 1661, *Arch. Md.*, 3:433. Jennings, "Glory, Death, and Transfiguration," 27–28.

22 Beeckman to Stuyvesant, October 26, 1661, *NYHMDPD*, 243. For a different account of these events, see William G. Duvall, "Smuggling Sotweed: Augustine Herrman and the Dutch Connection," *Maryland Historical Magazine* 98 (2003): 399–401.

23 "A Proclamacon for the better observacon of the Acte for Navigacion," January 31, 1661/2, *Arch. Md.*, 3:446–47.

24 "Private Instructions to Col.. R. Nicolls," April 23, 1664, *DRCHNY*, 3:57 (quotation); Michael J. Braddick, "The English Government, War, Trade, and Settlement, 1625–1688," in *The Origins of Empire*, ed. Nicholas Canny, vol. 1 of *The Oxford History of the British Empire*, ed. Wm Roger Lewis (Oxford: Oxford University Press, 1998), 302–8; Lawrence A. Harper, *The English Navigation Laws: A*

Seventeenth-Century Experiment in Social Engineering (New York: Octagon Books 1964), 59–60.

25 Krugler, *English & Catholic*, 220–21.

26 Jean Willemsz to Beeckman, recv. November 11, 1662, *NYHMDPD*, 312

27 Beeckman to Stuyvesant, November 24, 1662, *NYHMDPD*, 312.

28 Robert Ritchie, *The Duke's Province: A Study of New York Politics and Society, 1654–1691* (Chapel Hill: University of North Carolina Press, 1977), 12–13.

29 "Commission of Nicolas Varleth and Bryan Newton as envoys to Virginia," March 1, 1660, *DRCNHY*, 13:146–47; Warren M. Billings, *Sir William Berkeley and the Forging of Colonial Virginia* (Baton Rouge: Louisiana State University Press, 2004), 95–98, 102–8, 126–28; John R. Pagan, "Dutch Maritime and Commercial Activity in Mid-Seventeenth-Century Virginia," *VMHB* 90 (1982): 498; April Lee Hatfield, *Atlantic Virginia: Intercolonial Relations in the Seventeenth Century* (Philadelphia: University of Pennsylvania Press, 2004), 49–50.

30 [Sir William Berkeley], *A Discourse and view of Virginia* (n.p., 1663?), 6–7; Billings, *Sir William Berkeley*, 77–78, 141–44.

31 "The humble Remonstrance of *John Blande* of *London* Merchant, on the behalf of the Inhabitants and Planters in *Virginia* and *Mariland*," ca. 1676, CO 1/36, fol 142r–143r, TNA.

32 Billings, *Sir William Berkeley*, 220; Victor Enthoven and Wim Klooster, "The Rise and Fall of the Virginia-Dutch Connection in the Seventeenth Century," in *Early Modern Virginia: Reconsidering the Old Dominion*, ed. Douglas Bradburn and John C. Coombs (Charlottesville: University of Virginia Press, 2011), 111–13.

33 Lorena S. Walsh, *Motives of Honor, Pleasure, and Profit: Plantation Management in the Colonial Chesapeake, 1607–1763* (Chapel Hill: University of North Carolina Press for the OIEAHC, 2010), 147–49; Antoinette Sutto, *Loyal Protestants and Dangerous Papists: Maryland and the Politics of Religion in the English Atlantic, 1630–1690* (Charlottesville: University of Virginia Press, 2015), 82–89.

34 Letter of Lord Baltimore read at Maryland Council meeting, July 1, 1661, *Arch. Md.*, 3:427–28.

35 At His Majesty's Council for Foreign Plantations meetings of August 11 and August 25, 1662, CO 1/14, pp. 47, 49 (quotations), TNA.

36 Beeckman to Stuyvesant, February 1, 1663, *NYHMDPD*, 316 (quotations). Herrman's Maryland partners in this trade were Nathaniel Utie, Samuel Goldsmith, Henry Stockett, Charles James, and Richard Bennett. The men failed to supply all the tobacco they owed the City of Amsterdam. *Arch. Md.*, 49:299, 341–42.

37 "Deposition of Godefroy Meyer van Cloppenburgh before notary Hendrick Rosa," June 16, 1665, in I. N. Phelps Stokes, *The Iconography of Manhattan Island, 1498–1909* (New York: Robert H. Dodd, 1928), 6:19 ("of the best quality" and "Spanish wine"); Beeckman to Stuyvesant, October 26, 1661, *NYHMDPD*, 243 ("2 or 3000"); Orders of Charles Calvert, December 24, 1664, *Arch. Md.*, 49:342 ("best quality").

38 On Samuel Goldsmith, see *Arch. Md.*, 1:540. On Stockett, see *Arch. Md.* 1:540; J. D. Warfield, *The Founders of Anne Arundel and Howard Counties, Maryland: A Genealogical and Biographical Review from Wills, Deeds and Church Records* (Bowie, MD: Heritage Books, 1995), 93–96. On Charles James, see *Arch. Md*, 49:180–81. On Richard Bennett, see J. Frederick Fausz, "Richard Bennett (bap. 1609–ca. 1675)," *Encyclopedia Virginia* (Virginia Foundation for the Humanities, July 17, 2014), www.encyclopediavirginia.org. On Fendall's Rebellion, see Krugler, *English & Catholic*, 192–221.

39 *Arch. Md.*, 3:418–19, 433; *Arch. Md.*, 49:342.

40 *Arch. Md.*, 41:62, 263, 579.

41 Beeckman to Stuyvesant, December 28, 1663, *NYHMDPD*, 340–41; Weslager, *The English on the Delaware*, 189–95.

42 "At His Majesty's Council for Foreign Plantations," December 7, 1663, CO 1/14, p. 53 (quotations), TNA. See also council meetings of July 24, 1663, December 6, 1663, and January 19, 1663/4, CO 1/14, pp. 53, 54, 55, TNA; *DRCHNY*, 3:57; Ritchie, *The Duke's Province*, 9–20; Megan Lindsay Cherry, "The Imperial and Political Motivations behind the English Conquest of New Netherland," *Dutch Crossing* 34, no. 1 (2010): 77–94.

43 Donna Merwick, *Stuyvesant Bound: An Essay on Loss across Time* (Philadelphia: University of Pennsylvania Press, 2013), 103–14; Ritchie, *The Duke's Province*, 20–24.

44 "Commission to Sir Robert Carr to reduce the Dutch," September 3, 1664, *DRCHNY*, 3:70 (first and second quotations); Nicolls to the Secretary of State Lord Arlington, October 1664, *DRCHNY*, 3:69–70; Carr to Nicolls, October 13, 1664, *DRCHNY*, 3:73–74 (third quotation); *Arch. Md.*, 5:416–17; Weslager, *The English on the Delaware*, 186–202.

45 Petition to Philip Calvert, December 10, 1664, and Orders of Charles Calvert, December 24, 1664, *Arch. Md.*, 49:299, 342 (quotations); *Arch. Md.*, 2:282; Henry M. Miller, "'To Serve the Countrey': Garret Van Sweringen and the Dutch Influence in Early Maryland," in *From De Halve Maen to KLM: 400 Years of Dutch-American Exchange*, ed. Margriet Bruijn Lacy, Charles Gehring, and Jenneke Oosterhoff (Münster: Nodus Publikationen, 2008), 88–92.

46 Nicolls to the Secretary of State, October 1664, *DRCHNY*, 3:69; Peter R. Christoph and Florence A. Christoph, eds., *New York Historical Manuscripts: English. Books of General Entries of the Colony of New York, 1664–1688* (Baltimore: Genealogical Publishing, 1982), 1:35–37, 68, 75, 82–83, 105, 106; Dennis J. Maika, "'We shall bloom and grow like the Cedar of Lebanon': Dutch Merchants in English New York City, 1664–1672," *De Halve Maen* 84, no. 1 (2011): 9–11.

47 Cathy Matson, "Commerce after the Conquest: I, Dutch Traders and Goods in New York City, 1664–1764," *De Halve Maen* 59 (1987): 8–12; Christian J. Koot, *Empire at the Periphery: Anglo-Dutch Trade, English Colonists, and the Development of the English Empire, 1621–1713* (New York: New York University Press, 2011), 108–16.

48 "Articles of Agreement Between James Fookes and Ann Hack," May 6, 1665, and
    "Deposition of Augustine Herman," May 27, 1667, both in Accomack County
    Order Book, 1666–70, microfilm reel no. 78, fol. 30, LV (quotation); *RNA*, 6:120;
    Hatfield, *Atlantic Virginia*, 50; Dennis J. Maika, "Jacob Leisler's Chesapeake
    Trade," *De Halve Maen* 68 (1994): 9–14.
49 Herrman, "Memorandum or Journall," June 13, 1681, BMP, Ms. 1556, pp. 1–6,
    MdHS; Louis Dow Scisco, "Notes on Augustine Herman's Map," *Maryland
    Historical Magazine* 33, no. 4 (1938): 343–45.
50 Herrman, "Memorandum or Journall," June 13, 1681, BMP, Ms. 1556, p. 4, MdHS;
    Land patents, June 17, 1671, December 1, 1675, and July 13, 1676, in *Original Land
    Titles in Delaware Commonly Known as the Duke of York Record* (Wilmington,
    DE: Sunday Star Print, 1903), 101–2, 150, 181; *NYHMDPE*, 56; *Arch. Md.*, 17:
    485–87.
51 "Proposals of Mr. John Carr Concerning Delaware with Orders Thereon," 1671,
    NYHMDPE, 26; Christoph and Christoph, eds., *Books of General Entries of the
    Colony of New York*, 1:423–24; *DRCHNY*, 12:480–81.
52 *Arch. Md.*, 5:113–14; Bartlett Burleigh James and J. Franklin Jameson, eds., *Journal
    of Jasper Danckaerts* (New York: Charles Scribner's Sons, 1913), 127–28.
53 Francis Nicholson to the Board of Trade, March 27, 16[9]7, *Arch. Md.*, 23:87.
54 Richard Grubb and Associates, "Phase I (Identification-Level) Archaeological
    Survey U.S. Route 301, Levels Road Mitigation Site, St. Georges Hundred, New
    Castle County, Delaware, Parent Agreement 1417, Task 8," June 2011, 3–15, 3–26,
    www.deldot.gov.
55 "Philadelphia and Baltimore Land and Water New Line Packets," *Philadelphia
    Gazette and Universal Daily Advertiser*, April 29, 1794, 2 (supplement).
56 *RNA*, 7:12–3, 29, 30; *RNA*, 5:386; *RNA*, 6:33.
57 *Arch. Md.*, 3:528–9; Act of Naturalization, May 1666, CO 5/728, 113–14, TNA; *Arch.
    Md.*, 51:132; *Arch. Md.*, 1:462.
58 *NYHMDPD*, 212–14.
59 "An Act of Preventing Servants & Criminall persons from Runing out of this
    Province," April 30, 1669, *Arch. Md.*, 2:224–26; *NYHMDPE*, 113.
60 Ephraim Herrman to Matthias Nicolls, January 17, 1679/80, *NYHMDPE*, 291.
61 James and Jameson, *Journal of Jasper Danckaerts*, 115; Edward Bennett Mathews
    "History of the Boundary Dispute Between the Baltimores and the Penns
    Resulting in the Original Mason and Dixon Line," in *Report on the Resurvey of the
    Maryland-Pennsylvania Boundary Part of the Mason and Dixon Line* (Harrisburg:
    Harrisburg Publishing, State Printer, 1909), 128–30.

CHAPTER 4. THE PATRON AND THE ENGRAVER

1 *London Gazette*, March 30–April 2, 1674, issue no. 873, verso. Sarah Tyacke,
   London Map-Sellers: 1660–1720 (Tring, Hertfordshire: Map Collector Publications,
   1978), xv–xvi. Though the map is dated 1673 and though every scholar who has

written about the map place its publication date in 1673, it probably appeared for sale only in March 1674 (it was common for advertisements to appear in the *Gazette* only weeks after maps' publication). Because the English continued to follow the habit of marking the new year on March 25, the printer used 1673 when publishing it. Moreover, the king issued a copyright for the work in January 1674, and this copyright is included on all extant copies of the printed map, meaning the map was not published until after January 1674. The plates may have been largely finished by that date, however, as the copyright seems to be squeezed into the bottom left corner. "Grant to Augustine Herman of the privilege of the sole printing of his map of Virginia and Maryland," January 21, 1674, SP 44/36, 323–24, TNA.

2 Abraham Ortelius, *Theatrum orbis terrarum: The theatre of the whole world: Set Forth by That Excellent Geographer Abraham Ortellis* (London, 1606 [i.e. 1608?]),7. On the power of prints, see Michael Gaudio, *Engraving the Savage: The New World and Techniques of Civilization* (Minneapolis: University of Minnesota Press, 2008), ix–xi, xvii–xxii; William B. MacGregor, "The Authority of Prints: An Early Modern Perspective," *Art History* 22, no. 3 (1999): 393–99; Peter Parshall, "Art and the Theater of Knowledge: The Origins of Print Collecting in North European," *Harvard University Art Museum Bulletin* 2, no. 3 (1994): 7, 14–15, 25–26; Benjamin Schmidt, *Inventing Exoticism: Geography, Globalism, and Europe's Early Modern World* (Philadelphia: University of Pennsylvania Press, 2014), 98–105, 127–29, 153–55.

3 Antony Griffiths, *The Print in Stuart Britain, 1603–1689* (London: British Museum Press, 1998); Adrian Johns, *The Nature of the Book: Print and Knowledge in the Making* (Chicago: University of Chicago Press, 1998), 58–186. Contrast with Schmidt, *Inventing Exoticism*, esp. 25–161; Kevin Sharpe, *Reading Authority & Representing Rule in Early Modern England* (London: Bloomsbury Academic, 2013), 8, 19–24.

4 Gaudio, *Engraving the Savage*, xvii–xix; MacGregor, "The Authority of Prints," 401–5; Chandra Mulerji, *From Graven Images: Patterns of Modern Materialism* (New York: Columbia University Press, 1983), 98–116; Bruno Latour, *Science in Action: How to Follow Scientists and Engineers through Society* (Cambridge, MA: Harvard University Press, 1987), 29. Contrast this interpretation of the power and authority of printed images with those of cartographic scholars who typically argue that the act of reproduction diminished the status of printed maps; see, for example, Catherine Delano-Smith, "The Map as Commodity," in *Plantejaments I Objectius D'Una Història Universal de la Cartografia*, ed. David Woodward, Catherine Delano-Smith, and Cordell D. K. Yee, (Barcelona: El Institut, 2001), 95.

5 Herrman, "Memorandum or Journall," June 13, 1681, BMP, Ms. 1556, p. 3, MdHS (first quotation). Herrman cites two now-missing letters from Lord Baltimore relating the compliments of the king, dated September 3, 1670, and November 12, 1670. "Money Warrant for 40l. to Cecil Lord Baltimore," December 12 1671, T

51/19, p. 27, TNA; Governor Charles Calvert to Cecil, Lord Baltimore, April 26, 1672 in *Calvert Papers, Number One*, Maryland Historical Society, Fund Publication no. 28 (Baltimore, 1889), 272; Lord Baltimore to William Blathwayt, March 18, 1681, quoted in Jeannette D. Black, *The Blathwayt Atlas*, vol. 2 *Commentary* (Providence, RI: Brown University Press, 1975), 116n16.

6 "Grant to Augustine Herman of the privilege of the sole printing of his map of Virginia and Maryland," January 21, 1674, SP 44/36, pp. 323–24, TNA.

7 "Instructions to Sir Robert Carr for the Reducing of Delaware Bay, and Settling the People there under his Majesties Obedience," 1664, *NYHMDPE*, 1–2 (quotation); C. A. Weslager, *The English on the Delaware: 1610–1682* (New Brunswick, NJ: Rutgers University Press, 1967), 212–15; Mark L. Thompson, *The Contest for the Delaware Valley: Allegiance, Identity, and Empire in the Seventeenth Century* (Baton Rouge: Louisiana State University Press, 2013),, 189–90; Jean R. Soderlund, *Lenape Country: Delaware Valley Society before William Penn* (Philadelphia: University of Pennsylvania Press, 2015), 132–33, 150–51.

8 James Rice, *Nature & History in the Potomac Country: From Hunter-Gatherers to the Age of Jefferson* (Baltimore: Johns Hopkins University Press, 2009), 138.

9 Lord Baltimore to Governor Charles Calvert, February 16, 1665/6, *Arch. Md.*, 15:18; Black, *The Blathwayt Atlas*, 2:113–14.

10 J. Thomas Scarf, *History of Maryland, from the Earliest Period to the Modern Day* (Baltimore, MD: J. B. Piet, 1879), 1:261–62.

11 Paul Philip Musselwhite, "Towns in Mind: Urban Plans, Political Culture, and Empire in the Colonial Chesapeake, 1607–1722," (Ph.D. diss, College of William and Mary, 2011), 106–8, 254–68.

12 Timothy Riordan, *The Plundering Time: Maryland and the English Civil War, 1645–1646* (Baltimore: Maryland Historical Society, 2004), esp. 4–6, 13–14, 18–19, 88–164; John D. Krugler, *English & Catholic: The Lords Baltimore in the Seventeenth Century* (Baltimore, MD: Johns Hopkins University Press, 2004), 166–221; Antoinette Sutto, *Loyal Protestants and Dangerous Papists: Maryland and the Politics of Religion in the English Atlantic, 1630–1690* (Charlottesville: University of Virginia Press, 2015), 26–80.

13 "Denization of Augustine Herrman," January 28, 1660/61, *Arch. Md.*, 3:398–99 (first quotation);"An Ordinance of the Right Honble the Lord Proprietary of this Province of Maryld for the erecting of several Ports within the same," April 20, 1669, *Arch. Md.*, 5:47–48 (second quotation), 31–32; Lorena S. Walsh, *Motives of Honor, Pleasure, & Profit: Plantation Management in the Colonial Chesapeake, 1607–1763* (Chapel Hill: University of North Carolina Press for OIEAHC, 2011), 153, 183–84; Musselwhite, "Towns in Mind," 265–66.

14 Sutto, *Loyal Protestants and Dangerous Papists*, 9, 81–82, 104–25.

15 Antony Griffiths, *Prints and Printmaking: An Introduction to the History and Techniques* (Berkeley: University of California Press, 1996), 31; David Woodward,

"Techniques of Map Engraving, Printing, and Coloring in the European Renaissance," in *Cartography in the European Renaissance*, 592–94.

16 Louis Fagan, *A Descriptive Catalogue of the Engraved Works of William Faithorne* (London, 1888), 87–89.

17 Antony Griffiths, "Faithorne, William (c.1620–1691)," *Oxford Dictionary of National Biography* (Oxford: Oxford University Press, 2004), www.oxforddnb. com; Fagan, *A Descriptive Catalogue*, ix–xii.

18 November 7 and December 1, 1666, *Pepys Diary*, 359 (quotation), 393–94.

19 John Fitchett Marsh, "On the Engraved Portraits and Pretended Portraits of Milton," *Transactions of the Historical Society of Lancaster and Cheshire* 12 (1860): 152.

20 Jacob Kainen, Introduction to William Faithorne, *The Art of Graving and Etching by William Faithorne, New Introduction by Jacob Kainen* (New York: Da Capo Press, 1970), v–x.

21 Griffiths, *Prints and Printmaking*, 77–8.

22 Fagan, *A Descriptive Catalogue*, 43.

23 Griffiths, *The Print in Stuart Britain*, 14, 16–17, 125; Fagan, *A Descriptive Catalogue*, ix.

24 Quotations describing the engraving process from Faithorne, *The Art of Graving and Etching*, n.p. Griffiths, *Prints and Printmaking*, 31–38; Woodward, "Techniques of Map Engraving, Printing and Coloring in the European Renaissance," 592–97.

25 Faithorne, *The Art of Graving and Etching*, n.p.

26 Woodward, "Techniques of Map Engraving," 597; Griffiths, *Prints and Printmaking*, 38–39.

27 Somerset County, named for Mary, Lady Somerset, Cecilius, Lord Baltimore's sister-in-law, is missing from the map.

28 Governor Charles Calvert to Cecilius, Lord Baltimore, April 26, 1672. *Calvert Papers, Number One*, 272.

29 Krugler, *English & Catholic*, 6, 156–57.

30 Thomas Withinbrook's identity is unknown. There is no trace of him in either New Netherland or Maryland records or in seventeenth-century London. His name was not included in text of the king's proclamation granting Herrman the copyright in 1674, so why it is included on the copyright statement on the map is unclear. "Grant to Augustine Herman of the privilege of the sole printing of his map of Virginia and Maryland," January 21, 1674, SP 44/36, pp. 323–24, TNA.

31 Susan Stewart, *On Longing: Narratives of the Miniature, the Gigantic, the Souvenir, the Collection* (Durham, NC: Duke University Press, 1993), 151–63; Beth Fowkes Tobin, *Picturing Imperial Power: Colonial Subjects in Eighteenth-Century British Painting* (Durham, NC: Duke University Press, 1999), 25, 187–8, 213–25; Parshall, "Art and the Theater of Knowledge," 14–15.

32 Most recently, see Bernard Bailyn, *The Barbarous Years: The Peopling of British North America: The Conflict of Civilizations, 1600–1675* (New York: Borzoi Books by Alfred A. Knopf, 2012), 241.

33 Griffiths, *The Print in Stuart Britain*, 21–23, 193; David Piper, *The English Face*, ed. Malcolm Rogers (London: National Portrait Gallery, 1992), 113–17; Stephen Greenblat, Foreward to Frank Lestringant, *Mapping the Renaissance World: The Geographical Imagination in the Age of Discovery*, trans. by David Fausett (Berkeley: University of California Press, 1994), ix–xi.

34 T. Flatman, "TO my ingenious Friend, Mr. *Faithorne* on his Book," in Faithorne, *The Art of Graveing and Etching*, unpaginated front matter.

35 Piper, *The English Face*, 27; Marcia Pointon, *Hanging the Head: Portraiture and Social Formation in Eighteenth-Century England* (New Haven, CT: Yale University Press, 1993), 1, 5, 62–63.

36 Robert Hooke to Robert Boyle, August 25, 1664, in *The Works of the Honourable Robert Boyle*, ed. Thomas Birch (London, 1772), 6:487–88.

37 Pointon, *Hanging the Head*, 55.

38 Ian Roy, "Rupert, Prince and Count Palatine of the Rhine and Duke of Cumberland (1619–1682)," *Oxford Dictionary of National Biography* (Oxford: Oxford University Press, 2004), www.oxforddnb.com; John Evelyn, *Sculptura: or the History and Art of Chalcography and Engraving in Copper* (London, 1662), 145–48.

39 Katherine S. van Eerde, *Wenceslaus Hollar: Delineator of His Time* (Charlottesville: University Press of Virginia, 1970), 3, 6–12, 20–25, 35–41, 83.

40 Ibid., 59.

41 Thomas Harriot, *A brief and true report* (London, 1590).

42 Gaudio, *Engraving the Savage*, xii–xiii; Ute Kuhlemann, "Between Reproduction, Invention and Propaganda: Theodor de Bry's Engravings after John White's Watercolours," in *A New World: England's First View of America*, ed. Kim Sloan (London: British Museum Press, 2007), 82–92.

43 Thomas Woodcock and John Martin Robinson, *The Oxford Guide to Heraldry* (Oxford: Oxford University Press, 1988), 1, 4–5, 14–15; Pointon, *Hanging the Head*, 14, 22.

44 While their placement varies, these coats of arms are invariably located on landmasses, indicating imperial control over the land. Ken MacMillan, "Centers and Peripheries in English Maps of America, 1590–1685," in *Early American Cartographies*, ed. Martin Brückner (Chapel Hill: University of North Carolina Press for the OIEAHC, 2011), 82–83.

45 "Grant to Augustine Herman of the privilege of the sole printing of his map of Virginia and Maryland," January 21, 1674, SP 44/36, pp. 323–24 (quotations), TNA.

46 March 12, 1659/60, Journal of the Assembly, *Arch. Md.*, 1:388; Sutto, *Loyal Protestants and Dangerous Papists*, 41–42, 57, 76–77, 114–15, 160–61; Noeleen

McIlvenna, "Colonial Democrats," unpublished paper presented to Washington Early American Seminar, May 1, 2015, College Park, MD, 10–12.

47 Kevin Sharpe, "Restoration and Reconstitution: Politics, Society and Culture in the England of Charles II," in Sharpe, *Reading Authority & Representing Rule in Early Modern England* (London: Bloomsbury Academic, 2013), 194–200; Megan Cherry, "The Imperial and Political Motivations behind the English Conquest of New Netherland," *Dutch Crossing* 34, no. 1 (2010), 79–81, 87–90.

48 Schmidt, *Inventing Exoticism*, 28–33, 52, 69–74; Susan Scott Parrish, *American Curiosity: Cultures of Natural History in the Colonial British Atlantic World* (Chapel Hill: University of North Carolina Press for OIEAHC, 2006), 8, 16, 22, 105–08.

CHAPTER 5. THE CONSUMERS

1 For this and the paragraph above, see Laurence Worms, "The London Map Trade to 1640," in *Cartography in the European Renaissance*, 1695, 1712, 1714–15; Helen M. Wallis, "Geographie Is Better than Divinitie: Maps, Globes, and Geography in the Days of Samuel Pepys," in *The Compleat Plattmaker: Essays on Chart, Map, an Globe Making in England in the Seventeenth and Eighteenth Centuries*, ed. Norman J. Thrower (Berkeley: University of California Press, 1978), 4–19, 31–2; G. R. Crone, *Maps and Their Makers: An Introduction to the History of Cartography*, 5th ed. (Hamden, CT: Archon Books, 1978), 68–70; C. Delano Smith, "Map Ownership in Sixteenth-Century Cambridge: The Evidence of Probate Inventories," *Imago Mundi* 47 (1995): 67–70; Mary Sponberg Pedley, *The Commerce of Cartography: Making and Marketing Maps in Eighteenth-Century France and England* (Chicago: University of Chicago Press, 2005), 34, 81–82.

2 Peter Barber, "Mapmaking in England, ca. 1470–1650," in *Cartography in the European Renaissance*, 1608–9, 1666–68 (quotation 1608); Wallis, "Geographie Is Better than Divinitie," 3–4; Sarah Tyacke, *London Map-Sellers: 1660–1720* (Tring, Hertfordshire: Map Collector Publications, 1978), xi.

3 "Directions for Sea-Men, Bound for Far Voyages," *Philosophical Transactions* 1 (1665/66): 140–42 (quotation); Tony Campbell, "The Drapers' Company and Its School of Seventeenth Century Chart-Makers," in *My Head Is a Map: Essays & Memoirs in honour of R. V. Tooley*, ed. Helen M. Wallis and Sarah Tyacke (London: Francis Edwards and Carta Press, 1973), 81–87; Thomas R. Smith, "Manuscript and Printed Sea Charts in Seventeenth-Century London: The Case of the Thames School," in *The Compleat Plattmaker: Essays on Chart, Map, and Globe Making in England in the Seventeenth and Eighteenth Centuries*, ed. Norman J. W. Thrower (Berkeley: University of California Press, 1978), 46–55, 65–7;Tyacke, *London Map-Sellers*, xi–xii; Tyacke, "Chartmaking in England and Its Context, 1500–1660," in *Cartography in the European Renaissance*, 1731–34.

4 Tyacke, "Chartmaking in England and Its Context," 1746.

5 Seller, "Answer to some *Magnetical* Inquiries," *Philosophical Transactions* 2, no. 23 (1666–1667), 478–479; Coolie Verner, "John Seller and the Chart Trade in Seventeenth-Century England," in *The Compleat Plattmaker: Essays on Chart, Map, and Globe Making in England in the Seventeenth and Eighteenth Centuries*, ed. Norman J. W. Thrower (Berkeley: University of California Press, 1978), 127–57; Tyacke, *London Map-Sellers*, xii–xv.

6 *Term Catalogue* [London], Hillary, February 7, 1672, quoted in Verner, "John Seller and the Chart Trade," 135–36.

7 John Seller, *Praxis Nautica or Practical Navigator* (London, 1669).

8 Coolie Verner, Bibliographical Note, in *The English Pilot. London 1689: The Fourth Book* (Amsterdam: Theatrum Orbis Terrarum, 1967), v–xx; Verner, "John Seller and the Chart Trade," 139–40; Crone, *Maps and Their Makers*, 68; *The Tangier Papers of Samuel Pepys*, ed. Edwin Chappell (Colchester, UK: Printed by Ballantyne Press for the Navy Records Society, 1935), 107.

9 Verner, "John Seller and the Chart Trade," 143–55.

10 J. B. Harley, "Power and Legitimization in the English Geographical Atlases of the Eighteenth Century," in *Images of the World: The Atlas through History*, ed. John A. Wolter and Ronald E. Grim (Washington, DC: LOC, 1997), 189–90; Katherine Van Eerde, *John Ogilby and the Taste of His Times* (Kent, UK: Dawson, 1976), 95–121.

11 March 6–9, 1670/1, *London Gazette*, in Tyacke, *London Map-Sellers*, 4 (quotation); Verner, "John Seller and the Chart Trade," 136.

12 William B. MacGregor, "The Authority of Prints: An Early Modern Perspective," *Art History* 22, no. 3 (1999): 401–2; Robert Iliffe, "Author-Mongering: The 'Editor' between Producer and Consumer," in *The Consumption of Culture, 1600–1800: Image, Object, Text*, ed. Ann Bermingham and John Brewer (London: Routledge, 1995), 168–79.

13 Deborah E Harkness, *The Jewel House: Elizabethan London and the Scientific Revolution* (New Haven, CT: Yale University Press, 2007), 3, 57–8, 79–80, 127.

14 Ann Saunders, *The Art and Architecture of London: An Illustrated Guide* (Oxford: Phaidon, 1984), 68; Walter Thornbury and Edward Walford, *Old and New London: A Narrative of Its History, Its People and Its Places*, (London: Cassell, 1887), 1:495–503.

15 On coffeehouses and their patrons as discussed in this section, see Brian Cowan, *The Social Life of Coffee: The Emergence of the British Coffeehouse* (New Haven, CT: Yale University Press, 2005), 1–15, 89–99, 101–12, 169–77; Lawrence E. Klein, "Coffeehouse Civility, 1660–1714: An Aspect of Post-Courtly Culture in England," *Huntington Library Quarterly* 59, no. 1 (1996): 31–34, 36–43; Adrian Johns, *The Nature of the Book: Print and Knowledge in the Making* (Chicago: University of Chicago Press, 1998), 62–68, 111–13, 553–56; Steve Pincus, "'Coffee Politicians Does Create': Coffeehouses and Restoration Political Culture," *Journal of Modern History* 67, no. 4 (1995): 812, 818–22; Joseph Monteyne, *The Printed Image in Early Modern London: Urban Space, Visual Representation, and Social Exchange*

(Burlington, VT: Ashgate, 2007), 4, 19, 31–37, 39–41, 56–63; Nuala Zahedieh, *The Capital and the Colonies: London and the Atlantic Economy, 1660–1700* (New York: Cambridge University Press, 2010), 56, 69–70, 78, 97–99. For a broader discussion of London's burgeoning information culture, see Dror Wahrman, *Mr. Collier's Letter Racks: A Tale of Art & Illusion at the Threshold of the Modern Information Age* (New York: Oxford University Press, 2012), 41–47.

16 Harkness, *The Jewel House*, 2, 10–11, 98–141; Thomas Leng, "Epistemology: Expertise and Knowledge in the World of Commerce," in *Mercantilism Reimagined: Political Economy in Early Modern Britain and Its Empire*, ed. Philip J. Stern and Carl Wennerlind (New York: Oxford University Press, 2014), 99–101, 109–10; Monteyne, *The Printed Image in Early Modern London*, 83–85. William Petty used the term "political arithmetic" in his influential pamphlet *Political arithmetic* (London, 1690), which circulated in manuscript as early as the 1670s, and in *Another essay in political arithmetick, concerning the growth of the City of London* (London, 1683).

17 John Dunstall and John Sellers, *Scenes of the Plague in London with Statistical breakdown by parish for the years 1625, 1636, and 1665* (London, 1665–66); Monteyne, *The Printed Image in Early Modern London*, 73–85.

18 E. McSherry Fowble, *Two Centuries of Prints in America, 1680–1880: A Selective Catalogue of the Winterthur Museum Collection* (Charlottesville, VA, 1987), 35–37; Pedley, *Commerce of Cartography*, 68; David Woodward, "Techniques of Map Engraving, Printing, and Coloring in the European Renaissance," in *Cartography in the European Renaissance*, 601.

19 Bartlett Burleigh James and J. Franklin Jameson, ed., *Journal of Jasper Danckaerts* (New York: Charles Scribner's Sons, 1913), 297.

20 Accounts of the Lords of Trade, December 1674 to March 10, 1676, Add. Ms. 9767, fol. 15, BL (first quotation); Jeannette D. Black, *The Blathwayt Atlas*, vol. 2 *Commentary* (Providence, RI: Brown University Press, 1975), 110 (second quotation).

21 "Complaint from Heaven with a Huy & crye and a petitionout of Virginia and Maryland," [ca. 1676], CO 1/36, fol. 212r–218r, TNA.

22 Richard L. Kagan and Benjamin Schmidt, "Maps and the Early Modern State: Official Cartography," in *Cartography in the European Renaissance*, 661–69; Robert C. D. Baldwin, "Colonial Cartography under the Tudor and Early Stuart Monarchies, ca. 1480–ca. 1640," 1757–772," *Cartography in the European Renaissance*; Peter Barber, "Necessary and Ornamental: Map Use in England under the Later Stuarts, 1660–1714," *Eighteenth Century Life* 14, no. 3 (1990): 16–19; Ken MacMillan, "Sovereignty 'More Plainly Described': Early English Maps of North America, 1580–1625," *Journal of British Studies* 42, no. 4 (2003): 423–31, 435–46.

23 Patricia Seed, "Taking Possession and Reading Texts: Establishing the Authority of Overseas Empires," *WMQ* 3rd ser., 49, no. 2 (1992): 187–92, 195; MacMillan, "Sovereignty 'More Plainly Described,'" 426–31.

24 Michael J. Braddick, "The English Government, War, Trade, and Settlement, 1625–1688," in *The Origins of Empire*, ed. Nicholas Canny, vol. 1 of *The Oxford History of the British Empire*, ed. Wm Roger Lewis (Oxford: Oxford University Press, 1998), 296–304; Russell R. Menard, *Sweet Negotiations: Sugar, Slavery, and Plantation Agriculture in Early Barbados* (Charlottesville: University of Virginia Press, 2006), 29–48; Steven Pincus, "Popery, Trade and Universal Monarchy: The Ideological Context of the Outbreak of the Second Anglo-Dutch War," *English Historical Review* 107 (1992): 1–29.

25 For the use of maps to not only imagine but also produce empire, MacMillan, "Sovereignty 'More Plainly Described,'" 429–31, 446–47; Matthew H. Edney, "The Irony of Imperial Mapping," in *The Imperial Map: Cartography and the Mastery of Empire*, ed. James R. Akerman (Chicago: University of Chicago Press, 2009), 12–14, 17–18, 31–38.

26 Kagan and Schmidt, "Maps and the Early Modern State," 663–669 and Barber, "Mapmaking in England,," 1598–1609.

27 Ricardo Padrón, *The Spacious Word: Cartography, Literature, and Empire in Early Modern Spain* (Chicago: University of Chicago Press, 2004), 21–38; Antonion Barrera, "Empire and Knowledge: Reporting from the New World," *Colonial American Review* 15 (2006): 39–54. See also Harold J. Cook, *Matters of Exchange: Commerce, Medicine, and Science in the Dutch Golden Age* (New Haven, CT: Yale University Press, 2007).

28 William J. Bouwsma, *The Waning of the Renaissance, 1550–1640* (New Haven, CT: Yale University Press, 2000), 16–17, 67–69, 112–13, 116–23, 143–55, 189–90.

29 Braddick, "The English Government, War, Trade, and Settlement," 294–96, 302–08; Daniel A. Baugh, "Maritime Strength and Atlantic Commerce: The Uses of 'a Grand Marine Empire,'" in *An Imperial State at War: Britain from 1689 to 1815*, ed. Lawrence Stone (New York: Routledge, 1994), 185–93.

30 Benjamin Worsley, *The Advocate* (London,1652), 2–11; Josiah Child, *A New discourse on Trade* (London, 1693), 2–6, 91–101; Carew Reynel, *The True English Interest* (London, 1674), A8r; Jonathan Scott, *When the Waves Ruled Britannia: Geography and Political Identities, 1500–1800* (New York: Cambridge University Press, 2011), 56–68, 82–84, 96–97.

31 J. R. Tanner, ed., *Samuel Pepys's Naval Minutes*, Publications of the Navy Records Society, vol. 60 (London, Navy Records Society, 1926), 229–30, 345; Wallis, "Geographie is Better than Divinitie," 18–19, C. S. Knighton, "Pepys, Samuel (1633–1703)," in *Oxford Dictionary of National Biography*, ed. H. C. G. Matthew and Brian Harrison (Oxford: Oxford University Press, 2004), www.oxforddnb.com.

32 John Ogilby, *The Entertainment of his Most Excellent Majestie Charles II* (London, 1662), 43, 96, 101–10; Robert J. Mayhew, *Enlightenment Geography: The Political Languages of British Geography, 1650–1850* (New York: St. Martin's, 2000), 68–75; Eric Halfpenny, "The 'Entertainment' of Charles II," *Music & Letters* 38, no. 1 (1957): 32–33, 42–43.

33 Mayhew, *Enlightenment Geography*, 75.

34 Scott, *When the Waves Ruled Britannia*, 93–101, 125–26.

35 Circular letter from the King to merchant companies, January 11, 1676, SP 44/42, pp. 20–22, TNA; Zahedieh, *The Capital and the Colonies*, 163.

36 Circular Letter to the Lord Baltimore Lord Propriety of Maryland, April 10, 1676, CO 5/723, pp. 21–26, TNA; Lords of Trade and Plantations to Sir Jonathan Atkins, April 14, 1676, CO 29/2, pp. 37–44,TNA; Governor Sir Jonathan Atkins to the Lords of Trade and Plantations, July 4/14, 1676, CO 1/37, fol. 48r–55v, TNA; "The Lord Baltimore presents an answer to The Inqueries concerning Maryland, *viz.*," March 26, 1678, CO 5/723, pp. 35–45, TNA. Charles Andrews, *British Committees, Commissions, and Councils of Trade and Plantations, 1622–1675* (Baltimore, MD: Johns Hopkins University Press, 1908), 61–95; Alison Gilbert Olson, *Anglo-American Politics, 1660–1775: The Relationship between Parties in England and Colonial America* (Oxford: Clarendon Press, 1973), 39–51, 57–74.

37 The Lords of Trade and Plantations to Governor William Berkeley, April 6, 1676, CO 5/1355, p. 54 (quotation), TNA. Charles M. Andrews, *England's Commercial and Colonial Policy*, vol. 4, *The Colonial Period of American History* (New Haven, CT: Yale University Press, 1938), 180–89; Lawrence A. Harper, *The English Navigation Laws: A Seventeenth-Century Experiment in Social Engineering* (New York: Octagon Books 1964), 161–72.

38 This atlas is now in the collection of the John Carter Brown Library. Black, *The Blathwayt Atlas*, vol. 2 *Commentary*, 1–14.

39 "Journal of the Council for Plantations from the 3rd of August 1670, to the 20th of September 1672. Also of the Council for Trade & Plantations from the 13th of October 1672 to the 22th of December 1674," item 8539, Sir Thomas Phillipps Collection, LOC; Black, *The Blathwayt Atlas*, 2: 8–11.

40 "At the Committee of Trade and Plantations," July 30, 1678, CO 391/2, pp. 266, TNA; Accounts of the Lords of Trade and Plantations, June 24, 1677, to September 20, 1677, Add. Mss. 9767, fol. 41, BL; Black, *The Blathwayt Atlas*, 2: 56.

41 "At the Committee of Trade and Plantations," January 21, 1676, CO 391/1, p. 64, TNA. Lords of Trade and Plantations to Sir Jonathan Atkins, July 26, 1679, CO 29/2, p. 284, TNA; Black, *The Blathwayt Atlas*, 2: 4–5, 9, 27–28, 61–62, 110, 126, 134, 137, 141–42, 149–50, 181–82, 193–94, 203–4.

42 "The Lord Baltimore presents an answer to The Inqueries concerning Maryland, *viz.*," March 26, 1678, CO 5/723, p. 38–39, 40, TNA; Circular Letter to the Lord Baltimore Lord Propriety of Maryland, April 10, 1676, CO 5/723, p. 24 (final quotation).

43 Black, *The Blathwayt Atlas*, 2:86–87.

44 Journal of Trade and Plantations from February 1674 to March 1676, CO 391/1, TNA.

45 Price information from the *London Gazette* advertisements reproduced in Sarah Tyacke, *London Map-Sellers: 1660–1720* (Tring, Hertfordshire: Map Collector

Publications, 1978); Alexander Globe, *Peter Stent, London Printseller: Circa 1642–1665: Being a Catalogue Raisonné of His Engraved Prints and Books with an Historical and Bibliographical Introduction* (Vancouver: University of British Columbia Press, 1986), 45fn26.

46 Knighton, "Pepys, Samuel (1633–1703)."

47 John Seller, *Atlas maritimus, or, The sea-atlas* (London, 1675), 1v.

48 Lewes Roberts, *The Merchants Mappe of Commerce* (London, 1638).

49 March 20, 1660/61, and June 20, 1662, *Pepys Diary*, 2:56, 3:114–15.

50 Sarah Tyacke, Introduction, in *Catalogue of the Pepys Library at Magdalene College Cambridge*, vol. 4, *Music, Maps, and Calligraphy*, comp. Sarah Tyacke (Cambridge: D. S. Brewer, 1989), viii–xiv.

51 Ibid., x–xiv, 11.

52 John Dee, *The Elements of Geometrie of the Most Ancient Philosopher Euclide of Megara*, trans. H. Billingsley (London, 1570), preface, sig. A4r, quoted in John Gilles, "The Scene of cartography in *King Lear*," in *Literature, Mapping and the Politics of Space in Early Modern Britain*, ed. Andrew Gordon and Bernhard Klein (New York: Cambridge University Press, 2001), 122. On geographic literacy and education, see Kagan and Schmidt, "Maps and the Early Modern State," 678; Jonathan M. Smith, "State Formation, Geography and a Gentleman's Education," *Geographical Review* 86, no. 1 (1996): 94–95.

53 Peregrine Clifford, *Compendium Geographicum, Or, A More Exact, Plain, and Easie Introduction Into All Geography* (London, 1682), A3r,v; Smith, "State Formation, Geography, and a Gentleman's Education," 95–96; Bouwsma, *The Waning of the Renaissance*, 68–69, 189–90; Robert J. Mayhew, "Geography's English Revolutions: Oxford Geography and the War of Ideas, 1600–1660," in *Geography and Revolution*, ed. David N. Livingstone and Charles C.J. Withers (Chicago: University of Chicago Press, 2005), 249–50.

54 *London Gazette*, January 24–27, 1675/6, in Tyacke, *London Map-Sellers*, 14.

55 September 8, 1663, *Pepys Diary*, 4:301–2.

56 William Paterson Cummings, *The Southeast in Early Maps* (Chapel Hill: University of North Carolina Press, 1962), 148.

57 Scott, *When the Waves Ruled Britannia*, 146; Mayhew, *Enlightenment Geography*, 13–16, 26–28.

58 William Cuningham, *The cosmographical glasse* (London, 1559), preface, 3r (first quotation), 120 (second quotation).

59 Thomas Elyot, *The Book named the Governor*, ed. S. E. Lehmberg (New York: Dutton, 1962), 35; Peter Parshall, "Prints as Objects of Consumption in Early Modern Europe," *Journal of Medieval and Early Modern Studies* 28, no. 1 (1998): 28–30.

60 Robert Applebaum, "Anti-Geography," *Early Modern Literary Studies* 4, no. 2, Special Issue 3 (1998): 12.1–17 : purl.oclc.org, para. 2, 4, 11–13 (quotation).

61   Dee, *The Elements of Geometrie*, preface, sig. A4r, cited in Gilles, "The Scene of Cartography," 122.

62   Abraham Ortelius, *Theatrum orbis terrarum: The theatre of the whole world: Set Forth by That Excellent Geographer Abraham Ortellis* (London, 1606), unpaginated; John Loughman, and John Michael Montias. *Public and Private Spaces: Works of Art in Seventeenth-Century Dutch Houses* (Zwolle: Waanders Publishers, 2000), 54–59.

63   *Pepys Diary*, April 30, 1669, 9:537–39; *London Gazette*, March 20–24, 1672/3, in Tyacke, *London Map-Sellers*, 8; Wallis, "Geographie Is Better than Divinitie," 3–4, 17–24; Barber, "Necessary and Ornamental," 1–6; Pedley, *Commerce of Cartography*, 159–62, 164–66.

64   *Pepys Diary*, January 4, 1661/2 (first quotation), August 8, 1664 (second and third quotations), May 28, 1665, 3:3, 5:235–6, 6:109–111. Tyacke, Introduction, viii.

65   *Pepys Diary*, February 15, 1662/3, April 27, 1666 (first quotation), April 20, 1669 (subsequent quotations), 4:43, 7:101, 9:527; Kate Loveman, "Books and Sociability: The Case of Samuel Pepys's Library," *Review of English Studies* 61, no. 249 (2009): 217–23 (quotation, 218).

66   *Pepys Diary*, August 24, 1666 (quotation); April 27, 1666, 7:258, 111.

67   Will of Samuel Pepys, May 1703, quoted in Loveman, "Books and Sociability," 216.

68   Gilbert Cope and Augustine Herrman, "Copy of the Will of Augustine Herrman, of Bohemia Manor," *PMHB* 15, no. 3 (1891): 322, 324. Lee P. Phillips, *The Rare Map of Virginia and Maryland by Augustine Herrman First Lord of Bohemia Manor Maryland: A Bibliographical Account with Facsimile Reproduction from the Copy in the British Museum* (Washington, DC: W. H. Lowdermilk, 1911), 13.

69   Martin Brückner, "The Spectacle of Maps in British America, 1750–1800," in *Early American Cartographies*, ed. Martin Brückner, (Chapel Hill: University of North Carolina Press for the OIEAHC, 2011), 406–18.

70   "Complaint from Heaven with a Huy & crye and a petitionout of Virginia and Maryland," [ca. 1676?], CO 1/36, fol. 213r, TNA; Antoinette Sutto, *Loyal Protestants and Dangerous Papists: Maryland and the Politics of Religion in the English Atlantic, 1630–1690* (Charlottesville: University of Virginia Press, 2015), 120–21.

EPILOGUE

1   Jeannette D. Black, *The Blathwayt Atlas*, vol. 2 *Commentary* (Providence, RI: Brown University Press, 1975), 88–90, 82–5; Edward B. Mathews "The Maps and Map-Makers of Maryland," *Maryland Geological Survey* (Baltimore, MD: The Johns Hopkins University Press, 1898), 2:384–385.

2   Black, *The Blathwayt Atlas*, 2:75–81.

3   Coolie Verner, Bibliographical Note, in *The English Pilot, London 1689: The Fourth Book.* (Amsterdam: Theatrum orbis Terrarum, 1967), vi–x.

4 Donald H. Cresswell, "Colony to Commonwealth: The Eighteenth Century," in *Virginia in Maps: Four Centuries of Settlement, Growth, and Development*, ed. Richard Stephenson and Marianne McKee (Richmond: Library of Virginia, 2000), 52, 59, 77, 78, 104.

5 Gilbert Cope and Augustine Herrman, "Copy of the Will of Augustine Herrman, of Bohemia Manor," *PMHB* 15, no. 3 (1891): 321–26.

6 Thomas Čapek, *Augustine Herrman of Bohemia Manor* (Prague: State Printing Office, 1930), 28.

7 Townsend Ward, "Augustine Herman and John Thompson," *PMHB* 7, no. 1 (1883): 88 ("adventurous spirit"); John Lednum, *A History of the Rise of Methodism in America* (Philadelphia, 1859), 277 (other quotations).

8 *Baltimore Sun*, January 2, 1852, 4; Lednum, *A History of the Rise of Methodism*, 277 ("bolted, with"); George Alfred Townsend, "Herman of Bohemia Manor," in *Tales of the Chesapeake* (New York, 1880), 112, 114 (other quotations); George Johnston, *History of Cecil County* (Elkton, MD, 1881), 37; Ward, "Augustine Herman and John Thompson," 88–90.

9 J. S. Ingram, *The Centennial Exposition Described and Illustrated* (Philadelphia, 1876), 89, 251, 284, 363, 457, 626; Michael Kammen, *Mystic Chords of Memory: The Transformation of Tradition in American Culture* (New York: Vintage, 1993), 28–37, 93–95, 132–53, 200–22; John Bodnar, *Remaking America: Public Memory, Commemoration, and Patriotism in the Twentieth Century* (Princeton, NJ: Princeton University Press, 1992), 21–36 (quotation, 30); Richard Guy Wilson, "What Is the Colonial Revival?," in *Re-Creating the American Past: Essays on the Colonial Revival*, ed. Shaun Eyring, Kenny Marotta, and Richard Guy Wilson (Charlottesville: University of Virginia Press, 2006), 1–10.

10 Johnston, *History of Cecil County*, 38 (quotation); Philipa Lopate, "The Days of the Patriarchs: Washington Irving's *A History of New York*," 191–22, and Bartholomew F. Bland, "Imaging Dutch New York: John Quidor and the Romantic Tradition," 223–256, both in *Dutch New York: The Roots of Hudson Valley Culture*, ed. Roger Panetta (New York: Fordham University Press for the Hudson River Museum, 2009). For "Colonel Herman," see *Baltimore Sun*, January 2, 1852, 4. On Mount Vernon and Washington, see Lydia Mattice Brandt, "Re-Creating Mount Vernon: The Virginia Building at the 1893 Chicago World's Columbian Exposition," *Winterthur Portfolio* 43, no. 1 (2009): 79–81; 86–91, 94–97.

11 Eva Slezak, "Baltimore's Czech Community; The Early Years," *Czechoslovak and Central European Journal* 9, nos. 1–2 (1990): 106–7.

12 "The Great Bohemian: A Visit to the Old Manor All Honor to Augustine," *Baltimore Sun*, August 19, 1889, 4. Slezak, "Baltimore's Czech Community," 106–107.

13 Bodnar, *Remaking America*, 41–75; Kammen, *Mystic Chords of Memory*, 194–253; Kristin L. Hoganson, *Consumer's Imperium: The Global Production of American Domesticity, 1865–1920* (Chapel Hill: University of North Carolina Press, 2007),

212, 229–30; Kathleen Neil Conzen, David A. Gerber, Ewa Morawska, George E. Pozzetta, and Rudolh J. Vecoli, "The Invention of Ethnicity: A Perspective from the U.S.A.," *Journal of American Ethnic History* 12 (1992): 10–11, 22–24. Thomas Čapek address as reported in "The Great Bohemian," 4.

14   Thomas Čapek, *The Čechs (Bohemians) in America: A Study of Their, National, Cultural, Political, Social, Economic, and Religious Life* (Boston: Houghton Mifflin, 1920); Čapek, *Augustine Herrman*. It is possible to trace much of Čapek's research through his correspondence files now on deposit at the LOC: Thomas Čapek Collection Relating to Czechoslovakia and Czech Americans, Boxes 12–15, manuscript Division, LOC. On Czech-American authors' efforts to uncover ethnic persistence, see Joseph Opatrný, "Problems in the History of Czech Immigration to America in the Second Half of the Nineteenth Century," *Nebraska History* 74, nos. 3–4 (1993): 120–21.

15   Vlado Simko, "Baltimore's Czech Community," *Kosmas: Czechoslovak and Central European Journal* 25 (2012): 103–14; "Women's Work for Their Cities," *Harper's Bazaar* 43 (August 1909): 766; Annette Stott, *Holland Mania: The Unknown Dutch Period in American Art & Culture* (Woodstock, NY: Overlook Press, 1998), 95.

16   *Baltimore Sun*, August 19, 1889, 4; Hoganson, *Consumer's Imperium*, 212, 229–30; Conzen et al., "The Invention of Ethnicity," 10–11.

17   "Bohemian Manor: Pilgrimage to the Tomb of Augustine Hermen in Cecil County," *Baltimore Sun*, August 31, 1891, 6.

18   "The Augustine Hermann Monument," *Baltimore Sun*, June 16, 1892, 8. "Forecast for Baltimore and Vicinity," *Baltimore Sun*, September 3, 1906, 1; "At Herman's Old Home: Bohemians Make Pilgrimage to Bohemia Manor," *Baltimore Sun*, September 3, 1906, 12; "In Memory of Founder: Bohemians Plan to Pay Tribute to Augustine Herman," *Baltimore Sun*, July 31, 1907; "Bohemians on Outing: Excursion to Ocean City in Honor of Augustine," *Baltimore Sun*, August 12, 1907; "Herman's Memory Green," *Baltimore Sun*, October 10, 1901, 5.

19   "'Will Honor Herman': Bohemians Plan Monument for North Broadway," *Baltimore Sun*, March 15, 1908, 20.

20   "Augustine Herman Portrait Is Unveiled At Annapolis," *Baltimore Sun*, November 3, 1941, 5; E.V.B, "Augustine Herman Maryland's First Bohemian," *Baltimore Sun*, February 21, 1955, 12; "Augustine Herrman Day Is Proclaimed," *Baltimore Sun*, Ocotber 16, 1959, 15.

21   Miloslav Rechcigl, Jr., "The First Czech Settler in America," Embassy of the Czech Republic in Washington, DC, March 22, 2017, www.mzv.cz.

22   The SS *Augustine Herman* was built at the Bethlehem-Fairfield Shipyard in Baltimore and launched in November 1943. U.S. Merchant Marine, "Liberty Ships Built by Alabama Drydock & Shipbuilding Company, Mobile, Alabama, and Bethlehem-Fairfield Shipyard, Inc., Baltimore, Maryland, for U. S. Maritime Commission, 1941–1945," March 22, 2017, www.usmm.org.

INDEX

Page numbers in italics refer to figures

Christiana River (Minquas Kil) 107, 116

Coffeehouses, 186–189; Exchange Alley Coffee House, 188; Garaway's Coffee House, 186

Colonial revival, 221–225

Colson, John, 183

Committee of Trade and Plantations (Lords of Trade): as collector of maps, 201–203; origins of, 200–201; purchase of *Virginia and Maryland*, 5, 7, 191–192, 211, 214

Connecticut, 27, 34, 126, 127

Connecticut (Fresh) River, 18, 20, 34, 96

Cornelius, John, 39

Cornhill (London), 184, 186, 189, 197

Coymans, Coenraet, 18, 240n6

Cromwell, Oliver, 28, 121, 179

Cuningham, William, 83, 92, 209–210

Curaçao, 20, 21, 42, 43

Custis, Ann, 39

Custis, John, 39, 40, 122; geographic knowledge of, 90; trade with Augustine Herrman of, 41

Czech immigrant community: in Baltimore, 224–225; memorialization of Augustine Herrman, 225–228

Danckaerts, Jasper, 132, 135

Davis, John, 83, 84

Dead-reckoning. *See* Navigation

De Bry, Theodor, 60, 62, 170, 172

Dee, John, 189, 193, 205–206

De Laet, Johannes, 91, 92

Delaware, 15, 131

Delaware Bay. *See* Delaware (South) River

Delaware Landing, 132

Delaware (South) River, 15, 53; claims to, 17, 111–114, 120, 141–142; connected to Chesapeake Bay, 105, 114–116, 118, 124–126, 131–134; as depicted in maps, 67, 69, 78–79, 217–219; as depicted

in *Virginia and Maryland*, 56, 79, 98; settlement of, 105–111. *See also* New Amstel; New Sweden

Delmarva Peninsula. *See under* Chesapeake Bay; Delaware (South) River

D'Hinoyossa, Alexander, 114; diplomacy with Maryland of, 117–118; loss of property of, 128; migration to Maryland of, 129; new settlement of, 126, 128, 129; trade with Augustine Herrman of, 124–125; trade with Maryland of, 118, 120–121, 122

Die Speighel de Zeevaert. See also Waghenaer, Lucas Janszoon

Drake, Francis, 193, 197

A Draught of the Sea Coast and Rivers, of Virginia, Maryland, and New England, 66, 67

Dudley, Robert, 69, 71–72, 74, 205

Dunstall, John, 191

Dutch Brazil, 20

Dutch Republic (United Provinces): cultural ties to England, 45; economy of, 18, 21; English trade laws target trade of, 105, 119–120, 179, 196–197; geographic mindset in, 96–98; 104; immigrants in, 23; laws affecting women, 43; map and chart-making in, 55, 65–66, 74–81, 92–93, 179–180, 182–183, 205; maritime nature of, 38; merchants' trade of, 18, 19, 25, 27; New York City trade, 130; objects in England colonies, 45–46, 49–51; overseas expansion of, 2, 19–20; territory claimed by, 15, 52; trade in Chesapeake of, 29–31, 36–37, 39. *See also* Amsterdam; Anglo-Dutch trade; Anglo-Dutch Wars; New Amstel; New Amsterdam; New Netherland; West India Company (WIC)

Dyer, John, 34

Pennsylvania, 106, 127, 133, 135, 218
Pepys, Elizabeth, 206
Pepys, Samuel, 1, 182; use of maps, 182, 183, 196, 197, 204–206, 210–214; *Virginia and Maryland*, 3, 5, 7, 192, 211; William Faithorne, 148
Pepys Library (Magdalene), 1, 3, 213
Pepys's Library (Buckingham Street), 212, 213
Petty, William, 189
Philadelphia, 133, 141
Philadelphia Centennial International Exposition, 223
Philipse, Frederick, 23
Playing cards: maps on, 206
Plymouth (colony), 26
Povey, John, 203
Potomac River, 4, 15, 44, 219,
Powhatan people, 59, 100, 208
Prague, 167, 226
Preservation movement. *See* Colonial revival
Prince Rupert (of the Rhine), 167, 168
Printing, 155–158
Prints, power of, 139–140
Printz, Johan, 18, 42
A Prospect of the Most Famous Parts of the World (Speed), 179, 182, 204

Raleigh, Sir Walter, 193
Rappahannock River, 4, 39, 59–60
A regiment for the sea (William Bourne), 83
Rickards, John, 49, 50
Roanoke River, 208
Rotterdam, 20, 28–29, 37, 39
Royal Exchange, (London) 184–187
Rutters. *See* Waggoners

Sassafras River, 112, 115
Saxton, Christopher, 97
Scarborough, Edward, 33, 39, 40, 143

Seller, John, 83, 204; *The Coasting Pilot*, 3, 205; early life of, 181; shops of, 182, 189–190, 211; *The English Pilot*, 3, 182–184, 197, 199; Samuel Pepys, 205; *Scenes of the Plague*, 190, 191; *Virginia and Maryland*, 137, 145, 202, 217–218
Slavery: slave trade, 20, 40, 194; enslaved people, 23, 43, 88, 128, 134
Sluyter, Peter, 132, 135,
Smith, John: *Map of New England*, 66, 166; as mapmaker, 67, 72, 87–88, 90; *Virginia Discouvered and Discribed*, 16, 57–63, 99–100, 103–104, 172–173, 205 207, 217
Smuggling: in Maryland, 37, 118, 119–120, 123–126, 128–133; in New Netherland, 24, 130; in New Sweden, 109–110; in Virginia, 35–37, 38–40, 121–123. *See also* Navigation Acts; Tobacco; *and individual locations*
Somerset County (Virginia) 143, 159
Spain, 19, 20, 34, 76, 193
Spesutie Island, 116, 125
SS Augustine Herman, 228, 271n22
Stam, Arent Cornelisz, 29
Stam, Dirck Cornelisz, 29
St. Augustine's Creek, 131
Steenwyck, Cornelius, 126, 130
St. Eustatius, 20
St. Lawrence River, 63, 65
St. Martin, 20
St. Mary's City (Maryland), 29, 45, 117, 129
Stockett, Henry, 125
Stringer, John, 40, 41
Stuyvesant, Anna, 35
Stuyvesant, Petrus: Anglo-Dutch trade, 30, 122; Augustine Herrman, 33, 42, 44, 52, 91, 251n34; border dispute with Maryland, 15, 111–113; in colonial revival, 222; conflict with New England, 27–28; conflict with New Sweden, 108, 110–111; as Director-General of New

Netherland, 23–25; surrender of New Netherland, 127–128
Surveying, 81–83, 86–87, 100, 103
Susquehanna River, 107, 115, 208, 218
Susquehannock people, 107–108, 109–110, 113, 115, 117–118; depiction of, 60, 172; fort of, 109
Swanendael, 106, 107

Thames School, 93, 158, 161, 180–181, 202
Thornton, John, 180, 183, 218–220
Tiddeman, Mark, 220
Tobacco, 50, 101, 133, 143; Augustine Herrman trader of, 33, 35–42, 90, 125–127, 129–130; changing market for, 105, 122–124, 144; commercial policy regarding, 31, 119–120, 132; Dutch cruising trade in, 20, 28–29; New England trade, 26; New Netherland trade, 27, 30; New Sweden trade, 18, 109–110; pipes, 27, 45; Swanendael, 106–107. *See also* Anglo-Dutch trade; individual colonies
Townsend, George, 222
Tsenacommacah, 59, 60, 100

Utie, Nathaniel, 111–112, 125–126

Van Beeck, Johannes, 35, 40
Van Nas, Abraham, 117
Van Sweringen, Gerrit, 120, 128, 129
Varleth (var. Varlet), Anna, 36; furniture of, 46, 49–51; property of, 38–39, 143; marriage of, 35, 49; naturalization of, 134; trade of, 35, 38–40, 42, 106, 130. *See also* Boot, Nicholas; Hack, George; Herrman, Augustine
Varleth (var. Varlet), Jannetje , 35, 43–44. *See also* Herrman, Augustine
Varleth (var. Varlet), Caspar, 35
Varleth (var. Varlet), Maria, 35
Varleth (var. Varlet), Nicholas, 43, 122
Varleth (var. Varlet), Pieter, 35

Vaughan, Grace, 41
Verbrugge, Gillis, 30–32
Verbrugge, Seth, 30–32
View of New Amsterdam, (Herrman), 88–89, *89*
Vingboons, Johannes, 78, 91, 92, 93. See also *Caert vande Svydt Rivier in Niew Nederland*; *Pascaert van Nieuw Nederlandt, Virginia, ende Nieuw Engelandt.*
Virginia, 6, 175–176, 228; boundary dispute with Maryland, 53–54, 98, 123, 142–144; colonial revival, 223–224; as depicted in maps, 16, 57–68, 71–72, 79, 93–94, 103, 218–220 (*see also* individual maps); Dutch goods in, 44–51; Dutch trade in, 19, 25–31, 35–40, 42–43, 129–131 (*see also* Augustine Herrman; Chesapeake); importance of Anglo-Dutch trade in, 121–123, 130; Native American communities of, 100, 172; tobacco market in, 123–124. *See also* Augustine Herrman; Chesapeake; *Virginia and Maryland*
Virginia (Hall), 62–62, *63*
"Virginia" (manuscript chart, 1677), 93–94, *95*, 158–159
Virginia and Maryland (Moll), 220
Virginia and Maryland As it is Planted and Inhabited, 2, 1–5, *53*, 55–57, *71*, *73*, 116, 228; advertising of, 137–138; cartographic techniques used in, 67–74; as chorographical account, 207–210; copyright for, 141, 199; consumption of, 1–3, 191–193, 202–205, 211; depiction of Maryland's borders in, 141–144; derivatives of, 217–220; as distinguished from manuscript of, 7–12, 72, 88–90, 93–95, 140, 159–163, 176–177; drawing of, 92–95; as embodying English control, 8–9, 12–13, 138, 177–78; engraving of, 145–147, 151–155; gathering cartographic information for, 68–69, 82–92, 98–99;

ABOUT THE AUTHOR

Christian J. Koot is Associate Professor of History and the Director of American Studies at Towson University, where he teaches courses on Colonial and Revolutionary America.